COMPUTATIONAL METHODS FOR POPULATION PROJECTIONS: WITH PARTICULAR REFERENCE TO DEVELOPMENT PLANNING

COMPUTATIONAL METHODS FOR POPULATION PROJECTIONS: WITH PARTICULAR REFERENCE TO DEVELOPMENT PLANNING

Frederic C. Shorter
with programming assistance from
David Pasta

THE POPULATION COUNCIL
NEW YORK

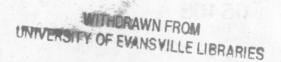

THE POPULATION COUNCIL
245 Park Avenue
New York, New York 10017

The Population Council is an organization established in 1952 for scientific training and study in the field of population. It endeavors to advance knowledge in the broad field of population by fostering research, training, and technical consultation and assistance in the social and biomedical sciences.

The Council acknowledges, with thanks, the funds received from the Ford Foundation, the United Nations Fund for Population Activities, the United States Agency for International Development, the World Bank, and other donors for the publication program of the Population Council.

Distributed for The Population Council by
Key Book Service, Inc.
425 Asylum Street
Bridgeport, Connecticut 06610

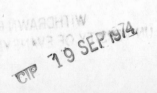

CONTENTS

PREFACE

This book was written out of necessity. It is laborious to the point of being painful to make repeated population projections on a desk calculator, even an electronic one. So the first step that led to this book was an untidy, but adequate, computer program for projections by five-year and annual intervals. At the State Planning Organization in Turkey, Ms. Samira Yener contributed many suggestions and gave the system its first test during the preparation of population projections for the Third Five-Year Plan of Turkey. Subsequently, an expert in clean and efficient programming, David Pasta, joined the author. Together we devised a system that is user-oriented, transportable, and capable of easy installation on a variety of computers.

Further opportunities to use the system arose in Iran, Egypt, El Salvador, Colombia, and Venezuela. Academic researchers in North America have also used the system as a convenient computational aid. For teaching about the growth and structure of human populations, the computing routine has proven simple to use and effective both for lecture illustrations and student problems. Having determined that the system functioned well in a wide range of applications, it was decided to expand the original notes for users to the present manual. The aim is to enable users to teach themselves how to make projections on the computer, and to guide them to solutions when particular problems are encountered.

Population projections are based on assumptions that must be prepared beforehand. Some new procedures for the preparation of the initial age distributions and other assumptions are included in this manual. One procedure involves the use of model age distributions that reflect the effect of past changes in mortality, fertility, and migration. Such models are useful for the detection and adjustment of severe age misreporting at the national level (Chapter Three). A procedure is also shown for adjusting urban or other local age distributions for age misreporting. This procedure is applicable whenever it may be assumed that urban age misreporting has the same characteristics as age misreporting in the country as a whole, but is of different intensity (Chapter Five).

Finally, there are a number of suggestions about the handling of migration in population projections in terms of both quantities and rates. A method for assignment of ages to migrants at the time of their migration is also shown. It is based on migration estimates made by classical survival procedures (Chapter Five).

Preparation of the book and associated FORTRAN programs was accomplished principally at the Office of Population Research, Princeton University, with support from a grant by the Ford Foundation. Encouragement and suggestions came from colleagues in the demographic and economic professions at home and abroad. Thus, the book is the result of the work of many persons. The authors have been privileged to draw together the contributions of others and to include them in this presentation of the subject as we understand it at this time.

INTRODUC- TION: THE USES OF POPULATION PROJECTIONS IN DEVELOPMENT PLANNING _____

This manual and its accompanying computer package are dedicated to those who have population projections to make. If the reader wants to make a population projection immediately, skip directly to Chapter One. If the reader is interested in learning about the place of population projections in development planning, continue reading below. If he or she needs to be refreshed on the logical structure of population projections, the mathematical appendix will be useful.

Demographic contributions to development planning typically consist of demographic information and alternative population projections. It may come as a surprise, however, to learn that until 1974 no more than one-half the development plans prepared in the third world were based on genuine projections of the population by age and sex. The future appears more promising since the number of plans that make use of population projections is increasing. Where such projections have been used, the typical procedure has been to select one projection from among "high," "medium," and "low" projections and to base the calculations of the plan on that projection.

Demographers have usually produced these projections on the basis of statistical observations concerning levels and trends in the basic demographic determinants of population change, insofar as these parameters were known. The main contribution of demographers has been to prepare current estimates of demographic conditions. The projections were usually described as "if, then" projections: "If such and such assumptions about fertility, mortality, and migration, then the future population will be so and so." Only the computations were "certified," not the results. Development planners then made a single choice from among the alternatives presented. As far as it goes, this approach to the use of population projections in planning is useful, but not nearly as powerful as recent thinking about the relationship of population to development suggests it could be.

DEMOGRAPHIC AND ECONOMIC MODELS

The logical relationship of population projections to development plans is shown schematically in Figure I.1, where two types of models are distinguished, demographic and economic. The selection of a particular population projection makes it possible to cross from the demographic model to the economic one, as shown in the upper part of the diagram. A major purpose of the present manual is to enable demographers to produce population estimates that match the units of time, place, and population subgroup in the economic model.

Across the bottom of the diagram, the effects of economic and social change on fertility, mortality, and migration are shown. Some elements of economic development are highly specific in their effects on demographic change. For example, the distribution of investments in construction and commodity production among cities affects internal migration and consequently the residential distribution of the population. The supply of health services, both public and private, and the distribution of eligibility for services (e.g., where people live in relation to where services are provided,

FIGURE I.1 Relationship Between Demographic and Economic Models in Development Planning

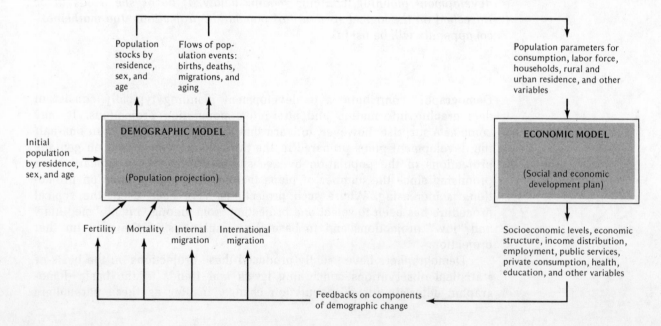

or the cost of services in relation to income) affect infant and adult survival. Fertility is influenced directly by the supply of, and access to, means of contraception and abortion. The economic and social environment for family formation also is specified by the development process and consequently affects fertility.

Feedbacks from the economic model to the demographic model logically require that population projections be revised on the basis of the results of the economic model. In terms of a planning sequence, the first demographic projection provides the basis for making a preliminary economic model, which provides, via its consequences, a basis for revising the assumptions of the demographic projection. Then a second iteration follows, with a second population projection, a second economic model, and, if necessary, a second revision of the assumptions for the demographic projection. Several iterations can produce a large gain in consistency between the demographic and economic models. If the iterations are carried out successfully, it becomes possible to say, "If the *plan*, then the population projection." This is a much stronger statement about consistency of the analysis than one that says, "If these assumptions about fertility, mortality, and migration, then this population projection."

LENGTH OF TIME PERSPECTIVE

Development plans usually refer to periods that are short relative to the processes of long-term change in populations. In a country with moderately high fertility (crude birth rate>40 per thousand population), about four-fifths of the population that will be alive five years from now is already alive. Alternative population projections for a five-year planning period are all the same for the population above age five, irrespective of different fertility regimes, if mortality and migration are identical in every one. At a national level, these conditions are satisfied in many countries. If the economic model is based exclusively on national population estimates, and if the time perspective is only five or ten years, the gain in consistency from making more than one projection would be negligible. However, planning is seldom confined to national estimates and implicitly requires a longer perspective, as will be explained below.

The spatial units of plans normally include regions, rural areas, and urban areas. In those parts of the developing world where the proportion of the population living in urban communities has already reached levels of 20 to 30 percent and economic growth is moderate to rapid, cities commonly receive one-third to two-thirds of their annual population increase from migration. The quantity of population change due to migration and its allocation among cities and regions is closely related to differences in economic and social development in the different communities. Consequently, population changes for periods as short as five years are determined to a substantial extent by migration. If projections are made for subdivisions of the national population, interaction between the economic and demographic models requires an iterative approach even within a five-year perspective.

International migration poses additional possibilities for national population changes. One set of determinants of the migration refers to foreign countries beyond the purview of the national plan. In a number of developing countries, population change is affected significantly by international migration because the labor force competes for jobs in extraterritorial labor markets. Policies of the national plan may affect job alternatives at home or the cost of moving from domestic to foreign labor markets. The effects of these policies on international migration should be worked out and considered when making migration assumptions. Thus, even within a short time perspective, migration feedbacks due to internal or international movements are reasons for making more than one round of projections and economic models.

Development plans guide the commitment of economic and organizational resources in the present for the purpose of production far into the future. Urban planning, educational planning, health planning, and many other kinds of planning are undertaken to determine whether immediate expenditures will provide facilities for production and service that will be justified by demands of the population in the future. It hardly seems necessary to stress that the same principles that require investment planners to look beyond the period of immediate commitments require development planners to do the same in relation to population. Errors in estimating the future size, characteristics, and distribution of a population give faulty signals to decision-makers that can lead to costly misallocations of resources. Although errors of prediction will always be present, population projections of more than five years, on the order of 25 or more years, are logically required to prepare sector plans of action for the immediate future.

The amount of interaction between the two models increases with the length of the time perspective, and the necessity of considering time periods of at least 25 years to prepare five-year plans leads to the conclusion that an interactive approach is unavoidable. Once this is accepted, a framework of analysis is needed within which to consider the effects on population projections of alternative economic and social policies that are planned for the immediate future. The field for maneuver in affecting population growth and distribution is not limited to public birth-control services, important as they are. Studies of the determinants of fertility, although still in their infancy, suggest that income, modes of production, distribution of education and income among families, and numerous other social and economic conditions are involved. Consequently, policies that affect these conditions are themselves determinants of population change in an important way.

Not only is fertility involved. Results of the international round of national censuses at the beginning of the 1970s cast doubt on the view that European levels of life expectancy are near at hand for most of the developing countries. Death rates still remain high in many parts of the developing world, especially among infants and young children. The impact of policies that distribute health and educational services more evenly, improve levels of nutrition, and affect the care of children may bring about changes in survival that are a major source of additional population growth. Thus, all such programs must be evaluated in terms of their demographic feedbacks.

AN INTERACTIVE PROCEDURE FOR PROJECTIONS

Whenever feedback effects occur and can be estimated, new population projections should be made. It is likely, therefore, that demographers will be required to compute and revise projections numerous times as interrelationships between the demographic and economic models are recognized. The labor of repeating computations after each round of changes in assumptions would be discouraging were it not for the electronic computer. Economists use the computer extensively in the computation of economic models and are in a position, therefore, to recompute on second, third, and fourth interactions without serious burden. Demographers are in the same position if their projections are done by computer.

Eventually, techniques of planning may reach a stage in which the interaction of the demographic and economic models can be contained within a single mathematical system, implemented on the computer and relatively simple to use in applied planning. That stage has not yet been reached, except with regard to relatively abstract models designed for exploratory research. Until a much more extensive knowledge of the nature of interaction across the top and bottom of the diagram is attained, there are advantages to working with two separate models. One can use the two models by thinking in an interactive framework and performing an evaluation of each iteration "on the desk" before deciding whether to make another pass through the two-model system. The aim is to put economists and demographers in a succession of situations in which they can better understand a range of relationships that are presently far from clear.

CHAPTER ONE: PROJECTIONS BY MODIFIED COHORT-COMPONENT METHOD

Wherever electronic computers are available, population projections can be made by package programs. The computer offers major savings in time as well as internal accuracy. The package programs described in this manual use methods of computation that are superior to those commonly used when calculations are performed on a desk calculator. In principle, computations done on the computer also can be done by hand, but in practice they are too laborious to be considered. Package programs are recommended, therefore, because they give a better product than hand procedures.

The programs are accessible to anyone who spends a few minutes learning how jobs are submitted on the computer and then follows the detailed instructions in this manual to make one or more projections of his own. It is not necessary to have prior experience with computers or programming in order to use this computational tool. The package includes a program named "FIVFIV," which makes population projections by five-year age groups spaced at five-year intervals of time. A second program, named "SINSIN," transforms the results of the FIVFIV projection into annual estimates of population arranged by single-year or other age groupings. SINSIN also calculates annual social and economic derivatives of the population projection on the basis of assumptions provided by the user.

On small computers, the work is done by executing FIVFIV and SINSIN sequentially in two steps. On moderate-sized or large computers, FIVFIV and SINSIN are combined into one program (SINSIN becomes a subroutine of FIVFIV), and the work is done in one step. It makes no substantive difference to the user which system is used. The instructions, which he prepares on punch cards, are the same for every system. Differences among computer installations require slightly different "job streams" of control cards, which are explained in Appendix Two.

FIVFIV PROJECTIONS

The basic approach to projections of the package programs is the cohort-component method, which takes separate account of the effects on population size and structure of fertility, mortality, and migration. It is a modified method in the sense that the effects of migration are projected integrally with fertility and mortality, rather than projected separately as in classical approaches to the problem.

A projection by the modified cohort-component method may refer to a country, a city, a province, or a region. It can be made whenever the minimum list of necessary assumptions about fertility, mortality, and migration are made. The main problem when making projections for local areas or subdivisions of the population is that assumptions about fertility, mortality, and migration cannot always be made. For such populations, projections by ratio methods may be the best that can be done. Discussion of ratio methods is deferred to a later chapter.

FIVFIV is used to make population projections by the modified cohort-component method. In order to learn how to use FIVFIV, first read this chapter and the one following. Probably all details will not be understood after a single reading, but that is not necessary. Next, try to make a projection on FIVFIV. The computer will print messages in response to errors. The user can teach himself from this point onward. A summary of user instructions and error codes is printed at the end of the book. It has page references pointing to those places in the book where clarification can be found.

Once the basic procedures of FIVFIV are mastered, a wide range of applications is possible. A very limited number are illustrated in this and subsequent chapters. The program SINSIN takes one a step further. It enables the FIVFIV results to be transformed into convenient annual projections. The use of SINSIN is explained in Chapter Four. Additional applications and options are explained in later chapters. Since instructions are transmitted to SINSIN through FIVFIV, it is best to learn the use of FIVFIV before going on to learn about SINSIN.

INSTRUCTIONS FOR FIVFIV

The user of FIVFIV must prepare a set of instructions on cards for each projection desired and give them to the computer. Each set of instructions consists of several "subjects," such as mortality, fertility, and migration, which refer to the particular projection. Each subject requires one or more cards to convey all necessary information about that subject to the computer. Thus, each subject may be understood as a subgroup of cards. The conclusion of each set of instructions is indicated by a final card with END PROJECTION punched in the first 14 columns.

An example of a set of instructions for one projection exactly as punched is shown below in Example 1.1. It is a listing of punched cards, one card for each row of print. The computer reads sets of instructions for one projection at a time. Upon reading the END PROJECTION card, it prints a detailed analysis of the assumptions on the printer and actually performs the projection. After it finishes, another cycle is begun by reading the next set of instructions. The computer continues to make one projection after another until no more instructions are found to process.

List of Subjects

Example 1.1 has the minimum necessary number of subjects: YEAR.TITLE, INIT.POP, MORTALITY, and FERTILITY. A full list of possible subjects is given below in what might be called a "natural" order, although any order is permissible. However, END PROJECTION always goes at the end.

YEAR.TITLE	
INIT.POP	
DATE.SHIFT	(optional)
SCALE	(optional)
MORTALITY	
MORT.SPLIT	(alternative to MORTALITY)
FERTILITY	
SEXRATIO	(optional)
MIGRATION	(optional)
FINDMIGRATION	(optional; alternative to MIGRATION)
STABLEXTEND	(optional)
PRODUCTION	(optional)
PUNCH.FIVE	(optional)
END PROJECTION	

EXAMPLE 1.1 Instruction Cards for a Projection

```
0         1         2         3         4         5         6         7         8
1234567890123456789012345678901234567890123456789012345678901234567890123456789012345678 90

YEAR.TITLE
YR.1984.ALTERNATIVE 7: CONSTANT FERTILITY DECLINING MORTALITY (POP IN THOUSANDS)
INIT.POP
INIT.F.A      2237.7    1884.8    1656.7    1430.8    1101.2     976.3     856.8
INIT.F.B       854.9     740.3     593.2     490.2     410.9     403.3     320.1
INIT.F.C       220.5     120.8
INIT.M.A      2257.7    1899.7    1700.8    1440.6    1090.3     970.2     846.8
INIT.M.B       844.9     735.2     595.2     483.1     405.8     400.1     315.9
INIT.M.C       219.5     118.7
MORTALITY
MORT.EZ.F       56.6      58.       60.       62.       64.       66.       68.
MORT.EZ.M       54.8      56.       58.       60.       62.       64.       66.
FERTILITY
TOTAL.FERT       6.1
FERDIST1.7      .015      .051      .049      .039      .028      .012      .006
FEND
END PROJECTION

1234567890123456789012345678901234567890123456789012345678901234567890123456789 01234567890
```

The set of instructions for each projection must contain every subject that is not optional. Additional subjects that may be given for execution by SINSIN will be explained in later chapters.

Arrangement of Cards

Each subject is announced to the computer by a "header" card such as those in the list above. The header card comes first and is followed by one or more "information" cards that relate to that subject. Certain subjects do not require information cards, but most do. Example 1.1 shows the header card, INIT.POP, which announces the subject of initial population, followed by six information cards that give the initial population for the projection. One subject header, with associated information cards, if any, follows another until END PROJECTION is reached.

Subjects other than END PROJECTION may be given in any order. Information cards must follow immediately after their respective header cards, although there is usually no restriction on the sequence within each group of information cards. However, information cards that form strings, as indicated by A, B, C or 1, 2, . . . n in their labels, must be kept in sequence so that the information will be processed in a correct order. For example, the information cards INIT.F.A, INIT.F.B, and INIT.F.C are a string of cards that give the initial female population in age groups arranged in ascending order of age.

Format of Instruction Cards

Keypunching for FIVFIV always begins in column 1. The name of the subject is punched on a header card that announces the subject to the computer, but gives no information about it. Information cards follow. They always begin in column 1 with a label that identifies what kind of information is on the card. The names of subjects (header cards) and labels (leftmost "words" on information cards) must be punched exactly as prescribed or the computer will not recognize them.

Quantitative information is given only on information cards, not on header cards, by punching numbers in numeric data fields to the right of the information label. A data field is a range of columns in which numbers are punched. The numeric data fields for FIVFIV are ten columns wide: columns 11–20, 21–30, and so on, continuing as far across the card as needed. The initial population shown in Example 1.1 was punched in this manner. It is good practice to "right-justify" all numbers in data fields, which means to place them against the right-most margin of the field. At times this seems like a bother, but experience has shown that punching errors are less frequent and, if made, are easier to locate. The habit of right-justification should be developed from the beginning.

Consider a field defined as columns 11–20. It is ten columns wide because it includes the initial and terminal columns. If the number, −1235.8, is right-justified in that field, punching will start with three empty columns (use space bar on the keypunch), followed by −1235.8 in the next seven columns. Minus signs must be punched (e.g., for out-migration); plus signs are not punched.

Decimal points are always punched in numeric data fields. Even whole numbers (e.g., 874.) should have a decimal point. This practice assures that the computer will not add extra unintended zeroes to the number if it is accidentally punched in the wrong columns of the field. The rule to remember is that whenever numeric data are placed in ten-column data fields, use decimal points and right-justify the numbers.

When numbers are embedded in labels on information cards, or arranged in any other manner different from the ten-column data fields, the symbol # will be used to show where the number should be punched. For example, #### indicates that a four-digit integer number, such as a year, is expected by the computer. Integers rather than decimal numbers are expected in places where ## appear. Do not punch a decimal point. If space is allowed for a larger number than the user wants to give, right-justify the smaller number. It may be easier than skipping over empty columns to punch leading zero(s) in those columns. Either practice is acceptable.

SUBJECTS FOR FIVFIV

The requirements for each subject are shown below. Some subjects are optional in their entirety; and some types of information within subjects are optional. If optional information is not given by the user, but is needed by the computer to make the projection, FIVFIV will use its own assumptions. Such assumptions are called *defaults*. Reliance on defaults by the user is justified only when his own assumptions are in agreement. Default values are given in connection with each subject where they could be used.

Although header cards are underlined in the exposition below, they cannot be punched with underlining. Punching always starts in column 1. Decimal points are often required in continuous strings of characters in order to assure correct column spacing; they do not necessarily indicate abbreviations. It pays to punch accurately and proofread carefully. The computer does not have the ability to correct even the most trivial errors.

YEAR.TITLE

YR.####.

This subject is used to assign an initial year to the projection and to give it a title. The year is punched in columns 4-7, replacing the ####. If the user prefers to designate years as 0, 5, 10, . . . 35, punch zero or leave the field blank (empty) and the starting year will be read by the computer as zero. The symbol # is always replaced, if not by a numeral, then by an empty space.

The remainder of the information card (columns 9-80) is used for a title. Start in column 9 and use any characters on the keypunch. The title will be printed on every page of output. A distinctly different title should be given to each projection in order to avoid confusion when there is output from several projections. Use different words, describe assumptions, or number the projections.

Save some space at the end of the title to add a parenthetical note about the units of measurement. The computer will process numbers as if they were in units of one. However, the user may punch populations in tens, hundreds, or thousands as he pleases. Any convenient unit may be selected. Punch the choice in the title so it will reappear on every page of output.

```
0         1         2         3         4         5         6         7         8
1234567890123456789012345678901234567890123456789012345678901234567890123456789 0
```

EXAMPLES OF YEAR.TITLE

*** TITLE INCLUDES NOTE ABOUT POPULATION UNITS ***

YEAR.TITLE
YR.1972.ALTERNATIVE 3: INFANT MORTALITY DECLINES RAPIDLY   (POP UNITS = 100)

*** DATES THE INITIAL POPULATION AS YEAR ZERO ***

YEAR.TITLE
YR.   0.SIMULATION 11: LET NRR BECOME 1.0 IN YEAR 10. CONSTANT THEREAFTER.

*** STARTS FROM YEAR ZERO AND PRINTS NO TITLE ***

YEAR.TITLE
YR.   .

```
1234567890123456789012345678901234567890123456789012345678901234567890123456789 0
```

INIT.POP

INIT.F.A	
INIT.F.B	Females, 16 or fewer age groups
INIT.F.C	
and	
INIT.M.A	
INIT.M.B	Males, 16 or fewer age groups
INIT.M.C	

The initial population is supplied on three information cards for females (coded F) and three for males (coded M). Either string of three cards may come first, but within each set, they must be arranged A, B, C.

The population data are in 16 five-year age groups: 0-4, 5-9, . . . 70-74, 75+. The 16 numbers are arranged on the cards as follows: A gets the first seven age groups, B gets the next seven, and C gets the last two. The fields start in column 11 of each card and are of width 10, i.e., columns 11-20, 21-30, . . . 71-80, across the card. Card C has only two age groups and hence only two fields, i.e., columns 11-20 and 21-30.

The population is expressed in any convenient units, such as thousands. The units are mentioned in the title as explained in the previous subject. There is a limitation on the size of numbers that can be handled by FIVFIV. If units are chosen so that the total of the initial population does not exceed 500,000.0, the resulting projection will usually have numbers within the allowable size. There is not much gain in accuracy by punching more than one digit after the decimal although the user may do so. It is not even necessary to give digits after the decimal point. However, the printed output of FIVFIV will show population figures with one decimal digit properly rounded.

When punching population numbers, never use commas. The computer, unlike literate man, does not appreciate the convenience of commas or spaces in numbers.

If the open interval at the upper end of the age distribution is less than 75+, do not use all the fields. For example, place data for 60+ in the field for 60-65, and leave the rest of the card empty. The computer will distribute the data for 60+ to the age groups 60-64, 65-69, 70-74, and 75+, by assuming the distribution of a stationary population above age 65. The mortality assumptions for the first projection interval cause a model life table to be selected and its distribution of $_nL_x$ values will be used. If the user prefers to use his own distribution assumptions, they should be applied to the population data prior to submission to the computer.

If the user wishes to assume a zero population for all age groups above a certain group, place a small number such as .0001 in the field for 75+. This will prevent FIVFIV from filling the true zero groups with numbers redistributed from a younger age group, and the small number placed in 75+ will be "forgotten" during computation.

```
0          1           2          3          4          5          6          7          8
1234567890123456789012345678901234567890123456789012345678901234567890123456789012345678901234567890

                              EXAMPLES OF INIT.POP

                   *** ACCEPTABLE PLACEMENT OF NUMERIC DATA ***
                    *** HOWEVER, RIGHT JUSTIFICATION RECOMMENDED ***

INIT.F.B          49.7       40.0       31.8       24.7       18.6       13.4        8.9
            *** OR ***
INIT.F.B          49.7       40.0       31.824.7              18.6       13.4        8.9


                   *** ERRONEOUS PUNCHING OF NUMERIC DATA ***

INIT.F.B.  (NOTE THE EXTRA DECIMAL)     31.8  (NOTE INVASION OF SECOND DATA FIELD)

INIT.F.B          49 7        40         .31.8     (NOTE OMITTED OR EXTRA DECIMALS)


                   *** AGE GROUPS 0-4, 5-9, . . . 75+. ONLY FEMALES SHOWN ***

INIT.POP
INIT.F.A         186.6      152.2      128.0      107.7       89.7       74.1       60.9
INIT.F.B          49.7       40.0       31.8       24.7       18.6       13.4        8.9
INIT.F.C           5.3        4.1
        *** MALES NEXT ***


                   *** OPEN AGE INTERVAL IS 60+ INSTEAD OF 75+ ***

INIT.POP
INIT.F.A         186.6      152.2      128.0      107.7       89.7       74.1       60.9
INIT.F.B          49.7       40.0       31.8       24.7       18.6       31.7
INIT.F.C                               (NOTE CARD INCLUDED WITH EMPTY DATA FIELDS)
        *** MALES NEXT ***


                   *** POPULATION SIZE IS NEGLIGIBLE OR ZERO ABOVE AGE 65 ***
                        *** PROVIDE SMALL NUMBER FOR AGE 75+ ***

INIT.POP
INIT.F.A         140.1      114.8      105.9       99.3       90.1       81.1       72.0
INIT.F.B          50.1       20.4       11.4        5.2        3.2        0.5
INIT.F.C                     .0001
        *** MALES NEXT ***

1234567890123456789012345678901234567890123456789012345678901234567890123456789012345678901234567890
```

INIT.POP   Alternative subject for repeating, extending, or overlapping projections

OLD.POP.####

The initial population does not need to be punched if this is not the first projection in a series and if its initial population comes from some year of the projection that immediately precedes this one. A single information card will indicate which year of the previous projection gives the starting population for this projection. Any FIVFIV projection year, which means one of the years spaced at five-year intervals, may be selected. The same initial year can be used again and again to make a series of alternative projections. Or an intermediate year, such as the one at the fifteenth year, may be selected so that the next projection will overlap the previous one. Or the terminal year of the previous projection may be used so that the next projection will extend the previous one for another 35 years. Punch the selected year in columns 9-12.

A full set of other subject cards is required, with one exception: do not move the starting date a second time (next subject). Review the previous subject, YEAR.TITLE, carefully since it may be necessary to change the year that is mentioned there as the first year, or the title may need to be changed, or both. The year given for YEAR.TITLE is usually the same as the one given for OLD.POP. If a series of alternative projections are all started from the same date, be sure to give distinctively different, or numbered, titles. Otherwise, it may be difficult to determine which printed output is the result of which assumptions.

If the immediately preceding projection fails for any reason, the computer will not be able to find the OLD.POP, and this projection will be skipped.

```
0         1         2         3         4         5         6         7         8
1234567890123456789012345678901234567890123456789012345678901234567890123456789012345678901234567890

                    EXAMPLES OF INIT.POP ALTERNATIVE

          *** STARTS FROM 1987 POPULATION OF PRCEDING PROJECTION ***

INIT.POP
OLD.POP.1987


          *** STARTS FROM POPULATION DATED ZERO IN PRECEDING PROJECTION ***

INIT.POP
OLD.POP.   0
          *** OR ***
INIT.POP
CLD.POP.


          *** POPULATION COPIED FROM YEAR 15 IN PRECEDING SIMULATION IS ***
               *** LABELED WITH A REAL DATE (1985) IN THIS ONE ***

YEAR.TITLE
YR.1985.ALTERNATIVE 4 FOR SECOND PLAN PERIOD   (POP IN THOUSANDS)
INIT.POP
OLD.POP.0015

12345678901234567890123456789012345678901234567890123456789012345678901234567890
```

DATE.SHIFT   Optional subject.   Default: No date shifting

YR.####.WEEK.##

Regardless of the year specified under the subject YEAR.TITLE, the projection will start from the population that is given as input on INIT.POP, and a date is implicitly attached to that input population. Often this date is the census date. If this date does not position the population exactly at midyear of the year mentioned with the title, the user may request such positioning by using DATE.SHIFT. The computer will estimate a midyear population for the year stated under YEAR.TITLE. To do this, the computer must be given the actual date of the INIT.POP. This is done on the information card, YR.####.WEEK.##. Shifting is accomplished by horizontal interpolation forward, or extrapolation backward in time, by age groups rather than by diagonal projection of cohorts. DATE.SHIFT should not be used over longer time periods than necessary. Therefore, the same base year for the projection is normally given for YEAR.TITLE as applies for INIT.POP, which is shown on the information card, YR.####. WEEK.##.

Date shifting always operates on the input population for that particular projection. If a projection starts from a population that is copied from a prior projection (alternative subject for INIT.POP immediately above), the input population is the copied one. It can be shifted, if desired, but no further shifting is necessary if it was already shifted for the prior projection.

```
0         1         2         3         4         5         6         7         8
1234567890123456789012345678901234567890123456789012345678901234567890123456789012345678901234567890

                        EXAMPLES OF DATE.SHIFT

   *** CENSUS TAKEN IN THIRD WEEK OF 1970:   SHIFT TO MIDYEAR OF SAME YEAR ***

YEAR.TITLE
YR.1970.REGION SOUTHWEST.  ALTERNATIVE 2.
DATE.SHIFT
YR.1970.WEEK.03

                *** SHIFT TO MIDYEAR OF PREVIOUS YEAR ***

YEAR.TITLE
YR.1969.REGION SOUTHWEST.  ALTERNATIVE 2.
DATE.SHIFT
YR.1970.WEEK.03

        *** MAKES PROJECTIONS BY FISCAL YEARS DEFINED AS JULY-JUNE YEARS ***
        *** THIRD WEEK OF CALENDAR YEAR 1971 IS 29TH WEEK OF FY 1971 ***
                *** SHIFT TO MIDYEAR OF FISCAL YEAR ***

YEAR.TITLE
YR.1971.FISCAL YEAR PROJECTION.  FY 1971 = JUL 70 TO JUN 71
DATE.SHIFT
YR.1971.WEEK.29

             *** CENSUS TAKEN IN 33RD WEEK OF SOLAR YEAR 1345 ***
                *** SHIFT TO MIDYEAR OF SOLAR YEAR CALENDAR ***

YEAR.TITLE
YR.1345.ASSUMPTION OF MOST RAPID ECONOMIC GROWTH  (POP UNITS=1000)
DATE.SHIFT
YR.1345.WEEK.33

1234567890123456789012345678901234567890123456789012345678901234567890123456789012345678901234567890
```

SCALE	Optional subject.	Default: No scaling
TOTAL.F	Desired total for females	
TOTAL.M	Same for males	

The input population may be increased or reduced by a scaling factor to produce total populations for males and females that are wanted by the user. Punch the desired totals in the first numeric data field (columns 11-20) of the two information cards. Scaling is done before date shifting by FIVFIV.

This subject allows one to submit an age distribution expressed as parts of one thousand or as percentages, and to scale that distribution to the desired population total. This is particularly useful when using model age distributions to distribute reported total populations by sex.

```
0          1          2          3          4          5          6          7          8
1234567890123456789012345678901234567890123456789012345678901234567890123456789012345678901234567890

                           EXAMPLES OF SCALE

      *** CREATES AN INPUT POPULATION FROM A PERCENTAGE DISTRIBUTION ***

INIT.POP
INIT.M.A        16.8        13.7        12.0        10.5         9.1         7.8         6.7
INIT.M.B         5.6         4.7         3.8         3.0         2.3         1.7         1.1
INIT.M.C          .7          .5
INIT.F.A        16.6        13.5        11.8        10.3         8.9         7.7         6.5
INIT.F.B         5.5         4.7         3.9         3.2         2.5         1.9         1.4
INIT.F.C          .9          .7
SCALE
TOTAL.F      12542.
TOTAL.M      12981.


          *** RAISES A CENSUS POPULATION TO A GIVEN TOTAL ***
                      *** ONLY FEMALES SHOWN ***

INIT.POP
INIT.F.A       1330.       1211.       1050.        815.        723.        542.        511.
INIT.F.B        491.        426.        341.        282.        243.        218.        186.
INIT.F.C        124.        101.              (FEMALE TOTAL IS 8594.)
        *** MALES NEXT ***
SCALE
TOTAL.F       9453.4
        *** MALES NEXT ***

1234567890123456789012345678901234567890123456789012345678901234567890123456789012345678901234567890
```

MORTALITY

either
MORT.LV.F
MORT.LV.M   Model levels for 7 periods
or
MORT.EZ.F
MORT.EZ.M   Expectation of life at birth ($\mathring{e}_0$) for 7 periods

This subject is used when whole model life tables are assumed. The use of split model life tables is explained under the next subject. The specification of level numbers, or average expectations of life at birth, enables FIVFIV to select the corresponding model life tables. Levels and values of $\mathring{e}_0$ may be expressed with as many decimal digits as desired.

Assumptions are punched for each of seven projection intervals: years 0-5, 5-10, . . . 30-35. Fields are the same as before, beginning with columns 11-20. Numbers should be right-justified with decimals punched.

If model levels are used to select life tables, the range is numbers 1.0 to 24.0 If $\mathring{e}_0$ is used, the limits are set by the range contained in the particular family of models. The user is able to select any one of the four regional families of model life tables ('East,' 'West,' 'North,' and 'South') prepared by A. J. Coale and P. Demeny. Models prepared by the user himself also may be used. The selection of the family of the life tables is explained later in this chapter.

If FIVFIV encounters empty fields, it assumes the mortality parameter of the preceding period. If mortality is assumed to be constant after the first or some subsequent period, the user may leave the rest of the card blank.

Male mortality may be estimated from female mortality, but not vice versa, by leaving all of the data fields blank on the male card. The computer will assign the same level of model life table to males as is assumed for females in each period. Assumptions must always be given for females, and the male card must always be included, even if empty.

```
0          1          2          3          4          5          6          7          8
1234567890123456789012345678901234567890123456789012345678901234567890123456789012345678901234567890


              EXAMPLES OF MORTALITY


         *** SELECTION IN TERMS OF MODEL LEVELS ***
      *** CONSTANT MORTALITY WILL PREVAIL WHERE FIELDS EMPTY ***

MORTALITY
MORT.LV.M          3.           3.5       4.0        4.5        5.0        5.5
MORT.LV.F          2.5          3.0       3.5        4.0        4.5        5.0


         *** SELECTION BY EXPECTATION OF LIFE AT BIRTH ***
     *** MALES EMPTY; HENCE WILL BE ASSIGNED SAME LEVEL AS FEMALES ***
       *** COMPUTER WILL DETERMINE MODEL LEVEL FOR FEMALES FROM E(0)

MORTALITY
MORT.EZ.F         32.       33.       34.       35.       41.       47.       53.
MORT.EZ.M


         *** CONSTANT MORTALITY AT SAME LEVEL FOR BOTH SEXES ***

MORTALITY
MORT.LV.F      11.5
MORT.LV.M

1234567890123456789012345678901234567890123456789012345678901234567890123456789012345678901234567890
```

MORT.SPLIT	Alternative to MORTALITY

either
CHILD.LV.F
CHILD.LV.M   Model levels for 7 periods
or
CHILD.IM.F
CHILD.IM.M   Infant mortality ($1000 \cdot {}_1q_0$) for 7 periods
and
ADULT.LV.F
ADULT.LV.M   Model levels for 7 periods
or
ADULT.E5.F
ADULT.E5.M   Expectation of life at age 5 ($\mathring{e}_5$) for 7 periods

When split mortality is assumed, a pair of cards is needed for mortality below age 5, and a pair for above age 5. Either pair may come first, and either sex may come first within a pair of cards. The data fields are arranged exactly as for MORTALITY.

The mode of selection may be levels for mortality below age 5, or above age 5, or both. If it is not convenient to specify levels, infant mortality rates (expressed as deaths per thousand births) may be used to select a segment of a life table for mortality below age 5. Above age 5, the expectation of life at age 5 ($\mathring{e}_5$) may be used. When segments of different models are selected below and above age 5, practically any plausible relationship between early childhood mortality and mortality at higher ages can be approximated. Thus, the deviant patterns of mortality at very young ages relative to older ages often found in developing countries are suitably represented by MORT.SPLIT.

Assumptions should be worked out separately for males and females if possible. If not, males may be estimated from females by leaving the data fields blank on the corresponding male card or cards. The male cards must be included, however.

Constant mortality is assumed by giving assumptions only for the first period and leaving the remainder of the card blank. Blank fields, except the first, are always assigned the assumptions of the preceding interval. Thus, the minimum necessary information is an assumption for females during the first period.

```
0         1         2         3         4         5         6         7         8
1234567890123456789012345678901234567890123456789012345678901234567890123456789012345678901234567890

                        EXAMPLES OF MORT.SPLIT

*** SELECTS UNDER AGE 5 BY INFANT MORTALITY AND OVER 5 BY LEVEL ***
      *** LETS MALE ASSUMPTIONS BE DETERMINED BY FEMALES ***
MORT.SPLIT
CHILD.IM.M
CHILD.IM.F     185.       168.3      151.2      134.0      116.8       99.2       82.
ADULT.LV.M
ADULT.LV.F      10.        11.        12.        13.        14.        15.        16.

*** SIMULATE EFFECT OF AN INCREASE IN SURVIVAL ONLY FOR PERSONS OVER AGE 5 ***
MORT.SPLIT
CHILD.LV.F      10.
CHILD.LV.M
ADULT.E5.F      10.        11.        12.        13.        14.        15.        16.
ADULT.E5.M
                                                                        (continued)
```

```
     *** SELECTS MORTALITY RATES OVER AGE  5 BY SPECIFYING E(5) ***
                    *** CONSTANT MORTALITY ***

MORT.SPLIT
CHILD.LV.F        12.
CHILD.LV.M        13.
ADULT.LV.F        56.5
ADULT.LV.M        55.5

12345678901234567890123456789012345678901234567890123456789012345678901234567890
```

FERTILITY

TOTAL.FERT	First card; total fertility for 7 periods
and	
FERDIST1.#	
FERDIST2.#	Age-specific fertility rates for ages 15-19, . . . 45-49
FERDISTn.#	
and	
FEND	Last information card; contains no data

Assumptions concerning fertility are needed in the form of age-specific fertility rates (ASFR) for women by five-year age groups from 15 to 49. The ASFRs may be from a standard schedule that sums to a total fertility of 1.0, or some other distribution. Assumptions about total fertility are given separately on the TOTAL.FERT card so that they may be varied from period to period or projection to projection without necessarily repunching the distribution of fertility by age of woman that is given on the FERDIST cards.

Total fertility for the seven projection intervals is shown on the first information card in the usual seven-field arrangement. If total fertility is to remain constant after the first or some other period, the rest of the data fields may be left blank. Fractional levels are acceptable.

The distribution of age-specific fertility is given on the FERDIST information cards. The computer will scale whatever is given to the total fertility shown on the TOTAL.FERT card for the same period. Therefore, users may submit a distribution of fertility by age (e.g., a standard distribution), or the actual age-specific fertility that is assumed, whichever they prefer. When information about the distribution of fertility by age of woman is scarce, a standard distribution referring to a population with similar marriage and birth-control characteristics may be used.

A fertility distribution by age is needed for each projection interval, but it is not necessary to punch seven cards if the distribution is held constant for more than one period. Replace the symbol # by a digit that shows the number of successive five-year projection intervals to which that particular distribution will apply. The specification of fertility distributions by age is independent of total fertility, which may or may not be changed from one period to the next. The FERDIST cards are placed in sequence and numbered from 1 to n as indicated. The FERDIST cards will cover seven periods altogether. Hence, the numbers that replace the symbol # should add to 7.

A final card, FEND, with no data, is always necessary to close this subject.

```
0         1         2         3         4         5         6         7         8
1234567890123456789012345678901234567890123456789012345678901234567890123456789 0
```

EXAMPLES OF FERTILITY

*** ONE STANDARD SCHEDULE OF ASFR COMBINED WITH CHANGUNG TF ***
*** FERTILITY CONSTANT AFTER THIRD PERIOD ***

```
FERTILITY
TOTAL.FERT      5.0         4.0         3.0
FERDIST1.7     .018        .042        .056        .044        .028        .010        .002
FEND
```

*** SAME ASSUMPTIONS WRITTEN DIFFERENTLY: USER MULTIPLIED STANDARD SCHEDULE ***
*** OF ASFR BY TF. NOTE THE CONVENIENCE OF PRIOR METHOD ***

```
FERTILITY
TOTAL.FERT      5.0         4.0         3.0
FERDIST1.1     .090        .210        .280        .220        .140        .050        .010
FERDIST2.1     .072        .168        .224        .176        .112        .040        .008
FERDIST3.5     .054        .126        .168        .132        .084        .030        .006
FEND
```

*** SAME ASSUMPTIONS WRITTEN DIFFERENTLY: DISTRIBUTION OF ASFR IN FIRST ***
*** PERIOD IS USED FOR LATER PERIODS ALSO ***

```
FERTILITY
TOTAL.FERT      5.0         4.0         3.0
FERDIST1.7     .090        .210        .280        .220        .140        .050        .010
FEND
```

*** DISTRIBUTION OF ASFR CHANGES TWICE ***

```
FERTILITY
TOTAL.FERT      6.0         5.8         5.6         5.4         5.0         4.5         4.0
FERDIST1.4     .018        .042        .056        .044        .028        .010        .002
FERDIST2.2     .024        .048        .055        .040        .024        .007        .002
FERDIST3.1     .029        .055        .054        .037        .020        .004        .001
FEND
```

*** ANALYTICAL PROJECTION APPROXIMATING ZERO BIRTHS ***
*** ASSUME SMALL TF AND ANY FERDIST ***

```
FERTILITY
TOTAL.FERT     .000001
FERDIST1.7      .1          .1          .1          .1          .1          .1          .1
FEND
```

```
1234567890123456789012345678901234567890123456789012345678901234567890123456789 0
```

SEXRATIO	Optional subject.	Default: Sex ratio=105.
MPERHUNDF	Sex ratio	

The sex ratio of births is expressed as a number of males per hundred females. It is punched in the first numeric data field (columns 11-20) and may be carried to one or more decimal digits if desired. The default value is normally accepted unless there is accurate information available to show a different sex ratio or if the population is Black. The sex ratio of Black populations may be assumed to be 103.

```
0         1         2         3         4         5         6         7         8
12345678901234567890123456789012345678901234567890123456789012345678901234567890

                        EXAMPLE OF SEXRATIO
          *** REPLACE CONVENTIONAL 105.0 WITH LOCAL ESTIMATE ***

SEXRATIO
MPERHUNDF      105.73

12345678901234567890123456789012345678901234567890123456789012345678901234567890
```

MIGRATION	Quantity option.	Default: Zero migration
MIGLEVEL.F	Female quantities for 7 periods	These two cards, in either
MIGLEVEL.M	Males. Annual levels.	order, must come first.
and		
MIGRFn.#.A		
MIGRFn.#.B	Female distributions of migration by age. *n* sets	
MIGRFn.#.C		
and		
MIGRMn.#.A		
MIGRMn.#.B	Male distributions of migration by age. *n* sets	
MIGRMn.#.C		
and		
MEND	Last information card; contains no data	

Migration assumptions may require many cards or only a small number, depending upon how often the age distribution of migrants for one or the other sex changes. Since each sex is processed separately by the computer, it does not matter whether sets of male or female cards are placed first.

The yearly level of net migration during each five-year period is punched by sex on the first two information cards. Out-migration is shown by negative numbers. Empty data fields are read as zeroes. Quantities must be punched for every period if the assumption is not zero. The quantity of migrants should be expressed in the same units as the population (e.g., hundreds or thousands).

In order to give the distribution of migrants by age, a three-card set is necessary to cover the standard 16 age groups. A set is needed for each sex with data punched in data fields exactly as for the initial population. Following the same principle as for fertility distributions, migrant distributions may apply to more than one five-year period, in which event duplicate cards do not have to be punched.

The sets of information cards for age distributions are numbered sequentially from 1 to *n* in column 6. If only one distribution is used for the entire projection, there will be only one set with *n* replaced by 1. If the age distribution changes to a second and then a third one, there will be three sets, *n* being replaced by 1 in the first, 2 in the second, and 3 in the third. In order to tell the computer for how many five-year periods to use each set, a number replaces the symbol #.

The distribution of migrants by age will be scaled up or down as necessary to bring the total into agreement with the yearly level on the MIGLEVEL card for the corresponding sex and time period. Therefore, distributions can be given as percentages of a total, or as actual quantities, or as distributed in a previous projection that may add to any total whatsoever. MIGLEVEL assumptions will determine the total of migrants.

The number of male and female data cards may be the same or different, since the age distribution does not need to be changed at the same dates for both. However, both will usually change together. If there is no migration during certain periods, any distribution, including zeroes, can be given in order to provide assumptions for all seven periods.

Positive and negative values may appear together in the age structure. If migration is assumed, the algebraic total for the age structure must be non-zero. A good practice when both negative and positive values are assumed is to punch the actual positive and negative numbers by age group on the MIGR cards. Then make sure there is a small net balance. The net balance goes on the MIGLEVEL card. For example, suppose that the net balance is zero and that migration is distributed among three age groups as follows: +50.0, −20.0, and −30.0. Replace the first number by an approximation, 50.01, and show a net balance of migration of .01 on the MIGLEVEL card. If a number much smaller than .01 is used for the net balance, losses of precision during computation by the computer may distort the original assumption.

```
0         1         2         3         4         5         6         7         8
1234567890123456789012345678901234567890123456789012345678901234567890123456789012345678901234567890

          EXAMPLES OF MIGRATION (QUANTITY OPTION)

      *** NET MIGRATION VARIES FRCM POSITIVE TO NEGATIVE ***
            *** CONSTANT DISTRIBUTION BY AGE ***

MIGRATICN
MIGLEVEL.F      100.        75.        50.        25.        0.        -50.       -50.
MIGLEVEL.M      150.       100.        50.         0.        0.        -75.       -80.
MIGRF1.7.A        9.         8.         7.         7.       20.         25.        20.
MIGRF1.7.B        5.         2.         1.         1.        0.          0.         0.
MIGRF1.7.C        0.         0.
MIGRM1.7.A       11.        10.        14.        20.       25.         25.        20.
MIGRM1.7.B       12.         8.         4.         1.
MIGRM1.7.C                                (NOTE EMPTY FIELDS ARE SAME AS ZEROS)
MEND


      *** DISTRIBUTICN OF MIGRANTS BY AGE VARIES TWICE ***
          *** NEGATIVES ALLOWED.  ONLY FEMALES SHOWN ***

MIGRF1.1.A       13.         9.         7.         7.       20.         25.        20.
MIGRF1.1.B        5.         1.        -3.        -2.       -1.         -1.
MIGRF1.1.C                                (NOTE FIRST SET FOR ONE PERIOD)
MIGRF2.1.A        9.         8.         7.         7.       20.         25.        20.
MIGRF2.1.B        5.         2.         1.         1.
MIGRF2.1.C                                (NOTE SECOND SET FOR ONE PERIOD)
MIGRF3.5.A        4.         3.         2.         2.       14.         25.        25.
MIGRF3.5.B       15.         8.         2.
MIGRF3.5.C                                (NOTE THIRD SET FOR FIVE PERIODS)

1234567890123456789012345678901234567890123456789012345678901234567890123456789012345678901234567890
```

MIGRATION	Rates option. Alternative to quantities
RATES	First card; contains no data
and	
MIGRFn.#.A	
MIGRFn.#.B	Female migration per thousand population for 16 age groups;
MIGRFn.#.C	n sets
and	
MIGRMn.#.A	
MIGRMn.#.C	Male migration per thousand population for 16 age groups;
MIGRMn.#.D	n sets
and	
MEND	

The RATES card is used to declare that the migration assumptions are in the form of migration rates instead of quantities of migrants as in the previous subject. Migration rates are defined as net numbers of migrants (positive means inward and negative means outward) per thousand population in the age-sex group. There are 16 rates for each sex corresponding with the standard 16 five-year age groups. Rates may be zero, punched as 0., or left empty.

The symbols n and # have the same meaning as in the previous subject. Sets of rates are numbered 1,2, . . . n. The length of the time period to which any one set of rates applies is given by #, measuring time in five-year projection periods. Thus, 2 would indicate two five-year projection periods.

```
0         1         2         3         4         5         6         7         8
1234567890123456789012345678901234567890123456789012345678901234567890123456789012345678 90

                        EXAMPLES OF MIGRATION (RATES OPTION)

                 *** MIGRATION CONCENTRATED IN WORKING AGES ***
             *** ALWAYS EXPRESSED AS NET MIGRANTS PER THOUSAND POPULATION ***

MIGRATION
RATES
MIGRF1.7.A                             1.7       5.3       4.0       2.0        .50
MIGRF1.7.B
MIGRF1.7.C
MIGRM1.7.A                   5.1       8.7      20.4      35.0      34.1       12.0
MIGRM1.7.B         7.8       3.1       1.1
MIGRM1.7.C
MEND
            *** FEMALE RATES CHANGE TWICE AND ARE ZERO IN LAST PERIOD ***
                    *** MALES CONSTANT ALL PERIODS ***
MIGRATION
RATES
MIGRM1.7.A        36.6      51.1      58.5      37.5      45.0      46.1       33.3
MIGRM1.7.B        40.1      39.6      31.3      15.9      10.9       5.0        3.0
MIGRM1.7.C         2.0       1.0
MIGRF1.2.A        16.0      23.2      34.0      24.6       8.3       9.0       17.6
MIGRF1.2.B        13.9       8.4       8.7       8.6       9.9       8.0        8.0
MIGRF1.2.C         7.0       6.0
MIGRF2.4.A        38.38     53.57     58.75     36.59     18.17     26.28      38.23
MIGRF2.4.B        32.22     20.35     20.06     28.36     15.34     14.00      12.00
MIGRF2.4.C        10.00      8.00
MIGRF3.1.A
MIGRF3.1.B              (NOTE EMPTY FIELDS SIGNIFY ZERO RATES)
MIGRF3.1.C
MEND

12345678901234567890123456789012345678901234567890123456789012345678901234567890
```

FINDMIGRATION	Optional subject. Default: Zero migration
TARGETPOP	Total population at dates 5, 10, . . . 35
MPERHUNDF	Sex ratio of migrants, 7 periods

These two cards, in either order, must come first.

and	
MIGRFn.#.A	
MIGRFn.#.B	Female distributions by age. n sets
MIGRFn.#.C	
and	
MIGRMn.#.A	
MIGRMn.#.B	Male distributions by age. n sets
MIGRMn.#.C	
and	
MEND	Last information card; contains no data

When this subject is used, the total population to be reached at each projection date is assumed, and the program computes the amount of migration (positive or negative) to attain the total population. The subject is usually used to make projections of the urban population when a rate of increase in urban population is assumed directly. The total population that will be reached at each projection date is estimated by the user and then punched on the TARGETPOP card. There are seven data fields corresponding with dates 5, 10, . . . 35. Use the same units as elsewhere for the population (e.g., thousands or hundreds). If any of the seven fields are left empty, the next preceding target will be assumed.

The sex ratio of total male to total female migrants also must be given. It refers to all ages combined. The sex ratio is expressed as a number of males per hundred females and may be given for up to seven periods on the MPERHUNDF card. If not given for all periods, the last value will be assumed for the empty fields. Either one of the two initial information cards may be given first. Next come the MIGR cards.

The age distribution of migrants at time of migration is assumed on the MIGR cards. They are prepared in exactly the same way as for the MIGRATION subject. There must be a non-zero distribution by age for both sexes for all seven periods.

```
0         1         2         3         4         5         6         7         8
1234567890123456789012345678901234567890123456789012345678901234567890123456789090
```

EXAMPLES OF FINDMIGRATION

```
       *** MAKE A PROJECTION FOR 15 YEARS (3 TARGETS AT 5, 10, 15) ***
FINDMIGRATION
TARGETPOP    3051.5    3728.4    4528.9    (NOTE EMPTY FOR DATES NOT WANTED)
MPERHUNDF     150.      130.      118.
MIGRF1.7.A    2.45      3.51      3.86      2.28      .87      1.11      1.58
MIGRF1.7.B    1.38       .69       .49       .60      .37       .35       .30
MIGRF1.7.C     .25       .20
MIGRM1.7.A    2.35      3.43      4.08      2.62     2.27      2.20      1.42
MIGRM1.7.B    1.78      1.52       .91       .38      .26       .25       .24
MIGRM1.7.C     .23       .30
MEND
```

```
          *** IF ALL MIGRANTS ARE MALES, USE LARGE NUMBER FOR MPERHUNDF ***

FINDMIGRATION
TARGETPOP      3051.5      3728.4      4528.9
MPERHUNDF      999999.                          (NOTE EMPTY FIELDS TAKE PRECEDING VALUE)
MIGRF1.7.A        1.          1.          1.          1.
MIGRF1.7.B              (NOTE USE OF ANY NON-ZERO DISTRIBUTION FOR FEMALES)
MIGRF1.7.C              (NOTE NON-ZERO DISTRIBUTION NECESSARY FOR BOTH SEXES)
MIGRM1.7.A        1.          1.
MIGRM1.7.B
MIGRM1.7.C
MEND


          *** IF ALL MIGRANTS ARE FEMALE, USE SMALL MPERHUNDF ***

MPERHUNDF      .00001
          *** INCLUDE NON-ZERO M AND F MIGR CARDS ***

1234567890123456789012345678901234567890123456789012345678901234567890123456789 0
```

STABLEXTEND   Optional subject.   Default: No extension

This subject will cause the projection to be extended an additional 35 years
with no change in assumptions concerning fertility, mortality, and migration. The
assumptions for the extension come from the last five-year period of the unextended
projection.

More than one STABLEXTEND header card may be given in the set of
instructions. For each card given, the projection will be extended another 35 years.
No information cards are given with this subject.

```
0         1         2         3         4         5         6         7         8
1234567890123456789012345678901234567890123456789012345678901234567890123456789 0
```

EXAMPLES OF STABLEXTEND

```
          *** INVESTIGATE HOW A STABLE POPULATION IS REACHED ***
              *** PROJECTION OF (4 X 35) = 140 YEARS ***

YEAR.TITLE
YR.1975.HYPOTHETICAL STABILIZATION OF POPULATION AT GRR OF 0.8
INIT.POP
OLD.POP.1975
STABLEXTEND
STABLEXTEND
STABLEXTEND
MORTALITY
MORT.LV.F      22.
MORT.LV.M
FERTILITY
TOTAL.FERT     1.64      (NOTE TF=2.05*0.8=1.64)
FERDIST1.7     .008      .032      .054      .050      .034      .018      .004
FEND
END PROJECTION


1234567890123456789012345678901234567890123456789012345678901234567890123456789 0
```

PRODUCTION   Optional subject.

Errors in user input typically cause FIVFIV to terminate only the projection involved and to pass on to the next set of projection instructions. For large-scale production runs, where a number of projections are made with multiple copies or special paper, the user may prefer to stop execution if any error is detected, so as not to waste more time and paper on subsequent projections. Inclusion of PRODUCTION within the first set of instructions to which it applies will end all subsequent projections if any error is found in this or any subsequent projection. The PRODUCTION card needs to be included only once.

No information card is needed for this subject.

```
0          1          2          3          4          5          6          7          8
1234567890123456789012345678901234567890123456789012345678901234567890123456789012345678901234567890

                         EXAMPLE  OF  PRODUCTION

          *** USUALLY IS FIRST CARD OF FIRST PROJECTION OF A SERIES ***

PRODUCTION
YEAR.TITLE
YR.1982.METROPOLITAN AREA 7.   ALTERNATIVE 'B'.   (POP UNITS = 100)
   *** REST OF INSTRUCTIONS FOLLOW ***

123456789012345678901234567890123456789012345678901234567890123456789012345678901234567890
```

PUNCH.FIVE   Optional subject.   Default: No punched projection

This subject will cause a deck of cards containing the FIVFIV projection results to be punched. The subject header can be included more than one time, in which event more than one deck will be punched. These punched cards are different from those passed to SINSIN, and are optional. The PUNCH.FIVE option may be used to transfer the output of the FIVFIV model to a planning model.

Before using PUNCH.FIVE, note whether the local installation of FIVFIV and SINSIN provides for communication between the two programs by punched cards (Job Stream 2 in combination with Job Stream 1, as explained in Appendix Two, page 135). If so, do not use PUNCH.FIVE in the same projection as SINSIN subjects (REGROUP and others, explained in later chapters). SINSIN subjects and PUNCH.FIVE may be used in the same run provided they appear in different projections. Hence, to use both, duplicate the instruction cards for the projection and give them once with PUNCH.FIVE and once with SINSIN subjects. There is no restriction on when to use PUNCH.FIVE if using Job Streams 3 or 4 (see Appendix Two, page 136).

No information card is needed for this subject.

```
0          1          2          3          4          5          6          7          8
1234567890123456789012345678901234567890123456789012345678901234567890123456789012345678901234567890

                         EXAMPLE OF PUNCH.FIVE

     *** INCLUDES MIDPERIOD POPULATION, BIRTHS, DEATHS, AND MIGRANTS ***
              *** REQUESTS A DECK OF CARDS FROM FIVFIV ***

YEAR.TITLE
YR.1982.ALTERNATIVE 2:   BASIS FOR 20 YEAR STUDY OF DOMESTIC WASTE DISPOSAL
PUNCH.FIVE
    *** OTHER SUBJECTS IN ANY ORDER ***

123456789012345678901234567890123456789012345678901234567890123456789012345678901234567890
```

<u>END PROJECTION</u> **Always comes last**

This subject has no data. END PROJECTION <u>must be the last card in the set of instructions for one projection.</u> If omitted, the computer will continue to read instructions, taking them from the next projection. Thus, the next projection may be defective as well. There must be an END PROJECTION card after every set of projection instructions. The order of subjects prior to this card is optional with the user.

Additional subjects may be given to FIVFIV, to be passed by FIVFIV to SINSIN for execution. They are explained in subsequent chapters.

SELECTION OF LIFE TABLES

The user has a choice among four regional families of model life tables. Survival rates from the four families and certain other mortality information have been punched on decks of cards that are furnished with the package programs. The user selects one of these small decks of cards, according to the family he wants to use, and submits it to the computer along with his set (or sets) of instructions for projections. Ordinarily, the user will not want to substitute life-table survival rates different from those in the standard models, but if he does, an explanation of how to do so is given below.

The card deck of model life-table values consists of 72 cards for females (F) and 72 cards for males (M), either sex first. The models are arranged in ascending order starting with level 1, which corresponds with a life expectation at birth for females of 20.0 years, and rises at intervals of 2.5 years. The computer interpolates linearly between levels for all intermediate values. An example of the female part of the card deck is shown in Example 1.2.

EXAMPLE 1.2 Excerpt from 'South' Life-Table Deck for Females

```
0          1          2          3          4          5          6          7          8
1234567890123456789012345678901234567890123456789012345678901234567890123456789012345678901234567890

                     *** SHOWS MODEL LEVELS 1, 2, AND 24 ***

'SOUTH' F  1 0.57447 0.73046 0.92985 0.94323 0.92649 0.91543 0.91063 0.90657
'SOUTH' F  2 0.90368 0.90076 0.88425 0.84772 0.77684 0.66780 0.52977 0.36503
'SOUTH' F  3 0.22202  69300.   55531.   49192.   45845.   43943.   20.000  38.977
'SOUTH' F  4 0.60405 0.75838 0.93648 0.94835 0.93304 0.92290 0.91847 0.91468
'SOUTH' F  5 0.91181 0.90876 0.89316 0.85910 0.79308 0.69094 0.55948 0.40002
'SOUTH' F  6 0.24655  71551.   58633.   52685.   49544.   47760.   22.500  40.787
        *** CONTINUE ***
'SOUTH' F 70 0.96630 0.99647 0.99933 0.99924 0.99886 0.99845 0.99802 0.99742
'SOUTH' F 71 0.99619 0.99404 0.99040 0.98504 0.97592 0.95708 0.91668 0.83676
'SOUTH' F 72 0.56265  96774.   96550.   96436.   96369.   96324.   77.500  75.442
        *** MALES NOT SHOWN HERE ***

 1234567890123456789012345678901234567890123456789012345678901234567890123456789012345678901234567890
```

Cards are punched with a name of up to eight characters, including apostrophes, in the first eight columns. The first three cards refer to level 1, the next three to level 2, and so on, up to level 24. Each set of three cards holds a string of 24 values computed from a single model. The values in sequence are:

Order	Life-table notation	
1	$_5L_0 / (5l_0)$	
2–16	$_5L_{x+5} / {}_5L_x$	$(x = 0, 5, \ldots 70)$
17	T_{80} / T_{75}	
18–22	l_x	$(x = 1, 2, \ldots 5)$
23–24	$\dot{e}_x$	$(x = 0, 5)$

The user can substitute values from different life tables of his own choosing by repunching the cards for levels 1, 2, and so on, as far as desired. He can then ask under the subject MORTALITY for those same life-table values, or for values between them that will be computed by interpolation. He must select mortality by specifying levels.

For example, suppose a life table has been estimated for the local population in 1970, and another life table is selected from another source to represent mortality projected 20 years to 1990. The 1970 life table can be substituted for level 1 and the 1990 life table for level 2, as in Example 1.3. The projection for intervening periods is done by calling for fractional levels between levels 1 and 2, as in Example 1.4.

Included in the special life-table deck is a life table at level 24 that would produce no deaths. It could be used to make projections that show how much, or how little, the future size of a population that has already attained high life expectancy would be affected by further increases in longevity.

The rules for making one's own deck of life tables are as follows: Provide cards for the same number of levels, 24 for each sex. Unused levels may be empty. The deck must be labeled with the same name in the first eight columns, including apostrophes, if used (e.g., 'MY LT'), and the sex code M or F. The 144 cards must also be ordered by numbers 1 to 72 for each sex. The deck in Example 1.3 may be modified to fit any special needs.

PREPARATION OF JOB DECKS

Projections are obtained from the computer by submitting "jobs." The sequence of cards surrounding the FIVFIV program, life-table data, and user instructions is the "job stream." It varies slightly from installation to installation and has to be learned locally at the time the package is installed. The following is a typical job deck, arranged from first to last cards (alternative job decks for alternative computer systems are explained in Appendix Two):

      ** System control card(s)
    FIVFIV program deck
      ** System control card(s)
    Life-table data.   (One family; either sex first)
    Instructions for one projection
    Instructions for additional projections
    HALT card   (Punch HALT in columns 1–4)
      ** System control card(s)

EXAMPLE 1.3   Deck of Substitute Life-Table Cards

```
0           1           2           3           4           5           6           7           8
1234567890123456789012345678901234567890123456789012345678901234567890123456789012345678901234567890

'MY LT'  F  1 0.74474  0.87228  0.96556  0.97104  0.96204  0.95594  0.95313  0.95054
'MY LT'  F  2 0.94771  0.94412  0.93267  0.90961  0.86558  0.79466  0.69358  0.55827
'MY LT'  F  3 0.34197  81504.   73318.   69550.   67560.   66429.   37.500   50.846
'MY LT'  F  4 0.88895  0.96125  0.98603  0.98523  0.97998  0.97572  0.97236  0.96864
'MY LT'  F  5 0.96426  0.95810  0.94636  0.92742  0.89661  0.84916  0.77830  0.67648
'MY LT'  F  6 0.42345  90661.   88364.   87324.   86646.   86127.   55.000   58.698
'MY LT'  F  7
'MY LT'  F  8
'MY LT'  F  9
'MY LT'  F 10
'MY LT'  F 11
'MY LT'  F 12
'MY LT'  F 13
'MY LT'  F 14
       *** CONTINUE ***
'MY LT'  F 70 1.0      1.0      1.0      1.0      1.0      1.0      1.0      1.0
'MY LT'  F 71 1.0      1.0      1.0      1.0      1.0      1.0      1.0      1.0
'MY LT'  F 72 1.0      100000.  100000.  100000.  100000.  100000.  999999.  999999.
'MY LT'  M  1 0.73079  0.87567  0.96916  0.97446  0.96156  0.95366  0.95312  0.95005
'MY LT'  M  2 0.94216  0.93042  0.91304  0.88555  0.84081  0.77340  0.67637  0.54439
'MY LT'  M  3 0.33311  79632.   71878.   68301.   66384.   65326.   36.226   49.861
'MY LT'  M  4 0.87196  0.95941  0.98620  0.98536  0.97870  0.97392  0.97094  0.96591
'MY LT'  M  5 0.95792  0.94643  0.92904  0.90354  0.86569  0.81117  0.73552  0.63147
'MY LT'  M  6 0.39303  88864.   86523.   85498.   84826.   84327.   51.831   56.294
'MY LT'  M  7
'MY LT'  M  8
'MY LT'  M  9
'MY LT'  M 10
'MY LT'  M 11
'MY LT'  M 12
'MY LT'  M 13
'MY LT'  M 14
       *** CONTINUE ***
'MY LT'  M 70 1.0      1.0      1.0      1.0      1.0      1.0      1.0      1.0
'MY LT'  M 71 1.0      1.0      1.0      1.0      1.0      1.0      1.0      1.0
'MY LT'  M 72 1.0      100000.  100000.  100000.  100000.  100000.  999999.  999999.

1234567890123456789012345678901234567890123456789012345678901234567890123456789012345678901234567890
```

As many sets of instructions may be given as desired. The FIVFIV FORTRAN program and life-table data are supplied as part of the package (see Appendix Two). System control cards are standard at every computer center and can be learned by local inquiry. The HALT card causes the job to be completed in a normal manner on the computer. If omitted accidentally, FIVFIV computations will be made correctly, but there will be a nasty computer message on the last page of output.

ERRORS AND DIAGNOSIS

Almost invariably errors are the fault of the user. This is fortunate, because he can correct them. As an aid to diagnosis of errors, FIVFIV prints messages and does certain other things that may help. It checks the life-table

EXAMPLE 1.4 Instructions for Projections with MY LT

```
0         1         2         3         4         5         6         7         8
1234567890123456789012345678901234567890123456789012345678901234567890123456789 0

    *** SELECTS MORTALITY BY INTERPOLATION BETWEEN LEVELS OF 'MY LT' ***

YEAR.TITLE
YR.1975.SURVIVAL IMPROVES FROM CURRENT LEVELS TO COUNTRY X LEVELS IN 35 YEARS
MORTALITY
MORT.LV.F          1.        1.2       1.4       1.6       1.75      1.9       2.0
MORT.LV.M          1.        1.25      1.50      1.75      1.85      1.9       2.0


        *** PROJECTION FOR A POPULATION WITH NO DEATHS ***
            *** USE LEVEL 24 OF 'MY LT' ***

YEAR.TITLE
YR.   0.DEMONSTRATE GROWTH BY BIRTHS WITHOUT DECREMENTS IN COHORTS BY DEATHS
MORTALITY
MORT.LV.F          24.
MORT.LV.M

1234567890123456789012345678901234567890123456789012345678901234567890123456789 0
```

input to be certain that the cards are in correct order and, if not, prints a message indicating what went wrong. It examines the order of each set of instructions for a projection. If it expects a subject header and finds none or one that is not valid, it prints what it found, followed by a message. It also checks the information cards for valid labeling and makes other tests of validity. Most error messages are self-explanatory. When the FIVFIV message includes a code letter, look it up in Appendix Three.

The user can learn to use FIVFIV by starting with a first job and letting the computer tell him where to look for errors. Thus, to some extent, the machine can help the new user overcome errors and get satisfactory results. The main thing is not to fear imperfection when getting started. One quickly learns to fulfill the computer's demand for accuracy, and thus acquires an obedient and powerful tool.

Most errors are due to incorrect punching. Labels on cards must agree exactly with those prescribed in this manual. Column positioning of labels and data must be checked when particular cards seem to be causing trouble. An extra decimal point or a stray letter in a numeric data field may cause the entire job to terminate abruptly. Completely empty cards should never appear as extra cards anywhere in the job deck.

Suggestions concerning how to locate trouble in the user deck, if it occurs, are given in Appendix Three. A directory of all subjects is given in Appendix Four at the end of the book. A little experience with diagnosis and correction of errors builds confidence in running jobs and will enable the analyst to obtain valid population projections.

CHAPTER TWO: EXAMPLES OF NATIONAL PROJECTIONS _____

This chapter presents an example of how to make national projections by the modified cohort-component method. The example refers to Turkey. The purpose of the illustration is to show an analytical procedure, rather than to defend the particular assumptions and projections that are made. Since the projections differ in many details from those made by the State Planning Organization of that country for the Third Five-Year Plan (1972–1977), it should be clearly understood that these projections have no official standing.

There will be two projections: One refers to the implications of a laissez-faire population policy and the other to a positive population policy. The Third Five-Year Plan is based on the policy assumptions that there will be no special effort by the government to: (1) accelerate a fertility decline that is already in progress; (2) speed up the current pace of reorganization and extension of health services; or (3) interfere with the international movement of Turkish workers beyond the enforcement of normal travel formalities. The laissez-faire projection shows how the population will develop in the presence of such policies. It is assumed that economic development will continue at a high rate, and that is why a demographic transformation, even though a slow and costly one, is shown in spite of the laissez-faire policy.

The second projection will explore the implications of a positive population policy consisting of: (1) accelerated expansion of health services, particularly in relation to infants and young children, for whom mortality is heavy in Turkey; and (2) a vigorous program for making contraceptive and abortion services available to women of all groups and communities. Laissez-faire assumptions will be retained with respect to international migration. In order to tie these alternative sets of assumptions closely to planning alternatives in Turkey, it would be necessary to participate fully in on-the-spot studies, which has not been possible. Therefore, the projections are, as already stressed, primarily illustrative of a procedure, rather than precise predictions of what will happen if one set of policies rather than the other is followed.

A complete set of FIVFIV instructions for the two projections is shown in Example 2.1. The following discussion of each subject shows how the assumptions were prepared. The results of one of the projections is given as an illustration of output.

DATING AND WITHIN-YEAR POSITIONING

For planning purposes, a specific time period for the projection is selected. In Turkey, the five-year plan refers to 1972–1977. A long-term plan was also prepared for 1972–1995 in order to evaluate Turkey's prospects upon reaching the target date (1995) for full membership in the European Economic Community. Thus, the long-term plan refers to 23 years. Because that is scarcely long enough to evaluate economic-demographic interaction, a 30-year perspective will be used in the example that follows.

YEAR.TITLE

Although the planning period starts with the year 1972, the nearest preceding date for information about the population is 1970. A census was taken in that year, and a sample of census returns was tabulated and published.[1] Therefore, the FIVFIV projection will start from 1970 and be carried 35 years. SINSIN will be used at a later stage of the computations to generate annual estimates that can be fitted exactly to the 30-year long-term planning period from 1972 to 2002. The reference to "thousands" in the title shows that data will be submitted in that form, and consequently reported in the same units.

DATE.SHIFT

Economic variables include annual flows, such as gross national product, investment, and consumption. When population quantities are used as denominators in relation to annual flows, it is useful to have the population estimates refer to midyear. This is accomplished by positioning the starting date on midyear with this subject. The Turkish census was taken on October 25; hence, the instruction states week 43.

If population figures are wanted for the beginning of the year instead of midyear, they may be obtained by interpolating between successive annual estimates positioned at midyear. If large numbers of estimates are needed, so that hand calculation is too laborious, the computer can be "fooled" into providing estimates for the beginning of the year even though the output will continue to be labeled as "midyear." Add 26 weeks to the

---

[1] State Institute of Statistics, *25 Ekim 1970 Genel Nüfus Sayimi Ornekleme Sonuçlari* [Census of the population 25 October 1970, sampling results], Publication no. 659 (Ankara: State Institute of Statistics, 1972).

EXAMPLE 2.1   Instruction Cards for Projections A and B

```
0         1         2         3         4         5         6         7         8
1234567890123456789012345678901234567890123456789012345678901234567890123456789012345678 90

YEAR.TITLE
YR.1970.TURKEY 'A'  LAISSEZ-FAIRE POPULATION POLICY  (POP IN THOUSANDS)
DATE.SHIFT
YR.1970.WEEK.43
INIT.POP
INIT.F.A    2761.7   2384.8   2157.6   1930.9   1331.2   1076.2   1056.0
INIT.F.B    1054.9    850.9    683.7    484.5    559.9    444.4    392.2
INIT.F.C     232.7    201.9
INIT.M.A    2791.4   2456.6   2222.8   1885.2   1528.7   1165.4    989.7
INIT.M.B    1116.4    909.8    703.5    483.3    598.5    467.4    378.2
INIT.M.C     225.2    140.9
MORT.SPLIT
CHILD.LV.F    15.2     16.3     17.4     18.3     19.0     19.6     20.0
CHILD.LV.M    16.4     17.2     18.0     18.6     19.2     19.6     20.0
ADULT.LV.F    18.4     18.9     19.3     19.7     20.0     20.3     20.6
ADULT.LV.M    19.3     19.6     19.8     20.0     20.2     20.4     20.6
FERTILITY
TOTAL.FERT    5.45     5.13     4.80     4.48     4.15     3.83     3.50
FERDIST1.1    .015     .051     .049     .039     .028     .012     .006
FERDIST2.2    .015     .054     .051     .038     .026     .011     .005
FERDIST3.2    .015     .057     .054     .037     .024     .009     .004
FERDIST4.2    .015     .060     .057     .036     .022     .007     .003
FEND
MIGRATION
MIGLEVEL.M    -70.     -70.     -56.     -42.     -28.     -28.     -28.
MIGLEVEL.F    -30.     -30.     -24.     -18.     -12.     -12.     -12.
MIGRF1.7.A      6.       4.       2.       8.      20.      19.      17.
MIGRF1.7.B     14.       8.       1.       1.
MIGRF1.7.C
MIGRM1.7.A      3.       2.       1.       1.       6.      21.      36.
MIGRM1.7.B     17.       9.       3.       1.
MIGRM1.7.C
MEND
END PROJECTION
YEAR.TITLE
YR.1970.TURKEY 'B'.  POSITIVE POPULATION POLICY  (POP IN THOUSANDS)
INIT.POP
OLD.POP.1970
MORT.SPLIT
CHILD.LV.F    15.51    16.86    18.20    19.55    20.89    21.44    22.
CHILD.LV.M    16.54    17.69    18.84    19.99    21.14    21.57    22.
ADULT.LV.F    18.66    19.21    19.77    20.33    20.89    21.44    22.
ADULT.LV.M    19.43    19.86    20.29    20.71    21.14    21.57    22.
FERTILITY
TOTAL.FERT     5.3      4.4      3.4      2.8      2.5      2.5      2.5
FERDIST1.1    .015     .051     .049     .039     .028     .012     .006
FERDIST2.1    .015     .054     .051     .038     .026     .011     .005
FERDIST3.1    .015     .057     .054     .037     .024     .009     .004
FERDIST4.1    .015     .060     .057     .036     .022     .007     .003
FERDIST5.3    .015     .064     .060     .035     .019     .005     .002
FEND
MIGRATION
MIGLEVEL.F    -30.     -30.     -24.     -18.     -12.     -12.     -12.
MIGLEVEL.M    -70.     -70.     -56.     -42.     -28.     -28.     -28.
MIGRF1.7.A      6.       4.       2.       8.      20.      19.      17.
MIGRF1.7.B     14.       8.       1.       1.
MIGRF1.7.C
MIGRM1.7.A      3.       2.       1.       1.       6.      21.      36.
MIGRM1.7.B     17.       9.       3.       1.
MIGRM1.7.C
MEND
END PROJECTION

1234567890123456789012345678901234567890123456789012345678901234567890123456789012345678 90
```

date that otherwise would be placed on the information card, and this will move the positioning backward in time 26 weeks. Consider the following examples, in each of which 26 weeks has been added to move the population back to the beginning of the year:

Example	Year for start of projection YEAR.TITLE	For midyear estimates DATE.SHIFT	For beginning-of-year estimates DATE.SHIFT
	(1)	(2)	(3)
A	YR.1960	YR.1960.WEEK.15	YR.1960.WEEK.41
B	YR.1970	YR.1970.WEEK.43	YR.1971.WEEK.17
C	YR.1971	YR.1970.WEEK.43	YR.1971.WEEK.17

Example B shows that the addition of 26 weeks to the DATE.SHIFT card raises the year by one (column 3). The starting date of the projection becomes more distant (43 weeks) from the date of the initial data. It could be brought closer by specifying 1971 as the starting year, as in Example C. Then the distance would be only 9 weeks (52 − 43). It is desirable to minimize the time period over which date shifting is done because the interpolation procedure has some distorting effect on the age distributions, even if minor in nature. The same principles for obtaining beginning-of-the-year estimates may be used to position the estimates at other dates within the year.

ADJUSTMENT OF INITIAL POPULATION

The initial age distributions should be free of age misreporting. Unfortunately, census and survey age distributions seldom can be used exactly as reported because of age misreporting. If demographic analysis has shown the nature of the errors so that adjustments can be made, that should be done.[2] A population model also may be used to distribute the population by age and sex. Such models can be generated by FIVFIV as explained in Chapter Three.

INIT.POP

For Turkey, an analysis of the pattern of age misreporting in censuses is available.[3] Age-group correction factors by sex were estimated by a cohort survival method from the 1960 and 1965 censuses and applied to the sample tabulations of the 1970 census as shown in Table 2.2. The extent of undercoverage by the census was not estimated, but is believed to have been small. The adjusted age distribution provides the input values that are needed.

---

[2] United Nations, *Methods of Estimating Basic Demographic Measures from Incomplete Data*, Manual IV of "Manuals on Methods of Estimating Population," Population Studies, No. 42 (New York: United Nations, 1967), pp. 17–22. See also, Henry S. Shryock et al., *The Methods and Materials of Demography* (Washington, D.C.: US Bureau of the Census, 1971), pp. 214–229.

[3] Paul Demeny and Frederic C. Shorter, *Estimating Turkish Mortality, Fertility and Age Structure: Application of Some New Techniques*, Publication no. 1306 (Istanbul: Istanbul University, 1968), pp. 29–37.

TABLE 2.2 Adjustment for Age Misreporting: Population of Turkey as Reported in a Sample of the 1970 Census and as Adjusted (population in thousands)

Age groups	Reported[a]		Adjusted[b]	
	Males	Females	Males	Females
0–4	2587.5	2519.9	2791.4	2761.7
5–9	2668.7	2532.9	2456.6	2384.8
10–14	2417.3	2178.6	2222.8	2157.6
15–19	1895.3	1809.5	1885.2	1930.9
20–24	1533.8	1364.7	1528.7	1331.2
25–29	1115.5	1166.5	1165.4	1076.2
30–34	989.0	1132.4	989.7	1056.0
35–39	1132.7	1101.7	1116.4	1054.9
40–44	905.6	893.3	909.8	850.9
45–49	637.9	582.5	703.5	683.7
50–54	466.2	510.3	483.3	484.5
55–59	513.8	449.2	598.5	559.9
60–64	483.6	533.4	467.4	444.4
65–69	328.9	324.0	378.2	392.2
70–74	227.3	256.4	225.2	232.7
75+	159.9	248.4	140.9	201.9
Total	**18063.0**	**17603.5**	**18063.0**	**17603.5**

[a] Age unknowns have been distributed to age groups in the same proportions as persons of known ages.

[b] Adjusted by multiplication of each age group by an adjustment factor derived from a cohort survival analysis of the 1960 and 1965 censuses. The procedure is explained in Demeny and Shorter, 1968, pp. 29–34, 53–57.

The second projection in the example starts from population data saved from the first projection by using OLD.POP.1970. The saved population was the one shifted to midyear and hence requires no further shifting.

MORTALITY

Mortality rates during infancy and early childhood are higher in Turkey relative to mortality rates at older ages than in the standard families of model life tables. A similar situation may prevail in many developing countries.[4] Whenever it does, segments from two models, at different levels, may be joined in a single life table for the population projection. In Figure 2.3, the split-level character of Turkish mortality in the past is shown. The two alternative projections, A and B, both show a gradual narrowing of the gap. Information about mortality differentials in Turkey shows that the gap is greatest in the villages and almost nonexistent in the largest cities. If it is

[4] Arjun Adlakha, "Model Life Tables: An Empirical Test of Their Applicability to Less Developed Countries," *Demography* 9, no. 4 (November 1972): 589–601.

FIGURE 2.3   Observations and Projections of Mortality in 'East' Model Levels by Five-Year Periods, 1935–2005, Turkey

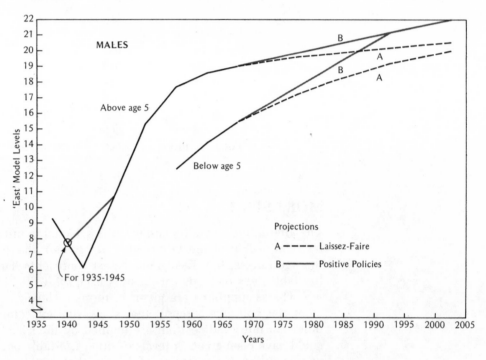

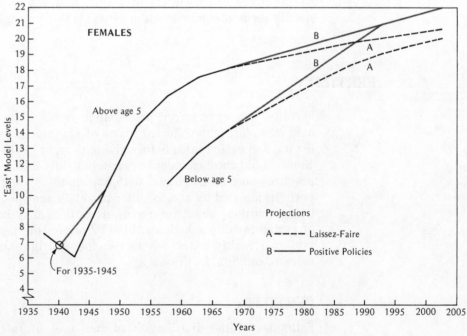

assumed that these cities lead the country in the sense that a growing proportion of the population will move to cities and that the educational, nutritional, and health-care conditions of the country will also change in the same direction, then a narrowing of the child mortality gap may be expected.

TABLE 2.4   Distribution of One Unit of Total Fertility: Turkey, 1966–1967

Age of woman	National total	City of Istanbul	Rural communities
(1)	(2)	(3)	(4)
15–19	.015	.015	.014
20–24	.051	.064	.049
25–29	.049	.060	.048
30–34	.039	.035	.039
35–39	.028	.019	.030
40–44	.012	.005	.013
45–49	.006	.002	.007
Total Fertility	**1.000**	**1.000**	**1.000**

MORT.SPLIT

The alternative mortality subject was selected in order to reflect the particular relationship of mortality rates below and above age 5. Within each of the age ranges, the 'East' model best represents Turkish mortality, so the life-table deck of cards for 'East' is used with FIVFIV for Turkey.[5]

The assumptions are given in terms of levels of model life tables. The computer will give a report that shows the expectation of life at birth and other mortality indices that are implied by the selected levels. Assumptions could have been given in terms of other life-table parameters, but since they were worked out in terms of levels, that is the most convenient way to specify them on the instruction cards for this example.

FERTILITY

Fertility assumptions are provided in terms of period fertility rates. The user may start with different forms of assumptions and transform them into the implied period rates before giving them to FIVFIV. For example, assumptions about future changes in marital fertility due to changes in birth-control practices may be combined with assumptions about future changes in proportions married by age, in order to obtain age-specific period fertility rates. Or assumptions about future cohort fertility may be rearranged in the form of period fertility schedules. FIVFIV allows the period rates to be factored into two multiplicative elements: the distribution of fertility by age of woman, and total fertility.

FERTILITY

Estimates of the distribution of one unit of total fertility by age were obtained from a national sample survey considered satisfactory to measure the distribution of childbearing by age (Table 2.4).[6] These estimates are the basis for the distributions shown on the FERDIST cards. The same source

[5] The mortality analysis for Turkey will be reported in detail in a forthcoming book by the author, *The Demography of Turkey.*

[6] School of Public Health, *Vital Statistics from the Turkish Demographic Survey, 1966–67* (Ankara: School of Public Health, 1970), appendix table 9.

TABLE 2.5   Estimation of Total Fertility from Crude Birth Rate: Turkey, 1965–1970 (population and births in thousands)

Age of woman	Midperiod female population	Distribution of one unit of total fertility	Births at TF = 1.0
15–19	1647.9	.015	24.72
20–24	1233.4	.051	62.90
25–29	1091.7	.049	53.49
30–34	1080.1	.039	42.12
35–39	978.5	.028	27.40
40–44	784.5	.012	9.41
45–49	595.9	.006	3.58
Total births at TF = 1.0			**223.63**

$$TF = (CBR \times \text{midperiod population}) \div 223.63$$

$$TF = (.0384 \times 33650) \div 223.63 = 5.78$$

Note: The CBR and midperiod populations for 1965–1970 were obtained by a reverse projection from the 1970 census.

could not be used to measure the level of births because substantial omissions of events in the survey would result in underestimation. Instead, an indirect approach was used.

A crude birth rate (CBR) was estimated for 1965–1970 by a form of reverse projection using census age distributions and estimates of infant and early childhood mortality during the period. The midperiod population for 1965–1970 was next calculated by age and sex. Multiplying the annual CBR by the total midperiod population gave an estimate of annual births. Then, on the assumption that births are distributed by age of woman as in Table 2.4, column 2, total fertility was calculated as 5.78 births. The computation is shown in Table 2.5.

This method of estimating total fertility, when only the crude birth rate is known, may prove useful in other situations. If a distribution by age of one unit of total fertility, as in Table 2.4, is not known, then a schedule may be borrowed from a country thought to have a similar mean age of marriage for women and similar prevalence of birth-control practices. Such a schedule will be needed in any event to provide assumptions about fertility rates for the FERDIST cards.

The assumptions for Turkey are that increases in birth control and increases in the mean age of marriage will cause a "peaking" in the distribution by age of childbearing. The more important of the two factors in Turkey has been birth control. A movement from the national schedule for 1966–1967 toward the Istanbul schedule (see Table 2.4) is assumed in the instructions. The assumptions about total fertility are shown in Figure 2.6 and punched on the TOTAL.FERT card.

INTERNATIONAL MIGRATION

In a national projection, migration refers to international migration. So far as Turkey is concerned, international migration is an important component

FIGURE 2.6   Observations and Projections of Total Fertility by Five-Year Periods, 1935–2005, Turkey

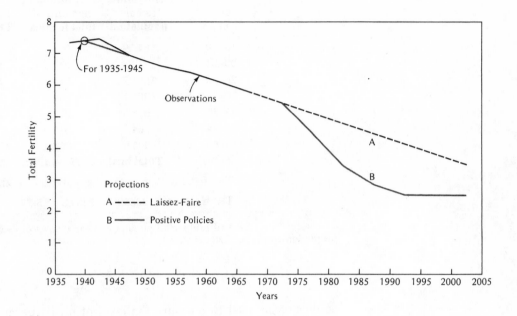

of population change. Western Europe, especially West Germany, draws on the Turkish labor market for residual supplies of unskilled and semi-skilled labor. There is a continuous flow of Turkish workers, including dependents, to Western Europe, and a backflow, the net balance being outward and much too large to be neglected in population projections for Turkey. The determinants of the net balance of emigration are found on the demand side. More than a million Turks have registered and are on the waiting lists ready to go if called.

On the demand side there are two major determinants at work: (1) the demand by West Germany for foreign labor; and (2) the competing supply of labor from other sending countries. Italy and Yugoslavia headed the list of sending countries in quantities of workers sent per year until 1972, but Turkey has now become the leading supplier of foreign labor. Other major sources are Greece, Spain, Portugal, and North African countries. Small changes in the rate of economic growth in Western Europe or in labor supplies from competing supplier countries are translated at the margin into volatile changes for Turkey. As a result of sensitivity to small changes elsewhere, projections of the balance of migration for Turkey are subject to major errors.

Based on studies by the State Planning Organization, the International Bank for Reconstruction and Development, and private assessments of prospects, a projection is made in Table 2.7. It provides uncertain estimates for the first five-year period and increasingly speculative estimates thereafter. The net balance of emigration declines after 1980 due to the assumption that constraints on Turkish immigration may be imposed by the receiving countries as the stock of Turkish workers rises, bringing with it social and political problems. In such circumstances, the Western European countries may diversify sources by reaching into additional surplus labor markets, such as Romania, the Arab countries, or Iran, whenever policies permit.

TABLE 2.7   Observations and Projections of Average Annual International Migration (net balances in thousands)

Observations	
1960–1965	− 34.5*
1965–1970	− 57.5*
Projections	
1970–1975	−100.
1975–1980	−100.
1980–1985	− 80.
1985–1990	− 60.
1990–1995	− 40.
1995–2000	− 40.
2000–2005	− 40.

Note: Negative figures signify net emigration.

* Observed on the basis of fragmentary statistics.

The sex and age composition of net migrants reflect the balance of flow in both directions. Information from sample surveys of departing workers and returnees and statistics on stocks of workers and dependents abroad were used to make assumptions about the composition by sex and age. The phase of rapid buildup in stocks abroad began in the late 1960s and is expected to continue throughout the 1970s. The age distribution of negative values (out-migration) dominates. However, a backflow is developing, and as this increases, the positive values of backflow will tend to make the net balance of emigration, which is negative, younger. A decline in the overall volume of emigration would have the same effect, because it would increase the relative weight of the older ages that characterize the backflow (positive values). These complexities are mentioned to draw attention to the need for separate analysis of the structure of the migration streams in both directions. Such an analysis has not yet been done for Turkey; hence, the assumptions about sex and age structure for the 1970s are retained for the entire duration of the projection.

MIGRATION

Assumptions about the amount of migration may be specified either in terms of quantities of net migrants or rates per thousand population. The quantity method is selected for Turkey because the net volume of emigration depends primarily on the external demand for workers and not on the size of the national base population of Turkey. The quantities from Table 2.7 are punched on the MIGLEVEL cards after division in the sex ratios that are shown in Table 2.8.

The assumptions about age structure, for each sex separately, from Table 2.8 go onto the MIGR information cards. Information may be given to FIVFIV either as shown in columns 2 and 3 or it may be scaled to any convenient total for a sex, as in columns 4 and 5. FIVFIV operates on each sex separately and utilizes the age structure to distribute by age whatever total quantity of net migration is given on the MIGLEVEL card for that sex. Thus, one set of MIGR cards for one age structure is sufficient even though

TABLE 2.8   Sex and Age Structure of Net Balance of International Migration

Age group at time of migration	Net migrants 1970-1975 (in thousands)		Scaled to 100 net emigrants	
	Males	Females	Males	Females
(1)	(2)	(3)	(4)	(5)
0–4	− 10.5	− 9.0	− 3	− 6
5–9	− 7.0	− 6.0	− 2	− 4
10–14	− 3.5	− 3.0	− 1	− 2
15–19	− 3.5	−12.0	− 1	− 8
20–24	− 21.0	−30.0	− 6	−20
25–29	− 73.5	−28.5	−21	−19
30–34	−126.0	−25.5	−36	−17
35–39	− 59.5	−21.0	−17	−14
40–44	− 31.5	−12.0	− 9	− 8
45–49	− 10.5	− 1.5	− 3	− 1
50–54	− 3.5	− 1.5	− 1	− 1
55–59	0.0	0.0	0	0
60–64	0.0	0.0	0	0
65–69	0.0	0.0	0	0
70–74	0.0	0.0	0	0
75 +	0.0	0.0	0	0
Total	**−350.0**	**−150.0**	**−100**	**−100**

Note: MIGR cards may be given either as in columns (2) and (3), or as in (4) and (5), with the same results. MIGLEVEL cards would specify −70. and −30., respectively, for males and females. Since all the age-group values have the same sign (−), no sign needs to be given on MIGR cards. When signs are mixed, use them.

the total level of migration changes from period to period, provided the assumption of constant age structure is the one intended.

INTERPRETATION OF RESULTS

When a projection, such as the one requested by the instruction cards of Example 2.1, is successful, the printed output will appear as in Example 2.9. An unnumbered page will precede the results with a list of all the subjects used to make the projection and error messages, if any. If the projection was unsuccessful, this leading page may be read with the help of Appendix Three, Error Diagnosis: Messages and Codes. If the projection was made successfully, the output may be interpreted with the following notes:

Assumptions (Page 1)

The page of assumptions begins with the title given by the user, followed by information about the dating and within-year positioning of the projection. If date shifting was done, the second line will mention that the projection refers to midyear dates. Subsequent pages do not repeat that information, so one must refer to the first page to determine the dating of the estimates. The year from which the projection starts is the one given on the YR.####. card. If the user mistakenly punches 1907 instead of 1970, FIVFIV will "believe" what is punched and make all computations as if 1907 were the actual date of the initial population.

Positioning of columns of figures is significant. If the figures are shown between years, they refer to exactly midperiod. If they are shown directly under a year label, they refer to that year only. This applies to all pages of the report.

The fertility assumptions include the sex ratio of births. The ratio will be the default value unless a different one was given by the user. A distribution by age of one unit of total fertility will be reported even when age-specific fertility rates are given as input on the FERDIST cards. The computer processes the input and transforms it into the standard form of output shown in the illustration. Thus, the report is not merely a repetition of the input information, but shows the assumptions that are implied.

Mortality assumptions are given by specifying parameters of life tables, which then cause the corresponding life-table data to be selected. The family that is used is reported. Asterisks show which parameters of the particular family were used to make the selection. If asterisks fail to appear where the user expects them, it means that there is something wrong with MORTALITY or MORT.SPLIT. Therefore, always read the page of assumptions carefully to be certain the projection is based on the assumptions that were given for it.

Parameters of the selected life tables other than the ones used to select them are also computed and shown. Instructions may be given on punch cards with any desired number of digits after the decimal point, but mortality reports are always printed to two significant places. Elsewhere, also, printed output has fixed numbers of decimal positions, but the user is free to introduce as much, or little, precision as he wishes when giving instructions to the computer.

A number of special indices are also computed and reported directly from the assumptions, independently of the projection itself. These include the gross reproduction rate (GRR), the net reproduction rate (NRR), and the mean age of childbearing (MEAN AGE).

If a user would like to make assumptions in terms of NRR, this can be done by first making two preliminary projections with given mortality and variable total fertility. If total fertility is held constant in one projection at a value f, and in the second projection at $(f+1)$, a linear expression for values of total fertility based on NRR can be written for each five-year projection period. Then any given assumption about NRR can be translated into an assumption about total fertility.

Migration (Page 2)

A report about migration assumptions is printed if any are made. The report shows the average yearly quantities of migration by age and sex unless the option to use rates of migration has been exercised. If so, only the rates themselves are shown.

Population Projection (Next 2 pages)

The basic FIVFIV projection is shown on the next two pages. The age labels refer to age groups 0–4, 5–9, . . . 75+. The indices at the bottom of the page are positioned on midperiod. The denominator for rates is in every instance a geometric mean of the initial and terminal populations unless one of these is approximately zero. If so, an arithmetic mean is used.

The analysis of the projection is continued on a final page that shows the same results expressed as percentages of the total population of each sex. If the results of the FIVFIV projection are passed to SINSIN for additional operations, a message to that effect appears at the bottom of the page. The user can also save the FIVFIV projection on cards by giving the instruction PUNCH.FIVE.

EXAMPLE 2.9   Complete FIVFIV Output for a National Population Projection

TURKEY 'A' LAISSEZ-FAIRE POPULATION POLICY   (POP IN THOUSANDS)   PAGE 1

INPUT POPULATION REFERS TO WEEK 43 OF YEAR 1970. IT IS SHIFTED TO MIDYEAR 1970.

FERTILITY ASSUMPTIONS

    SEX RATIO AT BIRTH: 105.0 MALES PER 100 FEMALES.

            DISTRIBUTION BY AGE OF ONE UNIT OF TOTAL FERTILITY

AGE	1970	1975	1980	1985	1990	1995	2000	2005
15	0.015	0.015	0.015	0.015	0.015	0.015	0.015	
20	0.051	0.054	0.054	0.057	0.057	0.060	0.060	
25	0.049	0.051	0.051	0.054	0.054	0.057	0.057	
30	0.039	0.038	0.038	0.037	0.037	0.036	0.036	
35	0.028	0.026	0.026	0.024	0.024	0.022	0.022	
40	0.012	0.011	0.011	0.009	0.009	0.007	0.007	
45	0.006	0.005	0.005	0.004	0.004	0.003	0.003	
5*TOT=TF	1.000	1.000	1.000	1.000	1.000	1.000	1.000	

            AGE SPECIFIC FERTILITY SCHEDULE

AGE	1970	1975	1980	1985	1990	1995	2000	2005
15	0.082	0.077	0.072	0.067	0.062	0.057	0.053	
20	0.278	0.277	0.259	0.255	0.237	0.230	0.210	
25	0.267	0.262	0.245	0.242	0.224	0.218	0.200	
30	0.213	0.195	0.182	0.166	0.154	0.138	0.126	
35	0.153	0.133	0.125	0.108	0.100	0.084	0.077	
40	0.065	0.056	0.053	0.040	0.037	0.027	0.024	
45	0.033	0.026	0.024	0.018	0.017	0.011	0.010	
5*TOT=TF	5.450	5.130	4.800	4.480	4.150	3.830	3.500	
GRR	2.659	2.502	2.341	2.185	2.024	1.868	1.707	
NRR	2.154	2.091	2.013	1.923	1.811	1.695	1.566	
MEAN AGE	29.350	28.975	28.975	28.525	28.525	28.075	28.075	

MORTALITY ASSUMPTIONS

		1970	1975	1980	1985	1990	1995	2000	2005
MODEL LEVELS	FROM 'EAST'	FAMILY	LIFE TABLES						
* UNDER 5	FEMALES	15.20	16.30	17.40	18.30	19.00	19.60	20.00	
* UNDER 5	MALES	15.40	17.20	18.00	18.60	19.20	19.60	20.00	
* OVER 5	FEMALES	18.40	18.90	19.30	19.70	20.00	20.30	20.60	
* OVER 5	MALES	19.30	19.60	19.80	20.00	20.20	20.40	20.60	
E(0)	FEMALES	59.18	61.34	63.32	65.00	66.27	67.42	68.33	
E(0)	MALES	57.36	58.81	60.13	61.15	62.17	62.92	63.67	
INF MORT	FEMALES	114.16	98.86	84.28	72.90	64.33	57.34	52.68	
INF MORT	MALES	117.92	105.39	93.28	84.61	76.08	70.57	65.06	
E(5)	FEMALES	64.84	65.53	66.08	66.63	67.05	67.49	67.93	
E(5)	MALES	62.42	62.76	62.98	63.21	63.45	63.69	63.93	

* TYPE OF MORTALITY INPUT

TURKEY 'A' LAISSEZ-FAIRE POPULATION POLICY (POP IN THOUSANDS)   PAGE 2

MIGRATION ASSUMPTIONS: QUANTITIES

YEARLY VALUES DURING FIVE-YEAR PERIODS

FEMALES

AGE	1970	1975	1980	1985	1990	1995	2000	2005
0		-1.8	-1.8	-1.4	-1.1	-0.7	-0.7	-0.7
5		-1.2	-1.2	-1.0	-0.7	-0.5	-0.5	-0.5
10		-0.6	-0.6	-0.5	-0.4	-0.2	-0.2	-0.2
15		-2.4	-2.4	-1.9	-1.4	-1.0	-1.0	-1.0
20		-6.0	-6.0	-4.8	-3.6	-2.4	-2.4	-2.4
25		-5.7	-5.7	-4.6	-3.4	-2.3	-2.3	-2.3
30		-5.1	-5.1	-4.1	-3.1	-2.0	-2.0	-2.0
35		-4.2	-4.2	-3.4	-2.5	-1.7	-1.7	-1.7
40		-2.4	-2.4	-1.9	-1.4	-1.0	-1.0	-1.0
45		-0.3	-0.3	-0.2	-0.2	-0.1	-0.1	-0.1
50		-0.3	-0.3	-0.2	-0.2	-0.1	-0.1	-0.1
55		0.0	0.0	0.0	0.0	0.0	0.0	0.0
60		0.0	0.0	0.0	0.0	0.0	0.0	0.0
65		0.0	0.0	0.0	0.0	0.0	0.0	0.0
70		0.0	0.0	0.0	0.0	0.0	0.0	0.0
75+		0.0	0.0	0.0	0.0	0.0	0.0	0.0
TOT		-30.0	-30.0	-24.0	-18.0	-12.0	-12.0	-12.0

MALES

AGE	1970	1975	1980	1985	1990	1995	2000	2005
0		-2.1	-2.1	-1.7	-1.3	-0.8	-0.8	-0.8
5		-1.4	-1.4	-1.1	-0.8	-0.6	-0.6	-0.6
10		-0.7	-0.7	-0.6	-0.4	-0.3	-0.3	-0.3
15		-0.7	-0.7	-0.6	-0.4	-0.3	-0.3	-0.3
20		-4.2	-4.2	-3.4	-2.5	-1.7	-1.7	-1.7
25		-14.7	-14.7	-11.8	-8.8	-5.9	-5.9	-5.9
30		-25.2	-25.2	-20.2	-15.1	-10.1	-10.1	-10.1
35		-11.9	-11.9	-9.5	-7.1	-4.8	-4.8	-4.8
40		-6.3	-6.3	-5.0	-3.8	-2.5	-2.5	-2.5
45		-2.1	-2.1	-1.7	-1.3	-0.8	-0.8	-0.8
50		-0.7	-0.7	-0.6	-0.4	-0.3	-0.3	-0.3
55		0.0	0.0	0.0	0.0	0.0	0.0	0.0
60		0.0	0.0	0.0	0.0	0.0	0.0	0.0
65		0.0	0.0	0.0	0.0	0.0	0.0	0.0
70		0.0	0.0	0.0	0.0	0.0	0.0	0.0
75+		0.0	0.0	0.0	0.0	0.0	0.0	0.0
TOT		-70.0	-70.0	-56.0	-42.0	-28.0	-28.0	-28.0

| GRAND TOTAL | | -100.0 | -100.0 | -80.0 | -60.0 | -40.0 | -40.0 | -40.0 |

TURKEY 'A' LAISSEZ-FAIRE POPULATION POLICY (POP IN THOUSANDS)   PAGE 3
POPULATION PROJECTION

FEMALES

AGE	1970	1975	1980	1985	1990	1995	2000	2005
0	2750.2	2913.2	3353.2	3748.3	4151.0	4392.4	4635.4	4797.2
5	2367.6	2652.0	2824.6	3274.9	3680.8	4092.2	4340.6	4595.3
10	2144.6	2348.7	2633.4	2807.6	3258.6	3665.5	4076.7	4325.7
15	1918.2	2123.9	2328.2	2614.3	2790.5	3242.2	3648.7	4059.9
20	1300.9	1880.5	2086.3	2294.8	2584.7	2765.4	3216.1	3622.3
25	1063.7	1257.6	1832.9	2044.3	2258.6	2553.6	2734.7	3184.3
30	1057.3	1023.3	1216.3	1792.1	2008.6	2227.9	2522.0	2703.4
35	1057.4	1018.2	986.0	1182.3	1757.2	1977.3	2195.8	2488.7
40	840.9	1021.4	984.3	957.1	1154.7	1725.8	1944.3	2161.6
45	675.4	814.0	991.6	957.8	933.6	1129.6	1691.1	1907.2
50	474.8	651.2	786.5	960.1	929.0	906.7	1098.3	1646.4
55	567.1	450.8	620.0	750.5	918.1	889.7	869.6	1055.1
60	440.0	524.2	418.1	576.6	699.8	857.9	833.2	816.3
65	392.3	386.6	462.9	370.6	513.2	624.7	768.3	748.7
70	228.1	315.5	313.1	376.9	303.4	421.8	515.9	637.5
75+	199.0	247.9	334.1	374.9	442.4	424.3	504.2	614.3
TOT	17477.7	19628.9	22171.5	25083.0	28384.4	31897.0	35595.1	39363.9

(continued)

```
      MALES
      AGE      1970      1975      1980      1985      1990      1995      2000      2005
       0      2772.9    3057.7    3504.9    3904.9    4308.6    4557.9    4800.1    4972.0
       5      2441.4    2683.1    2974.5    3428.6    3826.9    4241.9    4495.6    4748.5
      10      2209.5    2422.2    2663.6    2955.3    3409.1    3807.4    4221.4    4474.9
      15      1866.0    2190.6    2402.7    2643.8    2935.0    3387.5    3784.2    4196.8
      20      1509.6    1833.5    2155.6    2368.6    2610.6    2902.4    3351.8    3746.3
      25      1148.3    1443.1    1763.7    2092.1    2312.9    2562.5    2852.3    3298.2
      30       985.9    1033.4    1325.1    1662.1    2007.0    2245.9    2493.6    2781.3
      35      1133.8     878.0     925.5    1231.7    1583.0    1942.2    2178.9    2424.5
      40       901.4    1064.8     815.2     871.3    1181.2    1535.7    1889.4    2123.1
      45       694.2     853.3    1012.7     775.2     834.4    1140.6    1486.5    1832.2
      50       473.4     655.1     807.8     962.2     737.2     795.9    1090.0    1422.6
      55       610.0     438.2     608.0     751.1     896.1     687.4     743.0    1018.9
      60       463.3     545.9     392.8     545.7     674.9     806.4     619.4     670.5
      65       377.1     391.3     462.2     333.1     463.5     574.4     687.6     529.2
      70       221.5     290.0     301.9     357.3     258.1     360.0     447.4     536.9
      75+      137.3     204.7     280.0     321.1     376.9     336.1     388.4     471.8
      TOT    17945.5   19984.8   22396.2   25204.1   28415.4   31884.2   35529.5   39247.6

  GRAND TOTAL 35423.2   39613.7   44567.7   50287.1   56799.8   63781.2   71124.6   78611.4
```

```
                      MIDPERIOD INDICES FOR FIVE-YEAR TIME PERIODS
POPULATION SIZE        37459.9   42017.7   47341.1   53444.4   60189.4   67352.9   74774.4
YEARLY BIRTHS           1372.9    1547.8    1697.3    1852.1    1938.1    2027.2    2085.6
YEARLY DEATHS            434.8     457.0     473.4     489.5     501.8     518.6     548.3
NET YEARLY MIGRANTS    -100.0    -100.0     -80.0     -60.0     -40.0     -40.0     -40.0

                      YEARLY RATES PER THOUSAND POPULATION
GFR=BIRTHS/FEM(15-44)   177.3     175.0     167.8     158.6     143.8     132.1     121.2

BIRTH RATE               36.6      36.8      35.9      34.7      32.2      30.1      27.9
DEATH RATE               11.6      10.9      10.0       9.2       8.3       7.7       7.3
NATURAL INCREASE         25.0      26.0      25.9      25.5      23.9      22.4      20.6
NET MIGRATION            -2.7      -2.4      -1.7      -1.1      -0.7      -0.6      -0.5
POP INCREASE             22.4      23.6      24.2      24.4      23.2      21.8      20.0
```

TURKEY 'A' LAISSEZ-FAIRE POPULATION POLICY (POP IN THOUSANDS)   PAGE 4
POPULATION PROJECTION, PERCENTAGES

```
      FEMALES    1970      1975      1980      1985      1990      1995      2000      2005
       0        15.74     14.84     15.12     14.94     14.62     13.77     13.02     12.19
       5        13.55     13.51     12.74     13.06     12.97     12.83     12.19     11.67
      10        12.27     11.97     11.88     11.19     11.48     11.49     11.45     10.99
      15        10.97     10.82     10.50     10.42      9.83     10.16     10.25     10.31
      20         7.44      9.58      9.41      9.15      9.11      8.67      9.04      9.20
      25         6.09      6.41      8.27      8.15      7.96      8.01      7.68      8.09
      30         6.05      5.21      5.49      7.14      7.08      6.98      7.09      6.87
      35         6.05      5.19      4.45      4.71      6.19      6.20      6.17      6.32
      40         4.81      5.20      4.44      3.82      4.07      5.41      5.46      5.49
      45         3.86      4.15      4.47      3.82      3.29      3.54      4.75      4.85
      50         2.72      3.32      3.55      3.83      3.27      2.84      3.09      4.18
      55         3.24      2.30      2.80      2.99      3.23      2.79      2.44      2.68
      60         2.52      2.67      1.89      2.30      2.47      2.69      2.34      2.07
      65         2.24      1.97      2.09      1.48      1.81      1.96      2.16      1.90
      70         1.31      1.61      1.41      1.50      1.07      1.32      1.45      1.62
      75+        1.14      1.26      1.51      1.49      1.56      1.33      1.42      1.56
      TOT      100.00    100.00    100.00    100.00    100.00    100.00    100.00    100.00

      MALES      1970      1975      1980      1985      1990      1995      2000      2005
       0        15.45     15.30     15.65     15.49     15.16     14.30     13.51     12.67
       5        13.60     13.43     13.28     13.60     13.47     13.30     12.65     12.10
      10        12.31     12.12     11.89     11.73     12.00     11.94     11.88     11.40
      15        10.40     10.96     10.73     10.49     10.33     10.62     10.65     10.69
      20         8.41      9.17      9.62      9.40      9.19      9.10      9.43      9.55
      25         6.40      7.22      7.88      8.30      8.14      8.04      8.03      8.40
      30         5.49      5.17      5.92      6.59      7.06      7.04      7.02      7.09
      35         6.32      4.39      4.13      4.89      5.57      6.09      6.13      6.18
      40         5.02      5.33      3.64      3.46      4.16      4.82      5.32      5.41
      45         3.87      4.27      4.52      3.08      2.94      3.58      4.18      4.67
      50         2.64      3.28      3.61      3.82      2.59      2.50      3.07      3.62
      55         3.40      2.19      2.71      2.98      3.15      2.16      2.09      2.60
      60         2.58      2.73      1.75      2.16      2.38      2.53      1.74      1.71
      65         2.10      1.96      2.06      1.32      1.63      1.80      1.94      1.35
      70         1.23      1.45      1.35      1.42      0.91      1.13      1.26      1.37
      75+        0.77      1.02      1.25      1.27      1.33      1.05      1.09      1.20
      TOT      100.00    100.00    100.00    100.00    100.00    100.00    100.00    100.00
```

(continued)

	AGE	1970	1975	1980	1985	1990	1995	2000	2005
FEMALES	0-14	41.55	40.32	39.74	39.19	39.07	38.09	36.67	34.85
	15-64	53.76	54.84	55.25	56.33	56.49	57.30	58.31	60.07
	65+	4.69	4.84	5.01	4.47	4.44	4.61	5.02	5.08
MALES	0-14	41.37	40.85	40.82	40.82	40.63	39.54	38.04	36.17
	15-64	54.53	54.72	54.51	55.16	55.51	56.47	57.67	59.91
	65+	4.10	4.43	4.66	4.01	3.87	3.98	4.29	3.92
TOTAL	0-14	41.46	40.58	40.29	40.01	39.85	38.82	37.36	35.51
	15-64	54.15	54.78	54.88	55.75	56.00	56.89	57.99	59.99
	65+	4.39	4.63	4.83	4.24	4.15	4.30	4.66	4.50
MALES/FEMALES		1.027	1.018	1.010	1.005	1.001	1.000	0.998	0.997

CHAPTER THREE: MODEL DISTRIBUTIONS OF THE POPULATION BY AGE AND SEX ──────────

A problem commonly encountered when making population projections is that the age distribution of the census or survey that provides the initial population is distorted by age misstatement to such an extent that no practical means of adjusting it appears to be available. Smoothing by mathematical formula is usually unsatisfactory, because unevaluated biases are added at the same time as certain types of errors are reduced. If the reported size of the population can be accepted, and if demographic analysis has yielded a minimum amount of information about fertility and mortality in the recent past, it is possible to compute a population model that provides a more nearly accurate description of age composition than the reported one.

The justification for using models depends upon the theoretical observation that age distributions of populations not subject to migration are determined entirely by their histories of fertility and mortality. If migration has not been an important factor in the history of the population alive at the census date, and something of the past history of mortality and fertility is known, a population model will show the effect on age composition. Two circumstances in which models may be useful will be considered: (1) when no major changes in fertility or mortality appear to have occurred within the lifetimes of those alive at present; and (2) when a population has recently entered a period of declining mortality.

These two alternatives have been analyzed in the literature from the standpoint of stable and quasi-stable population theory. Coale and Demeny have recommended that a model stable population be used to approximate the age distribution in a wide range of instances of severely distorted age distributions.[7] Coale subsequently suggested that in instances of declining mortality certain adjustments be made to the stable model so that it would become a quasi-stable age distribution.[8] There is not, in practice, a great difference between the stable and quasi-stable age distributions, and either one is usually a much better description of the actual age distribution than the reported one that is distorted by age misstatement.

The theory of stable and quasi-stable models has evolved in terms of one-sex models. For population projections, a two-sex model is needed. The model for each sex separately has a definite total population associated with one unit of births of that sex at any given date. Since the births themselves are distributed between the two sexes in a given sex ratio, models for the two sexes separately can be combined if the sex ratio of births is specified.[9] The value of FIVFIV is that it can compute the two-sex models without laborious reference to tabulated one-sex models and adjustment and combination of those models. The range of assumptions about mortality and fertility acceptable to FIVFIV is sufficiently great to allow the computation of practically any type of nonstable two-sex model, including models with "split-level" mortality or with survival rates prepared by the user himself.

The examples given below show how FIVFIV may be used to generate first a stable model and subsequently a nonstable model that reflects the impact of declining mortality. Although not illustrated here, stable models that include an invariant regime of age- and sex-specific migration rates can also be generated by specifying the rates and holding them constant over time. Such models could be used to investigate the effects on urban age and sex structure of specified regimes of fertility, mortality, and urbanward migration. Thus, FIVFIV may be used to create virtually any model that would be of interest to the analyst.

POPULATIONS WITH STABLE AGE DISTRIBUTIONS

In a situation where only the total population count can be accepted, but the population is believed to have a stable age distribution owing to constant fertility and mortality, a stable population model would serve well as an initial population for projections. The stable model is approximated closely on FIVFIV by giving stable assumptions and extending the projection three additional cycles. Add three STABLEXTEND cards to the instructions, and the projection will extend to 140 years. This is ample time for the population to converge approximately on the exact stable model. To demonstrate this capability of FIVFIV, a rectangular age distribution is given in Example 3.1, and the population after 140 years is compared in Table 3.2 with the corresponding stable model calculated by Coale and Demeny. The

---

[7] United Nations, Manual IV, *Methods of Estimating Basic Demographic Measures from Incomplete Data*, p. 23.

[8] A. J. Coale, "Constructing the Age Distribution of a Population Recently Subject to Declining Mortality," *Population Index* 37, no. 2 (1971): 75–82.

[9] A. J. Coale and P. Demeny, *Regional Model Life Tables and Stable Populations* (Princeton, N.J.: Princeton University Press, 1966), p. 40.

EXAMPLE 3.1   Production of Stable Model from Rectangular Age Structure

```
0         1         2         3         4         5         6         7         8
1234567890123456789012345678901234567890123456789012345678901234567890123456789012345678901234567890

YEAR.TITLE
YR.    0.ESTIMATE A STABLE MODEL WITH 'WEST'.  GRR=3.   E(0) FEMALES = 30.
STABLEXTEND
STABLEXTEND
STABLEXTEND
INIT.POP
INIT.M.A         1.        1.        1.        1.        1.        1.        1.
INIT.M.B         1.        1.        1.        1.        1.        1.        1.
INIT.M.C         1.        1.
INIT.F.A         1.        1.        1.        1.        1.        1.        1.
INIT.F.B         1.        .1.       1.        1.        1.        1.        1.
INIT.F.C         1.        1.
SCALE
TOTAL.F      1000.
TOTAL.M      1000.
FERTILITY
TOTAL.FERT     6.15
FERDIST1.7     .018       .042      .056      .044      .028      .010      .002
FEND
MORTALITY
MORT.EZ.F      30.
MORT.EZ.M
END PROJECTION

1234567890123456789012345678901234567890123456789012345678901234567890123456789012345678901234567890
```

differences are on the order of hundredths of one percent by five-year age groups.

In order to prepare assumptions that will produce a stable model, the following steps are necessary:

1. The initial population may be any convenient set of punched cards that gives an initial population from some population. Convergence on a sex ratio for the population will be accelerated if SCALE is used to establish equal quantities of males and females at the start. In principle, however, it is only necessary to have a quantity of females of reproductive or lower age to initiate the convergence process.

2. The sex ratio at birth may be left at its default value of 105.0 males per one hundred females unless the stable model is for a Black population. In that event, a value of 103.0 can be given.

3. If the available measure of fertility is the gross reproduction rate (GRR), it can be converted to total fertility (TF) by using the assumed sex ratio of males to females at birth (s):

$$TF = GRR \cdot (1+s) \qquad \text{For GRR} = 3.0 \text{ and } s = 1.05, TF = 6.15.$$

4. If the starting point for fertility is a crude birth rate for the whole population (both sexes combined), it must be transformed to total fertility. A simple procedure for the transformation is to begin with two trial projections. Use a guess for total fertility that is probably too low for one projection, and a guess that is probably too high for a second one, and run both projections, one after the other, in a single job on the machine. In all respects other than total fertility, identical input should be given for both

TABLE 3.2 Approximation of Stable Model by FIVFIV Compared with Coale-Demeny Stable (percents)

Stable: 'West' Models; GRR = 30; $\overline{m}$ = 29; Sex
Ratio at Birth = 1.05; Female $\mathring{e}_0$ = 30.

Age groups	Year of projection by FIVFIV						Coale-Demeny Stable[a]
	0	5	35	70	105	140	
FEMALES							
0–4	6.25	13.30	15.51	15.50	15.40	15.40	15.42
5–9	6.25	5.72	12.00	12.61	12.52	12.50	12.50
10–14	6.25	6.34	10.12	11.21	11.28	11.25	11.25
15–19	6.25	6.34	9.09	9.91	10.12	10.12	10.12
20–24	6.25	6.26	8.82	8.78	8.94	8.98	8.98
25–29	6.25	6.19	8.75	7.90	7.84	7.88	7.89
30–34	6.25	6.13	8.64	7.09	6.86	6.86	6.86
35–39	6.25	6.08	3.95	6.14	5.97	5.92	5.92
40–44	6.25	6.03	4.16	5.01	5.12	5.08	5.07
45–49	6.25	5.98	3.93	3.99	4.30	4.32	4.30
50–54	6.25	5.87	3.64	3.31	3.52	3.58	3.58
55–59	6.25	5.66	3.29	2.91	2.82	2.87	2.88
60–64	6.25	5.32	2.83	2.48	2.18	2.16	2.17
65–69	6.25	4.86	2.24	1.94	1.55	1.50	1.50
70–74	6.25	4.28	1.58	.63	.95	.92	.91
75+	6.25	5.66	1.45	.58	.64	.66	.65
Total	**100.00**	**100.00**	**100.00**	**100.00**	**100.00**	**100.00**	**100.00**
MALES							
0–4	6.25	13.54	15.91	15.79	15.68	15.68	15.71
5–9	6.25	5.82	12.29	12.82	12.74	12.71	12.71
10–14	6.25	6.49	10.41	11.46	11.52	11.50	11.49
15–19	6.25	6.50	9.40	10.19	10.39	10.40	10.39
20–24	6.25	6.39	9.14	9.04	9.21	9.25	9.24
25–29	6.25	6.30	9.07	8.13	8.06	8.10	8.11
30–34	6.25	6.24	8.93	7.27	7.04	7.03	7.04
35–39	6.25	6.15	4.06	6.25	6.08	6.03	6.03
40–44	6.25	6.04	4.21	5.01	5.12	5.08	5.07
45–49	6.25	5.91	3.84	3.86	4.17	4.18	4.17
50–54	6.25	5.74	3.39	3.08	3.27	3.33	3.33
55–59	6.25	5.51	2.92	2.58	2.50	2.54	2.55
60–64	6.25	5.17	2.39	2.10	1.84	1.83	1.84
65–69	6.25	4.69	1.80	1.56	1.24	1.20	1.20
70–74	6.25	4.10	1.20	.47	.71	.69	.68
75+	6.25	5.39	1.03	.39	.43	.45	.45
Total	**100.00**	**100.00**	**100.00**	**100.00**	**100.00**	**100.00**	**100.00**
M/F	**1.0000**	**.9805**	**.9723**	**.9796**	**.9797**	**.9798**	**.9798**

[a] *Regional Model Life Tables and Stable Populations*, pp. 82, 178.

projections. They should both be extended by two STABLEXTEND cards. The resulting two models at year 105 (3×35) show what CBR is associated with each of the provisional values of total fertility. These results can be used to calculate by linear interpolation (or extrapolation) an assumption for total fertility that will yield approximately the assumed crude birth rate (b) if used in a final projection. Trials one and two are denoted by subscripts.

$$TF \doteq TF_1 + \left(\frac{b-b_1}{b_2-b_1}\right)(TF_2 - TF_1)$$

5. A standard distribution of fertility by age of woman is also needed for the FERTILITY input. A distribution with a mean age of childbearing of 29.0 years was taken from the Coale and Demeny volume and used in the example. Other distributions with other mean ages are reproduced in Table 3.4. Linear interpolation may be used to create specific schedules intermediate between any pair of given schedules. In order to determine which schedule to select if local information is scarce, criteria may be established by using information about proportions married by age of woman or children ever born by age of woman. Useful suggestions concerning how to select a fertility distribution are given in United Nations, Manual IV, *Methods of Estimating Basic Demographic Measures from Incomplete Data*, p. 24. As a last resort, an age-specific fertility schedule from another country may be given on the FERDIST card. (The computer will scale the input to one unit of total fertility if not done beforehand.)

6. The assumptions about mortality are furnished in any of the regular ways for FIVFIV. Whole model life tables or split models may be used. Males may be given a higher (lighter) level of mortality than females if neglect of female babies and women is a strong characteristic of the society, but on this point see the discussion of sex ratios that follows.

7. After the stable projection is made, input for the population projection itself may be prepared. On the last page of output the model age distributions are given in percentages of the total population by sex. The percentages themselves can be punched on the INIT.POP cards as the initial population for the projection. The next step is to use SCALE to bring the quantity of males and females into agreement with the total quantities assumed for each sex. The sex ratio of the model or the sex ratio of the enumerated population is chosen, depending upon judgment concerning which is likely to represent best the actual population. The sex ratio of the two-sex model is a logical result of the stable assumptions about fertility and mortality. Hence, if the enumerated sex ratio differs, the reasons for the discrepancy should be considered.

SEX RATIOS IN TWO-SEX MODELS

The sex ratio of a stable population is determined, in the absence of migration, entirely by the sex ratio at birth and the male and female survival functions. If the sex ratio in a two-sex model population differs from that of the enumerated population represented by the model, there is a strong presumption that either of two errors has occurred: either the male or female survival function has been selected incorrectly, or there has been sex-selective omission in the census. The only other possible cause, a deviant sex ratio of births, is improbable since accurately observed ratios show little variation among populations (except for Blacks, who appear to have somewhat lower ratios of male to female births than other populations).

It is possible for a population to have a higher-than-normal ratio of males to females (or females to males) when infanticide is practiced on a sex-selective basis or there is relative neglect in the care of female (or male) infants or older persons. Pravin Visaria has verified the existence of female neglect in several populations.[10] The author has noted that female survival in the Turkish population is less than what would be predicted by European experience. Irene Taeuber has also found evidence of female-selective infanticide in past Chinese censuses.

If the analyst is convinced that an enumerated sex ratio that is different from the sex ratio in a model is due to special risks that prevail for one sex, assumptions should be revised for the model. If female-selective infanticide is hypothesized, raise the sex ratio at birth, and reinterpret births in the model as "net births" after infanticide. The more common situation will involve relative neglect of one sex after birth. A heavier level of mortality may be specified for that sex. Either the entire survival function may be set at a lower level or a split model may be used with only the mortality below age 5 assumed at a lower level. By experimentation (successive trials), a combination of male and female mortality assumptions can be selected that produces a sex ratio in the model that corresponds approximately with the one considered to be correct.

NONSTABLE POPULATION MODELS

Once a population enters a period of persistent mortality decrease, the age distribution departs from that of a stable model and is said to take a quasi-stable form. FIVFIV enables the analyst to compute such quasi-stable models, as well as other forms of nonstable population models. The question of whether to use a nonstable model to estimate the sex and age distribution of a population when nonstable conditions prevail must be answered in relation to a particular statistical situation. An example of such a situation is provided by Iran. The population was enumerated in two censuses, 1956 and 1966. An evaluation of the two censuses leads to the following observations about the enumerated sex and age structure in 1966.

First, the sex ratio of the enumerated population rose from 103.6 males per hundred females in 1956 to 107.3 in 1966. Such a radical change, when there is no hint of massive sex-selective international migration, casts doubt on the accuracy of the sex ratios in both censuses. Neither census is shown by the reported sex ratio to be better than the other, and both are probably in error.

Second, the reported age distributions shown in Figure 3.3 are seriously distorted by errors. The 1956 census could not be plotted above age 40 as it was originally enumerated, because the census authorities evidently smoothed the distribution above that age prior to publication. If attention is first concentrated on the shapes of the female and male censuses in 1956 alone, massive deficiencies are noted below about age 20, and excesses above that age. If the cavities were due to heavy mortality (or a temporary decline in fertility) in the 1940s, they should reappear in the second census ten years later, but located ten years higher in the age distribution. There is some such upward shift of the cavity in the reported male distribution,

---

[10] Pravin M. Visaria, *The Sex Ratio of the Population of India* (New Delhi: Office of Registrar General, 1971).

FIGURE 3.3   Reported and Model Populations for Iran, 1966

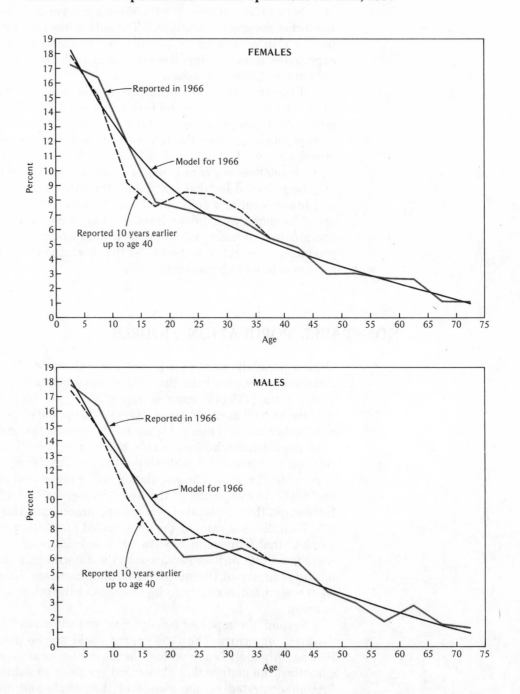

but it is ambiguous, because there is only a five-year shift, and there should be a ten-year movement if the deficiency were a real one.

The reported female age distributions are not as ambiguous and probably indicate what actually caused the cavities to appear in the censuses. In many Asian and African countries there is a well-documented tendency for females in the ages of puberty and marriage to be reported at higher ages. The effect is to vacate the teens and enlarge the twenties and thirties. Such upward transfers can be massive where there is a poor knowledge of age. In 1956, the Iranian census was severely distorted by such misreporting. In 1966, the magnitude of the distortions was still large but less than in 1956. The change is seen clearly in the female population, where there is no upward shift at all in the deficit age group between 1956 and 1966. There is only a reduction in the size of the cavity below age 20 and excess above that age.

Misreporting, and possibly omissions, also affected the male distributions. The deficiency in the age range 20–24, which became more serious in 1966, is not surprising considering the liability for military service in that age range. The age pattern of misreporting for males is also less predictable than for females, according to the experience of other populations having the Asian-African pattern of errors. The source of these response errors is the avoidance of certain ages and exaggeration of others that occurs when age is not a highly salient piece of information for the individual. Age is then attributed to persons during the census-taking on the basis of their marital or childbearing status.

If the age distributions for Iran were smoothed by any method that allowed the cavity at the ages that are on the threshold of entry into the labor force to remain, population projections would show a slowing down of entrants to the labor force. There is no solid evidence that such a deceleration was in prospect after 1966, because the irregularities of the age distribution conform well to expected patterns of age misreporting in such populations. This is especially evident in the female age distributions, and there is no reason to believe that males experienced different trends in births or mortality over time. A better approximation of the age structure than a smoothed one would be to compute a population model for the age distributions and use that. For Iran, the model cannot be a stable one, since it must reflect the effects of a recent decline in mortality.

The procedure for computing nonstable models has two steps: (1) computation of an initial model that has a stable age structure and represents the situation prior to the onset of changes in mortality (or fertility); and (2) projection from a stable model on the assumed date of destabilization up to the date of the census that will be adjusted by using the results. The second step may be likened to a simulation of population change after the departure from stable conditions.

Fertility

In the example for Iran, which is explained below in detail, fertility was held constant during both steps of the computation. The rate of growth of a population is sensitive to the mean age of childbearing independently of total fertility, because early childbearing shortens the length of generation and speeds up reproduction. Hence, it was important to make an estimate of $\bar{m}$, the mean age of childbearing, that would simulate the situation both before and during destabilization. Statistics in the 1966 census on the marital status of women were used to estimate a mean age of childbearing of 28.3 years.[11] A standard schedule for the distribution of births by age of woman was then computed as shown in the last column of Table 3.4.

---

[11] United Nations, Manual IV, *Methods of Estimating Basic Demographic Measures from Incomplete Data,* p. 24.

TABLE 3.4   Yearly Births by Age of Woman for One Unit of Total Fertility ($\overline{m}$ = mean age of childbearing in years)

Age	$\overline{m} = 27$	$\overline{m} = 29$	$\overline{m} = 31$	$\overline{m} = 33$	$\overline{m} = 28.3$[a]
15–19	.029	.018	.008	.002	.022
20–24	.055	.042	.032	.019	.047
25–29	.054	.056	.054	.047	.055
30–34	.037	.044	.050	.056	.041
35–39	.020	.028	.034	.046	.025
40–44	.004	.010	.018	.025	.008
45–49	.001	.002	.004	.005	.002
Total fertility	**1.000**	**1.000**	**1.000**	**1.000**	**1.000**

[a] Computed by interpolation between the first two columns.

Source: Coale and Demeny, *Regional Model Life Tables and Stable Populations*, p. 30.

An estimate of total fertility for the Iranian population was then made by following the procedures outlined in *Methods of Estimating Basic Demographic Measures* (pp. 22–29) for populations having distorted age distributions. The female population for 1966, and the rate of growth of the female population, provided the best available basis. The parameters used to make an estimate of total fertility were the following: (1) the proportion female under age 35 reported in the 1966 census, $C(35) = .756$; (2) the rate of increase in the female population for 1956–1966, $r^{1961} = .0262$; (3) an assumption that the decline in mortality for Iran prior to 1966 had a duration of 25 years, $t = 25$; and (4) an assumed rate of increase in 1941, prior to the departure from stability, of one percent per annum, $r^{1941} = .0100$. The last two assumptions were necessary in order to use quasi-stable estimation methods.

The estimate of total fertility that results from these standard computations is 6.7 children. Errors of estimation are reduced by the techniques used, but it is possible that the estimate just given is a minimum estimate of the actual level for fertility. The value of $C(15)$, which is the proportion of the population under age 15, would suggest an estimate for total fertility nearly 10 percent higher. The final selection of an estimate in the presence of inaccurate basic data always requires an exercise of judgment. In this instance, the estimate based on $C(35)$, namely TF = 6.7, is preferred because it is least affected by misreporting of age near the age of marriage in Iran, which is early for a significant proportion of the population. The estimate of total fertility is for 1966, but on the assumption of constant fertility, it may be attributed to earlier dates as well.

Mortality

Concerning mortality, estimates based on national data are only possible for the intercensal decade, 1956–1966. The estimates are based on a type of survival analysis that minimizes the errors of mortality estimation caused by age misreporting but is sensitive to changes in the extent of coverage by successive censuses.[12] In terms of 'West' model life tables, an expectation of life at birth for both sexes combined of 47.2 years (level 12.5) is indicated. In addition, heavier mortality for females might be expected in view of the

---

[12] United Nations, Manual IV, *Methods of Estimating Basic Demographic Measures from Incomplete Data*, pp. 8–12.

differential health care of women and female babies as compared with males.

The trend of reductions in death rates in Iran prior to 1956–1966 is not actually known. It is commonly believed by demographers in Iran that death rates began to decline in the 1940s. Prior to that time, the expectation of life at birth could have been 25–30 years, but the actual value must remain a matter of conjecture. Since the choice of initial level makes only a minor difference in the model age distribution for 1966, the choice of assumption is not critical. The trend of life expectancy, on the other hand, does influence the shape of the model. However, a plausible set of assumptions is likely to yield a better age distribution as a basis for projections after 1966 than the reported age distribution. Accordingly, the assumptions shown in Table 3.5 are made.

The preparation of assumptions for the computation of a nonstable model is now complete. The model was generated by using the instructions shown in Example 3.6. The stable population was computed with three STABLEXTEND cards; hence, the final year is 140 (35 + (3 × 35)). Year 140 was then used in OLD.POP. 140 to initiate the second projection. Since the second projection is to end in 1966, the initial date given under YEAR.TITLE for the second projection is YR.1931 (i.e., 1966 − 35 = 1931). However, destabilization is simulated only from 1941 as shown by the change in mortality assumptions after that date, beginning with the third five-year period.

The absolute population quantities in the printed output (Example 3.7) are a scalar multiple of the population represented by the model. Rates and ratios are valid without further manipulation. The model can be transformed into a more elegant simulation by scaling the 1931 input population so that absolute population quantities will also become valid for Iran. The scaling at 1931 will carry through to 1966 because the model is a scalar multiple of the population it represents. The procedure is to compute total males and females in 1931 for a second run on the computer as follows:

Total population in 1966

From the census	25078.9
From the model	14878.2

Scaling ratio = 25078.9/14878.2 = 1.6856

Population in 1931

Females in 1931 from the model	3826.7
Males in 1931 from the model	4069.2

Scale 1931 model females to 3826.7 × 1.6856 = 6450.29
Scale 1931 model males to 4069.2 × 1.6856 = 6859.04

The following subject and information cards will do the scaling. They are included during a rerun of the nonstable model. For the second run, all of Example 3.6 (both projections) is used a second time, plus the following cards, which become part of the instructions for the destabilization projection.

```
0         1         2         3         4         5         6         7         8
1234567890123456789012345678901234567890123456789012345678901234567890123456789012345678901234567890

SCALE
TOTAL.M    6859.04
TOTAL.F    6450.29

1234567890123456789012345678901234567890123456789012345678901234567890123456789012345678901234567890
```

TABLE 3.5   Mortality Assumptions for the Nonstable Model in Terms of 'West' Model Life Tables

	Model levels		Corresponding $\mathring{e}_0$	
Period	Males	Females	Males	Females
1931–1936	4.	3.	25.26	25.00
1936–1941	4.	3.	25.26	25.00
1941–1946	5.	4.	27.67	27.50
1946–1951	6.	5.	30.08	30.00
1951–1956	9.	8.	37.30	37.50
1956–1961	12.	11.	44.52	45.00
1961–1966	14.	13.	49.56	50.00

EXAMPLE 3.6   Instructions for Computation of a Nonstable Model

```
0          1          2          3          4          5          6          7          8
1234567890123456789012345678901234567890123456789012345678901234567890123456789012345678901234567890

YEAR.TITLE
YR.    0.MODEL FOR IRAN PRIOR TO DESTABILIZATION (POP SIZE IS NOMINAL)
STABLEXTEND
STABLEXTEND
STABLEXTEND
INIT.POP
INIT.F.A     2761.7     2384.8     2157.6     1930.9     1331.2     1076.2     1056.0
INIT.F.B     1054.9      850.9      683.7      484.5      559.9      444.4      392.2
INIT.F.C      232.7      201.9
INIT.M.A     2791.4     2456.6     2222.8     1885.2     1528.7     1165.4      989.7
INIT.M.B     1116.4      909.8      703.5      483.3      598.5      467.4      378.2
INIT.M.C      225.2      140.9
SCALE
TOTAL.F      1000.
TOTAL.M      1000.
FERTILITY
TOTAL.PERT     6.7
FERDIST1.7    .022       .047       .055       .041       .025       .008       .002
FEND
MORTALITY
MORT.LV.F      3.
MORT.LV.M      4.
END PROJECTION
YEAR.TITLE
YR.1931.DESTABILIZATION 1941-1966.   NOT SCALED BUT RATES RATIOS OKAY
INIT.POP
OLD.POP.0140
FERTILITY
TOTAL.PERT     6.7
FERDIST1.7    .022       .047       .055       .041       .025       .008       .002
FEND
MORTALITY
MORT.LV.F      3.         3.         4.         5.         8.        11.        13.
MORT.LV.M      4.         4.         5.         6.         9.        12.        14.
END PROJECTION

1234567890123456789012345678901234567890123456789012345678901234567890123456789012345678901234567890
```

EXAMPLE 3.7   Model for Iran Following Destabilization

DESTABILIZATION 1941-1966.   NOT SCALED BUT RATES RATIOS OKAY   PAGE 1

THE INPUT POPULATION IS DATED 1931

FERTILITY ASSUMPTIONS

   SEX RATIO AT BIRTH: 105.0 MALES PER 100 FEMALES.

          DISTRIBUTION BY AGE OF ONE UNIT OF TOTAL FERTILITY

AGE	1931	1936	1941	1946	1951	1956	1961	1966
15	0.022	0.022	0.022	0.022	0.022	0.022	0.022	
20	0.047	0.047	0.047	0.047	0.047	0.047	0.047	
25	0.055	0.055	0.055	0.055	0.055	0.055	0.055	
30	0.041	0.041	0.041	0.041	0.041	0.041	0.041	
35	0.025	0.025	0.025	0.025	0.025	0.025	0.025	
40	0.008	0.008	0.008	0.008	0.008	0.008	0.008	
45	0.002	0.002	0.002	0.002	0.002	0.002	0.002	
5*TOT=TF	1.000	1.000	1.000	1.000	1.000	1.000	1.000	

          AGE SPECIFIC FERTILITY SCHEDULE

AGE	1931	1936	1941	1946	1951	1956	1961	1966
15	0.147	0.147	0.147	0.147	0.147	0.147	0.147	
20	0.315	0.315	0.315	0.315	0.315	0.315	0.315	
25	0.369	0.369	0.369	0.369	0.369	0.369	0.369	
30	0.275	0.275	0.275	0.275	0.275	0.275	0.275	
35	0.167	0.167	0.167	0.167	0.167	0.167	0.167	
40	0.054	0.054	0.054	0.054	0.054	0.054	0.054	
45	0.013	0.013	0.013	0.013	0.013	0.013	0.013	
5*TOT=TF	6.700	6.700	6.700	6.700	6.700	6.700	6.700	
GRR	3.268	3.268	3.268	3.268	3.268	3.268	3.268	
NRR	1.301	1.301	1.422	1.540	1.877	2.188	2.384	
MEAN AGE	28.300	28.300	28.300	28.300	28.300	28.300	28.300	

MORTALITY ASSUMPTIONS   *Period of Destabilization*

MODEL LEVELS FROM 'WEST'		1931 FAMILY	1936 LIFE TABLES	1941	1946	1951	1956	1961	1966
UNDER 5	FEMALES	3.00	3.00	4.00	5.00	8.00	11.00	13.00	
UNDER 5	MALES	4.00	4.00	5.00	6.00	9.00	12.00	14.00	
* OVER 5	FEMALES	3.00	3.00	4.00	5.00	8.00	11.00	13.00	
* OVER 5	MALES	4.00	4.00	5.00	6.00	9.00	12.00	14.00	
E(0)	FEMALES	25.00	25.00	27.50	30.00	37.50	45.00	50.00	
E(0)	MALES	25.26	25.26	27.67	30.08	37.30	44.52	49.56	
INF MORT	FEMALES	305.19	305.19	279.36	255.73	195.18	146.12	118.31	
INF MORT	MALES	322.15	322.15	295.46	270.89	207.37	155.37	124.53	
E(5)	FEMALES	40.02	40.02	41.70	43.36	48.18	52.84	55.86	
E(5)	MALES	40.52	40.52	42.05	43.55	47.96	52.24	55.03	

* TYPE OF MORTALITY INPUT

DESTABILIZATION 1941-1966.   NOT SCALED BUT RATES RATIOS OKAY   PAGE 2
POPULATION PROJECTION

FEMALES — OLD.POP

AGE	1931	1936	1941	1946	1951	1956	1961	1966
0	609.3	639.4	671.1	738.6	814.3	962.0	1132.7	1317.3
5	481.7	505.5	530.5	568.1	636.5	732.5	893.5	1070.7
10	434.2	455.6	478.1	504.3	542.6	615.2	714.7	876.5
15	391.2	410.6	430.9	454.5	481.6	524.3	600.0	700.7
20	347.1	364.3	382.4	403.9	428.4	460.7	507.4	584.6
25	304.1	319.1	334.9	354.1	376.6	406.4	443.1	491.8
30	263.5	276.5	290.1	307.1	327.2	354.8	388.9	427.7
35	225.9	237.0	248.6	263.4	281.2	306.1	337.6	373.6
40	191.8	201.4	211.3	223.9	239.3	261.3	289.7	322.8
45	161.5	169.6	178.1	188.8	201.9	220.9	245.7	275.2
50	133.1	139.7	146.7	155.8	166.9	183.2	204.7	230.4
55	105.3	110.4	115.9	123.5	132.9	147.0	165.6	187.7
60	77.7	81.4	85.4	91.4	99.1	111.3	127.5	146.3
65	51.6	54.1	56.7	61.1	66.9	76.9	90.5	106.2
70	29.6	31.1	32.7	35.4	39.4	46.5	56.7	68.8
75+	19.0	20.0	21.0	23.1	26.2	32.3	41.8	54.2
TOT	3826.7	4015.9	4214.4	4496.9	4860.9	5441.5	6240.1	7234.5

(continued)

```
MALES
AGE      1931      1936      1941      1946      1951      1956      1961      1966
  0     631.8     663.0     695.8     766.4     845.8    1002.1    1183.0    1381.9
  5     508.8     533.9     560.3     598.7     670.1     768.7     937.7    1127.2
 10     463.3     486.3     510.3     537.6     576.6     651.5     753.0     923.0
 15     422.3     443.2     465.2     490.0     518.1     560.6     638.0     740.7
 20     378.1     396.8     416.5     439.4     465.1     497.9     544.1     622.9
 25     333.3     349.7     367.1     387.9     411.7     442.7     479.9     528.3
 30     290.6     304.9     319.9     338.4     360.1     389.2     424.7     464.2
 35     249.6     261.8     274.7     290.9     310.3     337.2     370.8     408.5
 40     209.9     220.4     231.2     245.2     262.2     286.7     317.9     353.5
 45     172.5     181.1     190.1     202.0     216.6     238.3     266.5     299.3
 50     137.3     144.2     151.4     161.2     173.5     192.1     216.9     246.1
 55     104.8     109.9     115.3     123.1     133.1     148.7     169.7     194.7
 60      74.9      78.5      82.3      88.1      95.8     108.3     125.3     145.8
 65      48.3      50.7      53.1      57.1      62.5      71.9      85.0     100.7
 70      26.9      28.3      29.7      32.2      35.6      41.9      50.9      61.8
 75+     16.7      17.6      18.5      20.2      22.8      27.7      35.4      45.3
 TOT   4069.2    4270.3    4481.5    4778.5    5159.8    5765.4    6598.8    7643.8

GRAND TOTAL  7895.8    8286.2    8695.9    9275.4   10020.7   11206.9   12838.9   14878.2
```

```
                  MIDPERIOD INDICES FOR FIVE-YEAR TIME PERIODS
POPULATION SIZE    8088.7    8488.6    8981.0    9640.9   10597.2   11995.2   13821.0
YEARLY BIRTHS       411.5     431.8     454.9     482.2     517.1     565.1     630.5
YEARLY DEATHS       333.4     349.9     339.0     333.1     279.9     238.7     222.6
NET YEARLY MIGRANTS   0.0       0.0       0.0       0.0       0.0       0.0       0.0

                    YEARLY RATES PER THOUSAND POPULATION
GFR=BIRTHS/FEM(15-44)  233.0   233.0     233.0     233.0     232.7     231.9     231.1

BIRTH RATE           50.9      50.9      50.6      50.0      48.8      47.1      45.6
DEATH RATE           41.2      41.2      37.7      34.6      26.4      19.9      16.1
NATURAL INCREASE      9.7       9.7      12.9      15.5      22.4      27.2      29.5
NET MIGRATION         0.0       0.0       0.0       0.0       0.0       0.0       0.0
POP INCREASE          9.7       9.7      12.9      15.5      22.4      27.2      29.5
```

```
DESTABILIZATION 1941-1965.  NOT SCALED BUT RATES RATIOS OKAY                PAGE  3
POPULATION PROJECTION, PERCENTAGES

FEMALES    1931      1936      1941      1946      1951      1956      1961      1966
  0       15.92     15.92     15.92     16.42     16.75     17.68     18.15     18.21
  5       12.59     12.59     12.59     12.63     13.09     13.46     14.32     14.80
 10       11.35     11.35     11.35     11.22     11.16     11.31     11.45     12.12
 15       10.22     10.23     10.23     10.11      9.91      9.63      9.61      9.69
 20        9.07      9.07      9.07      8.98      8.81      8.47      8.13      8.08
 25        7.95      7.94      7.95      7.87      7.75      7.47      7.10      6.80
 30        6.89      6.88      6.88      6.83      6.73      6.52      6.23      5.91
 35        5.90      5.90      5.90      5.86      5.78      5.63      5.41      5.16
 40        5.01      5.01      5.01      4.98      4.92      4.80      4.64      4.46
 45        4.22      4.22      4.23      4.20      4.15      4.06      3.94      3.80
 50        3.48      3.48      3.48      3.47      3.43      3.37      3.28      3.18
 55        2.75      2.75      2.75      2.75      2.73      2.70      2.65      2.59
 60        2.03      2.03      2.03      2.03      2.04      2.05      2.04      2.02
 65        1.35      1.35      1.35      1.36      1.38      1.41      1.45      1.47
 70        0.77      0.78      0.77      0.79      0.81      0.86      0.91      0.95
 75+       0.50      0.50      0.50      0.51      0.54      0.59      0.67      0.75
 TOT     100.00    100.00    100.00    100.00    100.00    100.00    100.00    100.00

MALES      1931      1936      1941      1946      1951      1956      1961      1966
  0       15.53     15.53     15.53     16.04     16.39     17.38     17.93     18.08
  5       12.50     12.50     12.50     12.53     12.99     13.33     14.21     14.75
 10       11.39     11.39     11.39     11.25     11.17     11.30     11.41     12.08
 15       10.38     10.38     10.38     10.25     10.04      9.72      9.67      9.69
 20        9.29      9.29      9.29      9.20      9.01      8.64      8.25      8.15
 25        8.19      8.19      8.19      8.12      7.98      7.68      7.27      6.91
 30        7.14      7.14      7.14      7.08      6.98      6.75      6.44      6.07
 35        6.13      6.13      6.13      6.09      6.01      5.85      5.62      5.34
 40        5.16      5.16      5.16      5.13      5.08      4.97      4.82      4.62
 45        4.24      4.24      4.24      4.23      4.20      4.13      4.04      3.92
 50        3.38      3.38      3.38      3.37      3.36      3.33      3.29      3.22
 55        2.57      2.57      2.57      2.58      2.58      2.58      2.57      2.55
 60        1.84      1.84      1.84      1.84      1.86      1.88      1.90      1.91
 65        1.19      1.19      1.18      1.19      1.21      1.25      1.29      1.32
 70        0.66      0.66      0.66      0.67      0.69      0.73      0.77      0.81
 75+       0.41      0.41      0.41      0.42      0.44      0.48      0.54      0.59
 TOT     100.00    100.00    100.00    100.00    100.00    100.00    100.00    100.00
```

(continued)

AGE	1931	1936	1941	1946	1951	1956	1961	1966
FEMALES 0-14	39.86	39.86	39.86	40.27	41.01	42.44	43.92	45.12
15-64	57.52	57.52	57.53	57.07	56.27	54.69	53.05	51.71
65+	2.62	2.62	2.62	2.66	2.73	2.86	3.03	3.17
MALES 0-14	39.42	39.42	39.42	39.82	40.55	42.01	43.55	44.90
15-64	58.32	58.32	58.32	57.89	57.10	55.53	53.86	52.38
65+	2.26	2.26	2.26	2.29	2.34	2.45	2.59	2.72
TOTAL 0-14	39.63	39.63	39.63	40.04	40.78	42.22	43.73	45.01
15-64	57.93	57.93	57.94	57.49	56.70	55.12	53.46	52.05
65+	2.43	2.44	2.43	2.47	2.53	2.65	2.81	2.94
MALES/FEMALES	1.063	1.063	1.063	1.063	1.061	1.060	1.057	1.057

EXAMPLE 3.8 Scaled Model for Iran
[Note: Other pages of the projection remain as in EXAMPLE 3.7]

```
IRAN. DESTABILIZATION 1941-1966.  SCALED TO SIZE IN 1966. (THOUSANDS)          PAGE  2
POPULATION PROJECTION
                    OLD. POP                          Period of Destabilization
        FEMALES
        AGE     1931      1936      1941      1946      1951      1956      1961      1966
          0    1027.1    1077.8    1131.1    1244.9    1372.6    1621.5    1909.3    2220.4
          5     812.0     852.1     894.2     957.6    1072.9    1234.7    1506.0    1804.8
         10     731.8     768.0     806.0     850.1     914.7    1037.0    1204.7    1477.4
         15     659.4     692.2     726.4     766.1     811.8     883.7    1011.3    1181.2
         20     585.1     614.1     644.6     680.8     722.2     776.5     855.3     985.3
         25     512.5     537.8     564.5     596.9     634.8     685.1     746.9     829.0
         30     444.2     466.0     489.0     517.6     551.6     598.1     655.5     720.9
         35     380.8     399.5     419.1     443.9     473.9     516.0     569.1     629.8
         40     323.3     339.4     356.1     377.4     403.3     440.5     488.4     544.1
         45     272.3     286.0     300.2     318.2     340.3     372.3     414.2     463.9
         50     224.3     235.5     247.3     262.6     281.3     308.8     345.0     388.3
         55     177.5     186.1     195.4     208.2     224.0     247.8     279.2     316.3
         60     131.0     137.2     143.9     154.0     167.0     187.6     214.8     246.6
         65      87.0      91.2      95.6     102.9     112.8     129.7     152.5     179.0
         70      49.9      52.5      55.0      59.7      66.3      78.4      95.6     115.9
        75+      32.0      33.7      35.4      38.9      44.2      54.5      70.5      91.3
        TOT    6450.3    6769.2    7103.8    7580.0    8193.6    9172.3   10518.3   12194.5

        MALES
        AGE     1931      1936      1941      1946      1951      1956      1961      1966
          0    1365.0    1117.5    1172.8    1291.9    1425.7    1689.1    1994.1    2329.4
          5     857.7     900.0     944.5    1009.2    1129.5    1295.7    1580.5    1900.0
         10     781.0     819.7     860.1     906.2     971.9    1098.1    1269.3    1555.8
         15     711.8     747.1     784.1     826.0     873.2     944.9    1075.4    1248.5
         20     637.3     668.9     702.1     740.7     784.0     839.2     917.2    1049.9
         25     561.8     589.5     618.7     653.8     694.0     746.2     808.9     890.5
         30     489.8     513.9     539.2     570.4     607.0     656.1     715.8     782.5
         35     420.7     441.4     463.0     490.3     523.0     568.5     625.0     688.5
         40     353.8     371.5     389.7     413.3     441.9     483.2     535.9     595.8
         45     290.7     305.3     320.5     340.4     365.1     401.6     449.2     504.5
         50     231.5     243.0     255.2     271.7     292.4     323.9     365.7     414.9
         55     176.6     185.2     194.4     207.6     224.3     250.6     286.0     328.2
         60     126.3     132.3     138.7     148.6     161.5     182.5     211.2     245.7
         65      81.4      85.4      89.5      96.2     105.4     121.3     143.3     169.7
         70      45.4      47.8      50.1      54.2      60.0      70.5      85.7     104.2
        75+      28.2      29.7      31.2      34.1      38.4      46.7      59.6      76.3
        TOT    6359.0    7198.1    7554.0    8054.6    8697.4    9718.1   11123.0   12884.4

   GRAND TOTAL  13309.3   13967.3   14657.8   15634.6   16891.0   18890.4   21641.3  (25078.8)
```

```
                   MIDPERIOD INDICES FOR FIVE-YEAR TIME PERIODS
POPULATION SIZE   13534.3   14308.4   15138.4   16250.7   17862.7   20219.1   23296.7
YEARLY BIRTHS       693.6     727.9     766.7     812.8     871.6     952.5    1062.8
YEARLY DEATHS       562.0     589.8     571.3     561.5     471.7     402.3     375.3
NET YEARLY MIGRANTS   0.0       0.0       0.0       0.0       0.0       0.0       0.0

                   YEARLY RATES PER THOUSAND POPULATION
GFR=BIRTHS/FEM(15-44) 233.0  233.0     233.0     233.0     232.7     231.9     231.1
                                             Destabilization
BIRTH RATE           50.9      50.9      50.6      50.0      48.8      47.1      45.6
DEATH RATE           41.2      41.2      37.7      34.6      26.4      19.9      16.1
NATURAL INCREASE      9.7       9.7      12.9      15.5      22.4      27.2      29.5
NET MIGRATION         0.0       0.0       0.0       0.0       0.0       0.0       0.0
POP INCREASE          9.7       9.7      12.9      15.5      22.4      27.2      29.5
```

When the new instructions are given to FIVFIV they produce population quantities that agree with the census total in 1966, as shown in Example 3.8. This step was not actually necessary in order to make population projections from 1966. The unscaled model (Example 3.7) provides a valid percentage distribution of the population by age and sex for 1966.

COMPARISON OF ENUMERATED AND MODEL POPULATIONS

The first thing to do after computing a nonstable model is to test its plausibility. It should be satisfactory, but if there have been any mistakes of judgment, reasoning, or punching of instructions, they may be detected at this stage.

The female ogives of the model (enumerated proportions to age x) are compared with those of the enumerated population in Figure 3.9. The differences, $C(x)$ Iran minus $C(x)$ Model, show a characteristic and expected pattern for populations with the Asian-African type of age misreporting. In particular, the reported and model ogives are reasonably well matched at ages 15 and 35 as shown by points near the zero line. If the ogive of the model lies generally above that of the enumerated population, the values of

FIGURE 3.9   Comparison of Ogives of Enumerated and Model Populations, Females, 1966

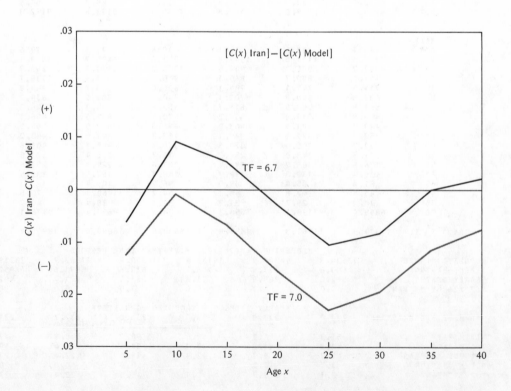

[C(x)Iran − C(x)Model] will lie below the zero line in the diagram. Such a deviant model is shown as a second and lower curve in the diagram. It was computed on the basis of a total fertility of 7.0. Whenever the curve is "too low," it indicates that fertility has probably been assumed at a higher level than justified by the enumerated age distribution. Whenever such a curve or its opposite ("too high") is found, the fertility assumptions should be reevaluated and possibly changed. The comparison just shown is one of the reasons why an estimate of total fertility for Iran of 6.7 is better than higher estimates.

If a population is affected by the Latin American type of age misreporting, which has more consistently patterned errors in the male than the female population, the analysis would be carried out on the male rather than the female population following the same procedures.

An extra dividend from the model is that it provides a sketch of population changes during destabilization in Iran for the period 1931–1966. The model shows, for example, that the crude birth rate is declining in Iran in spite of constant fertility. The reason for this is that increased survival during destabilization adds relatively more to population size (denominator of the CBR), than it does to births (numerator).

The sex ratio in the model for 1966 is 105.7 males per hundred females, as compared with 107.3 in the census. As mentioned earlier, the sex ratio in the 1956 census was only 103.6. If one were confident that a high ratio of males to females, as shown in the most recent of the two censuses, actually prevailed, a model with such a relationship could be created by changing the mortality assumptions by sex. In Table 3.4, a difference between males and females of one level has already been assumed. This is equivalent to 2.5 years of $\overset{\circ}{e}_0$ for females. If the differential were widened, the sex ratio in the model would increase. For a one-level differential as shown, the ratio is 105.7; for a two-level differential, recomputation of the nonstable model shows that the ratio would be 112.9. Thus, the sex ratio of the population is sensitive to differential mortality by sex and can be changed in the model by changing the mortality differential.

The sex ratio of the model is logically consistent with the rest of the assumptions, so it is the one to prefer when making population projections. Its acceptance implies that the reported 1966 population should be adjusted not only for age misreporting, but also for sex misreporting. This is accomplished in the second destabilization projection shown in Example 3.8.

If the destabilization model was not scaled to fit the actual census, the results of the unscaled model (see Example 3.7) could be used to make projections from 1966. First, the percentage age distribution of the 1966 model would be punched as the INIT.POP. Second, males and females would be raised to the actual 1966 population size, taking into consideration the sex ratio of the model.

$$\text{Males} = \begin{pmatrix} \text{Proportion male} \\ \text{in model for 1966} \end{pmatrix} \times \begin{pmatrix} \text{Enumerated population} \\ \text{of both sexes in 1966} \end{pmatrix}$$

$$= \frac{7643.8}{14878.2} \times 25078.9 = 12884.5$$

$$\text{Females} = 25078.9 - 12884.5 = 12194.4$$

Thus, the census of 1966 would be adjusted and given as input for a population projection in the following manner:

```
0          1           2           3           4           5           6           7           8
1234567890 1234567890 1234567890 1234567890 1234567890 1234567890 1234567890 1234567890 1234567890

INIT.POP
INIT.F.A        18.21       14.80       12.12        9.69        8.08        6.80        5.91
INIT.F.B         5.16        4.46        3.80        3.18        2.59        2.02        1.47
INIT.F.C         0.95        0.75
INIT.M.A        18.08       14.75       12.08        9.69        8.15        6.91        6.07
INIT.M.B         5.34        4.62        3.92        3.22        2.55        1.91        1.32
INIT.M.C         0.81        0.59
SCALE
TOTAL.M      12884.5
TOTAL.F      12194.4

1234567890 1234567890 1234567890 1234567890 1234567890 1234567890 1234567890 1234567890 1234567890
```

In each country, the quality of age and sex data and the feasibility of reducing systematic inaccuracies by adjustments must be assessed according to the specific statistical information available. Stable and nonstable models are a means by which information about fertility and mortality may be used to evaluate the reported age and sex structure. The main point about models is that the reported age distributions do not have to be used alone as if nothing else were known that can provide information about age and sex structure. It is especially hazardous to use reported distributions for projections, even if smoothed by mathematical formulas, when age misreporting is a strong possibility. Although models do not provide accurate estimates of age structure, they do yield statements in terms of standard demographic indices of the implications of assumptions about fertility and mortality that are a suitable basis for population projections when nothing better is available.

CHAPTER FOUR: ANNUAL DETAIL AND SPECIAL AGE GROUPS _____

The projections that are made by FIVFIV can be transformed into 15-year (or longer) annual projections. In addition, the five-year age groups can be distributed to single-year age groups and recombined into special age groups defined by the user of the package programs. These tasks are performed by SINSIN, which functions as an integral part of the system.

Standard distribution procedures have long been used to subdivide five-year population quantities into smaller age groups. The use of Sprague multipliers is an example (see page 126). These methods work reasonably well over age distribution ranges that are smoothly graduated and are not at the extremities of age. At the lowest ages, the single-year age distribution is under the influence of a sharply curving schedule of survival rates. The curvature of the age distribution at the lowest ages, therefore, is not estimated well by multipliers that use the curvature at higher ages as weights. This problem is not as serious at the upper extremities of age because the change in curvature is less marked.

In order to provide a better basis for distribution by single-year age groups over the first six years, stable population models are computed by SINSIN and their distributions are assigned to the population at low ages. The system of Sprague multipliers is used at higher ages, and results of the two methods are merged where they come together.

Another improvement on standard systems of distribution and interpolation is that SINSIN operates on cohorts. Rather than interpolating horizontally to make annual population estimates for age groups between five-year estimates for the same age groups, it interpolates diagonally along the single-year cohort vectors. The entire system is linked to FIVFIV in such a way that numerical consistency is retained between SINSIN output and FIVFIV output. The detailed procedures of distribution and interpolation are described in Appendix One.

ANNUAL PROJECTIONS BY SINSIN

The tasks that SINSIN can perform are numerous. In this chapter, the basic one of preparing annual detail will be described. An illustration of annual estimates for one sex is shown in Example 4.1. Similar pages of estimates are produced by SINSIN for the other sex and for both sexes combined.

EXAMPLE 4.1 Annual Projection for One Sex

TURKEY 'A' LAISSEZ-FAIRE POPULATION POLICY (POP IN THOUSANDS)   PAGE 6

POPULATION PROJECTION FOR FIFTEEN YEARS

MALES

AGE	1970	1971	1972	1973	1974	1975	1976	1977	1978	1979	1980	1981	1982	1983	1984	1985
0	2773.	2855.	2918.	2970.	3016.	3058.	3138.	3235.	3335.	3429.	3505.	3605.	3711.	3803.	3869.	3905.
5	2441.	2481.	2528.	2581.	2634.	2683.	2723.	2776.	2838.	2904.	2975.	3039.	3122.	3222.	3330.	3429.
10	2209.	2261.	2304.	2343.	2381.	2422.	2467.	2514.	2563.	2612.	2664.	2716.	2770.	2824.	2884.	2955.
15	1866.	1935.	2005.	2072.	2135.	2191.	2240.	2283.	2322.	2361.	2403.	2446.	2493.	2542.	2592.	2644.
20	1510.	1577.	1642.	1705.	1768.	1833.	1901.	1969.	2036.	2099.	2156.	2205.	2248.	2287.	2326.	2369.
25	1148.	1189.	1244.	1308.	1376.	1443.	1506.	1568.	1630.	1696.	1764.	1833.	1902.	1970.	2034.	2092.
30	986.	960.	956.	970.	998.	1033.	1077.	1132.	1194.	1259.	1325.	1394.	1462.	1529.	1596.	1662.
35	1134.	1108.	1053.	983.	919.	878.	857.	854.	868.	892.	926.	972.	1029.	1095.	1164.	1232.
40	901.	944.	994.	1040.	1067.	1065.	1037.	982.	915.	855.	815.	793.	790.	805.	833.	871.
45	694.	733.	763.	789.	818.	853.	895.	943.	988.	1014.	1013.	986.	933.	868.	811.	775.
50	473.	483.	516.	565.	614.	655.	691.	719.	744.	773.	808.	847.	894.	937.	963.	962.
55	610.	587.	543.	490.	451.	438.	447.	479.	524.	570.	608.	640.	667.	690.	717.	751.
60	463.	472.	500.	532.	550.	546.	522.	480.	434.	402.	393.	403.	434.	474.	512.	546.
65	377.	368.	354.	351.	363.	391.	418.	451.	476.	480.	462.	425.	380.	344.	328.	333.
70	221.	263.	294.	307.	304.	290.	242.	217.	220.	250.	302.	297.	324.	353.	369.	357.
75+	137.	150.	163.	176.	190.	205.	220.	236.	251.	266.	280.	292.	302.	310.	317.	321.
TOTAL	17946.	18364.	18776.	19182.	19584.	19985.	20380.	20837.	21338.	21862.	22396.	22893.	23460.	24055.	24644.	25204.

SELECTED AGE GROUPS (POPULATION AND PER CENT OF TOTAL)

AGE	1970	1971	1972	1973	1974	1975	1976	1977	1978	1979	1980	1981	1982	1983	1984	1985
0-14	7424.	7596.	7750.	7894.	8031.	8163.	8327.	8524.	8735.	8945.	9143.	9360.	9602.	9850.	10082.	10289.
%	41.37	41.36	41.28	41.15	41.01	40.85	40.86	40.91	40.94	40.91	40.82	40.89	40.93	40.95	40.91	40.82
15-64	9786.	9988.	10215.	10454.	10696.	10936.	11173.	11409.	11656.	11922.	12209.	12520.	12852.	13198.	13549.	13904.
%	54.53	54.39	54.40	54.50	54.61	54.72	54.82	54.75	54.62	54.53	54.51	54.69	54.78	54.87	54.98	55.16
65-75	736.	781.	811.	834.	857.	886.	880.	904.	947.	996.	1044.	1014.	1006.	1008.	1013.	1012.
%	4.10	4.25	4.32	4.35	4.38	4.43	4.32	4.34	4.44	4.56	4.66	4.43	4.29	4.19	4.11	4.01
6-11	2852.	2899.	2948.	3002.	3061.	3121.	3179.	3237.	3303.	3374.	3447.	3520.	3604.	3704.	3818.	3937.
%	15.89	15.79	15.70	15.65	15.63	15.62	15.60	15.53	15.48	15.43	15.39	15.37	15.36	15.40	15.49	15.62
18-23	1943.	2022.	2100.	2178.	2257.	2338.	2418.	2494.	2564.	2628.	2685.	2736.	2784.	2832.	2884.	2939.
%	10.82	11.01	11.18	11.35	11.52	11.70	11.86	11.97	12.02	12.02	11.99	11.95	11.87	11.77	11.70	11.66
13-15	1251.	1292.	1327.	1355.	1379.	1401.	1423.	1447.	1474.	1503.	1533.	1563.	1593.	1624.	1656.	1687.
%	6.97	7.03	7.07	7.07	7.04	7.01	6.98	6.94	6.91	6.88	6.84	6.83	6.79	6.75	6.72	6.69
20-29	2658.	2766.	2886.	3013.	3144.	3277.	3406.	3537.	3667.	3795.	3919.	4038.	4150.	4257.	4360.	4461.
%	14.81	15.06	15.37	15.71	16.06	16.40	16.71	16.97	17.18	17.36	17.50	17.64	17.69	17.70	17.69	17.70
0-18	8945.	9173.	9384.	9581.	9767.	9941.	10141.	10369.	10610.	10851.	11083.	11336.	11617.	11905.	12178.	12426.
%	49.84	49.95	49.98	49.95	49.87	49.74	49.76	49.76	49.72	49.63	49.49	49.52	49.52	49.49	49.42	49.30
5-7	1491.	1515.	1547.	1581.	1615.	1643.	1663.	1696.	1740.	1782.	1828.	1868.	1926.	1997.	2060.	2115.
%	8.31	8.25	8.24	8.24	8.24	8.22	8.16	8.14	8.15	8.15	8.16	8.16	8.21	8.30	8.36	8.39
6-6	497.	506.	514.	527.	538.	548.	556.	566.	580.	594.	609.	622.	644.	666.	687.	705.
%	2.77	2.76	2.74	2.75	2.75	2.74	2.73	2.71	2.72	2.72	2.72	2.72	2.75	2.77	2.79	2.80

[Handwritten annotations: "Means 65+" pointing to 65-75 row; "User's Selections" bracketing the lower group of age selections]

Instructions are given to SINSIN by including them within the original instructions given to FIVFIV. The computer prepares special output from FIVFIV (on cards, tape, or disk), which is passed as input to SINSIN. Thus, the user only has to think about one set of instructions for FIVFIV, which may include additional work for SINSIN or not as he wishes.

The main subject for SINSIN is REGROUP. It must always be used if SINSIN is used at all. The cards are prepared according to the usual conventions for punching of instruction cards (see Chapter One).

<u>REGROUP</u>   (Required for all SINSIN runs)

GROUPS.##-##.##-##.##-##.##-##.##-##.##-##.##-##.
(Column 80 for print code)

SINSIN will reassemble population by the special age groups that are mentioned where the symbols ##-## are located. The user may specify as many groups as desired up to seven groups. SINSIN will also print complete single-year age distributions, if requested as explained later.

All symbols ## must be replaced by numbers of the same size or left empty. For example, GROUPS.11–13.09–11. 2– 3. is acceptable, but GROUPS.2–11. is not. The card may be left blank after the last age group that is punched.

When the upper limit of an age group is the same as the lower limit, a single-year age group will be printed. However, the age group 00–00 will not be printed by itself as a special age group. The highest possible age group is 75, which is an open age interval and always means 75 and over. Thus, the range 70–75 will group the population aged 70 and over. The range 75–75 will group 75 and over. It is not necessary to request standard five-year age groups, or 0–14, 15–64, and 65+, because these age groups will be computed and printed whether requested or not.

The default for special age groups takes two forms, depending upon whether the decimal point is included after the label GROUPS. If no special age groups are wanted, punch the decimal point (GROUPS.), and no age groups will be printed. Alternatively, the decimal point can be omitted (GROUPS), and a default list of age groups will be printed. The default groups are as follows: 7–11, 12–14, 15–17, 18–21, and 20–44. Whether special age groups are wanted or not, a card for GROUPS must be included.

The single-year age distributions that are prepared by SINSIN as an intermediate step during computation are not normally printed. However, if the number "1" is punched in column 80 of the GROUPS card, ages 5 and over will be printed. A code of "2" in column 80 will cause the distribution from age 0 upwards to be printed. Printing by SINSIN is for each sex separately and both sexes combined.

```
0         1         2         3         4         5         6         7         8
1234567890123456789012345678901234567890123456789012345678901234567890123456789 0
```

EXAMPLES OF REGROUP

*** REQUESTS ANNUAL PROJECTION WITHOUT SPECIAL AGE GROUPS ***

REGROUP
GROUPS.   (NOTE INCLUSION OF DECIMAL AFTER GROUPS, BUT NO AGE GROUPS FOLLOW)

*** REQUESTS SPECIAL DEFAULT AGE GROUPS ***

REGROUP
GROUPS   (NOTE OMISSION OF DECIMAL AFTER GROUPS)

(continued)

```
            *** SPECIFIES SOME SPECIAL AGE GROUPS ***

REGROUP
GROUPS. 06-12. 18-23. 13-15. 20-29. 00-18. 05-07. 06-06.


            *** PRINTING CONTROL IN COLUMN 80 ASKS ***
            *** FOR ALL SINGLE-YEAR AGE GROUPS ***

REGROUP
GROUPS. 18-23. 20-29.                                              2

12345678901234567890123456789012345678901234567890123456789012345678901234567890
```

Single-Year Age Distributions

Single-year age distributions can be requested by punching a printing code (1 or 2) in column 80 of the GROUPS card. Single-year age distributions such as the one shown in Example 4.2 should be used cautiously. Diligent distribution and interpolation yield relatively smooth and orderly arrays of numbers, but the results come from essentially arbitrary procedures.

EXAMPLE 4.2   Single-Year Age Distribution for One Sex

```
STABLE MODEL. TF=6.7. MORTALITY=WEST LEVEL 3.                            PAGE  4
SINGLE YEAR AGE GROUPS
```

FEMALES

AGE	0	1	2	3	4	5	6	7	8	9	10	11	12	13	14	15
0	402.	406.	410.	414.	418.	422.	426.	430.	434.	438.	443.	447.	451.	456.	460.	465.
1	332.	339.	341.	344.	346.	349.	356.	358.	361.	363.	366.	373.	376.	379.	381.	384.
2	301.	308.	311.	313.	315.	316.	319.	326.	328.	330.	332.	337.	342.	344.	346.	348.
3	284.	290.	294.	296.	297.	299.	300.	304.	310.	312.	313.	317.	327.	326.	327.	329.
4	272.	277.	281.	285.	284.	286.	287.	289.	292.	299.	300.	303.	309.	319.	313.	315.
5	264.	268.	272.	275.	278.	277.	278.	280.	282.	285.	291.	293.	299.	305.	310.	305.
6	257.	260.	263.	267.	269.	270.	269.	272.	275.	278.	283.	280.	291.	295.	298.	297.
7	251.	254.	257.	259.	262.	264.	265.	264.	268.	272.	277.	277.	273.	287.	290.	290.
8	246.	249.	251.	254.	256.	258.	260.	261.	262.	266.	271.	272.	272.	269.	283.	284.
9	241.	243.	246.	248.	250.	252.	255.	257.	259.	260.	265.	267.	268.	269.	269.	278.
10	236.	238.	241.	243.	246.	247.	250.	252.	254.	257.	260.	262.	264.	265.	267.	273.
11	231.	234.	236.	239.	241.	243.	245.	247.	250.	252.	255.	257.	259.	261.	263.	267.
12	227.	229.	231.	234.	236.	238.	240.	242.	245.	247.	250.	252.	254.	256.	259.	262.
13	222.	225.	227.	229.	231.	233.	236.	238.	240.	242.	245.	247.	249.	251.	254.	257.
14	218.	220.	222.	225.	226.	229.	231.	233.	235.	237.	240.	242.	245.	247.	249.	252.
15	213.	215.	218.	220.	222.	224.	226.	228.	231.	233.	235.	237.	240.	242.	244.	247.
16	209.	211.	213.	215.	217.	219.	221.	223.	226.	228.	230.	232.	234.	237.	239.	242.
		206.	208.	210.	213.	215.	217.	219.	221.	223.	225.	227.	229.	232.	234.	237.
			204.	206.	208.	210.	212.	214.	216.	218.	220.	222.	224.	226.	229.	231.
				201.	203.	205.	207.	209.	211.	213.	215.	217.	219.	221.	223.	226.
					198.	200.	202.	204.	206.	208.	210.	212.	214.	216.	218.	220.
						195.	197.	199.	201.	203.	205.	207.	209.	211.	213.	215.
							192.	194.	196.	198.	200.	202.	204.	206.	208.	210.
								189.	191.	193.	195.	197.	199.	201.	203.	204.
54	64.									186.	188.	190.	192.	193.	195.	197.	199.
55	61.	61.									183.	185.	187.	188.	190.	192.	194.
56	58.	59.	59.									180.	182.	183.	185.	187.	189.
57	55.	56.	56.	57.									177.	178.	180.	182.	184.
58	52.	53.	53.	54.	54.									173.	175.	177.	179.
59	49.	50.	50.	51.	51.	52.									170.	172.	174.
60	46.	47.	47.	48.	48.	49.	49.									167.	169.
61	43.	41.	44.	45.	45.	46.	46.	46.									164.
62	41.	38.	38.	42.	42.	43.	43.	43.	44.							
63	38.	36.	35.	35.	39.	40.	40.	40.	41.	41.						
64	35.	33.	32.	33.	34.	37.	37.	37.	38.	38.	38.					
65	32.	30.	29.	30.	31.	34.	34.	34.	35.	35.	35.	36.				
66	29.	29.	27.	27.	29.	31.	31.	32.	32.	32.	32.	33.	33.			
67	27.	27.	27.	25.	26.	28.	28.	29.	29.	29.	30.	30.	30.	30.		
68	24.	24.	24.	25.	23.	26.	26.	26.	26.	27.	27.	27.	27.	27.	28.	
69	22.	22.	22.	22.	23.	23.	23.	23.	24.	24.	24.	24.	25.	25.	25.	25.
70	20.	20.	20.	20.	20.	21.	21.	21.	21.	21.	22.	22.	22.	22.	22.	23.
71	17.	17.	17.	18.	18.	18.	18.	19.	19.	19.	19.	19.	19.	20.	20.	20.
72	15.	15.	15.	15.	16.	16.	16.	16.	16.	17.	17.	17.	17.	17.	18.	18.
73	13.	13.	14.	14.	14.	14.	14.	14.	14.	14.	15.	15.	15.	15.	15.	16.
74	12.	12.	12.	12.	12.	12.	12.	12.	13.	13.	13.	13.	13.	13.	13.	13.
75+	50.	50.	51.	51.	52.	52.	53.	53.	54.	54.	55.	55.	56.	57.	57.	58.

Occasionally, one will even discover illogical increases in the size of a single-year cohort, reading diagonally as the cohort ages. Unless there is in-migration, increase is impossible. The increase in such an instance is due to distribution procedures that are an imperfect substitute for original data in the form of single-year age groups and projections by single years. An error of this type, if it occurs at all, usually appears where distributions made by Sprague multipliers at five-year intervals of time do not permit the formation of logically acceptable diagonals. Unexpected irregularities may occur in such instances, particularly if they involve population below age 10 where LaGrange interpolation along diagonals is merged with stable models. It is recommended, therefore, that analysts attach no significance to patterns in the estimates that could be the result of arbitrary distribution or interpolation procedures.

The chief purpose of SINSIN is to provide the user with a means for projecting populations by calendar years and by age groups other than the standard five-year groupings. The elegance of voluminous output by single-year age groups should not be misunderstood as evidence of precision when the original input is by five-year age groups and probably was inaccurate even in that aggregated form. Regrouping into multiple-year age groups should be done whenever possible.

Machine-Readable Output

The single-year age distributions that are computed by SINSIN can be used as input for planning models. If machine-readable input is wanted, SINSIN can be ordered to produce a deck of cards (or a file on disk or tape) that contains the single-year age distributions for years 0 to 15. The subject to use for this purpose is PUNCH.SINGLE. It is similar in effect to PUNCH. FIVE. One causes the five-year age groups from the FIVFIV array for 35 years to be output, and the other causes the single-year age groups from the SINSIN array for 15 years to be output. Whether the output is on cards, tape, or disk is determined at the time the package is installed (see references to logical unit numbers for KPFIV and KPSIN in Appendix Two).

PUNCH.SINGLE   Optional subject.   Default: No punched projection

This subject will cause a deck of cards containing the single-year SINSIN projection for 15 years to be punched. The subject header can be included more than one time, in which event more than one deck will be punched.
No information card is needed for this subject.

```
          0         1         2         3         4         5         6         7         8
1234567890 1234567890 1234567890 1234567890 1234567890 1234567890 1234567890 1234567890

                         EXAMPLE OF PUNCH.SINGLE

                      *** ALWAYS INCLUDES REGROUP ***

PUNCH.SINGLE
REGROUP
GROUPS.                                                                          2

1234567890 1234567890 1234567890 1234567890 1234567890 1234567890 1234567890 1234567890
```

Annual Output for Thirty-Five Years

The standard output of SINSIN is for 15 years. It fills a page with columns of estimates. If additional years are wanted, SINSIN can be ordered to provide annual detail for the entire 35-year projection period. This is done by making three projections starting with years 0, 10, and 20. Use OLD.POP without any more date shifting for years 10 and 20. Assumptions about fertility, mortality, and migration have to be moved forward in time to match the starting dates 10 and 20, respectively. The results are three projections with three corresponding sets of SINSIN output (A, B, and C) dated as shown schematically below:

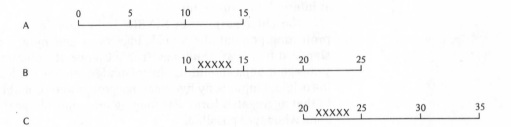

The symbols XXXXX show overlaps in the output. The overlapping parts of B and C should be scissored and discarded. The SINSIN estimates will then match in A and B for year 15, and in B and C for year 25. The SINSIN estimates will also match the FIVFIV projection at all five-year dates. The FIVFIV projections beyond year 35, which will be produced as a by-product, can be disregarded. Assumptions for those later years have no effect on the SINSIN distributions for earlier years.

Chapters Six and Seven explain additional computations with SINSIN that require dated assumptions about ratios and age-specific rates for variables. The form of the assumptions in those chapters makes them independent of the starting date for the projection. Hence, instruction cards for the subjects explained there (SUBDIVIDE and AGESEXSPEC) can be duplicated and used in the sets of instructions for all three projections, A, B, and C.

Example 4.3 shows how an annual projection for 35 years is made. It is marked to show how the second (Part B) and third (Part C) projections are dated 10 and 20 years later, respectively, in relation to the first projection (Part A). When the output is obtained, some differences in detail will be noticed where interpolated years overlap: specifically, years 11–14 and 21–24. Such minor differences are unavoidable since the distribution and interpolation processes take into account the FIVFIV projection only for the particular 15 years that are included in each SINSIN operation. The result of running the three projections shown in Example 4.3 and scissoring and pasting up the results is shown in Example 4.4.

MEASUREMENT OF POPULATION STOCKS AND FLOWS

A word about stocks and flows in population projections may be useful. Projections show stocks of population at specified dates. It is often valuable

EXAMPLE 4.3   Instructions for an Annual Overlapping Projection of 35 Years

```
0          1          2          3          4          5          6          7          8
1234567890 1234567890 1234567890 1234567890 1234567890 1234567890 1234567890 1234567890

YEAR.TITLE
YR.1970.TURKEY 'B'   POSITIVE POPULATION POLICY   (POP IN THOUSANDS)   PART A
DATE.SHIFT
YR.1970.WEEK.43
INIT.POP
INIT.F.A      2761.7     2384.8     2157.6     1930.9     1331.2     1076.2     1056.0
INIT.F.B      1054.9      850.9      683.7      484.5      559.9      444.4      392.2
INIT.F.C       232.7      201.9
INIT.M.A      2791.4     2456.6     2222.8     1885.2     1528.7     1165.4      989.7
INIT.M.B      1116.4      909.8      703.5      483.3      598.5      467.4      378.2
INIT.M.C       225.2      140.9
MORT.SPLIT
CHILD.LV.F     15.51      16.86      18.20      19.55      20.89      21.44      22.
CHILD.LV.M     16.54      17.69      18.84      19.99      21.14      21.57      22.
ADULT.LV.F     18.66      19.21      19.77      20.33      20.89      21.44      22.
ADULT.LV.M     19.43      19.86      20.29      20.71      21.14      21.57      22.
FERTILITY
TOTAL.FERT      5.3        4.4        3.4        2.8        2.5        2.5        2.5
FERDIST1.1      .015       .051       .049       .039       .028       .012       .006
FERDIST2.1      .015       .054       .051       .038       .026       .011       .005
FERDIST3.1      .015       .057       .054       .037       .024       .009       .004
FERDIST4.1      .015       .060       .057       .036       .022       .007       .003
FERDIST5.3      .015       .064       .060       .035       .019       .005       .002
FEND
MIGRATION
MIGLEVEL.F     -30.       -30.       -24.       -18.       -12.       -12.       -12.
MIGLEVEL.M     -70.       -70.       -56.       -42.       -28.       -28.       -28.
MIGRF1.7.A       6.         4.         2.         8.        20.        19.        17.
MIGRF1.7.B      14.         8.         1.         1.
MIGRF1.7.C
MIGRM1.7.A       3.         2.         1.         1.         6.        21.        36.
MIGRM1.7.B      17.         9.         3.         1.
MIGRM1.7.C
MEND
REGROUP
GROUPS
END PROJECTION
```

```
YEAR.TITLE
YR.(1980).TURKEY 'B'   POSITIVE POPULATION POLICY  (POP IN THOUSANDS)   PART B
INIT.POP                     } Use OLD.POP without date shifting
OLD.POP.(1980)
MORT.SPLIT
CHILD.LV.F     18.20      19.55      20.89      21.44      22.00       ← move two periods
CHILD.LV.M     18.84      19.99      21.14      21.57      22.00          to left
ADULT.LV.F     19.77      20.33      20.89      21.44      22.00
ADULT.LV.M     20.29      20.71      21.14      21.57      22.00
FERTILITY
TOTAL.FERT  move   3.4       2.8        2.5
FERDIST 1.1  up    .015      .057       .054       .037       .024       .009       .004
FERDIST 2.1  two   .015      .060       .057       .036       .022       .007       .003
FERDIST 3.5  periods .015    .064       .060       .035       .019       .005       .002
FEND
MIGRATION
MIGLEVEL.F      -24.      -18.       -12.       -12.       -12.       ← move two periods to
MIGLEVEL.M      -56.      -42.       -28.       -28.       -28.         left   19.        17.
MIGRF 1.7 A  Move up   6.      4.         2.         8.         20.
MIGRF 1.7 B  only if  14.      8.         1.         1.
MIGRF 1.7 C  necessary.
MIGRM 1.7 A  not      3.      2.         1.         1.         6.         21.        36.
MIGRM 1.7 B  needed  17.      9.         3.         1.
MIGRM 1.7 C  here because distribution same all periods.
MEND
REGROUP
GROUPS
END PROJECTION
```

```
YEAR.TITLE
YR.(1990).TURKEY 'B'   POSITIVE POPULATION POLICY  (POP IN THOUSANDS)   PART C
INIT.POP
OLD.POP.(1990)
MORT.SPLIT
CHILD.LV.F     20.89      21.44      22.    ← Move four periods to left
CHILD.LV.M     21.14      21.57      22.
ADULT.LV.F     20.89      21.44      22.
ADULT.LV.M     21.14      21.57      22.
FERTILITY
TOTAL.FERT      2.5
FERDIST 1.7     .015      .064       .060       .035       .019       .005       .002
FEND
MIGRATION
MIGLEVEL.F      -12.      -12.       -12.    ← move four periods to left
MIGLEVEL.M      -28.      -28.       -28.
MIGRF 1.7 A      6.       4.         2.         8.         20.        19.        17.
MIGRF 1.7 B     14.       8.         1.         1.
MIGRF 1.7 C
MIGRM 1.7 A      3.       2.         1.         1.         6.         21.        36.
MIGRM 1.7 B     17.       9.         3.         1.
MIGRM 1.7 C
MEND
REGROUP
GROUPS
END PROJECTION
```

```
12345678901234567890123456789012345678901234567890123456789012345678901234567890
```

to estimate annual flows of persons into certain age ranges as well. By attaining certain ages, individuals become eligible for primary school, for work, for compulsory military service, and for marriage. These flows can be estimated approximately from SINSIN projections.

Consider, for example, the excerpt in Figure 4.5 from a page of SINSIN output. If the original projection was positioned on midyear (if DATE.SHIFT was used), the estimates of population are stocks at midyear of the years shown. If not positioned on midyear of calendar years, the date of the original input population may be interpreted as the "midyear" of a statistical year selected arbitrarily.

The age labels show the initial age of each one-year age range. The label 18 refers to persons who have completed 18 years, but have not yet attained 19 full years. The population estimate refers to persons distributed between exact ages 18 and 19. If one wished to relabel the estimates with exact dates and exact age ranges, they would be as shown in italics.

Aging of a population cohort over time can be traced diagonally. A convenient approximation of the annual flow across any age boundary is the one-year age group centered on that boundary at the midpoint of the time interval. That is the general rule, which will now be illustrated.

1. The annual flow of persons attaining exact age 20.5 during the year labeled "1" is the one-year group of persons averaging 20.5 years of age at midyear, namely 409.

2. If one wanted to estimate the annual flow of persons attaining exact age 20, the one-year age group centered on age 20 could be approximated by taking the average of two groups, one centered on exact age 19.5 and the other on exact age 20.5, namely $(415+409)/2=412$.

3. Different time periods can be defined. If the annual flow is measured from midyear to midyear, the estimate centers on the beginning of the year. For example, the annual flow of persons attaining age 20 centered on January 1 of year 4 is approximated by averaging the one-year age groups on either side of this midpoint, namely $(428+426)/2=427$.

4. Following these principles for approximation, the SINSIN output enables one to construct a time series of entrants into particular age ranges. Annual entrants to the age range 21 and over is simply the mean of the rows printed for ages 20 and 21; they are 401½, 406, 410½, 415½, and 421½, respectively, for years 0 through 4.

A caution may be added. The stock of persons shown for age group 0 is not a measure of annual births. Individuals in the age group are distributed between exact ages 0 (birth) and 1, and are the survivors of previous births, not the annual quantity of births.

The same principles for measuring flows from SINSIN estimates of stocks can be applied to FIVFIV output. A larger element of approximation is involved, however, because the age groups refer to five years of age, and the time intervals are five years. For example, an estimate of the annual number of persons attaining age 17.5 in year 5 would be the age group 15–19 in year 5 divided by 5 to annualize the result. To estimate the annual number attaining age 15 would necessitate averaging of the age groups above and below that exact age and dividing by 5, namely, $(P(10-14)+P(15-19))/(2\times5)=$ flow at age 15. The linearity assumptions that are implicit in this procedure would make such estimates less useful than those that could be obtained from SINSIN output.

EXAMPLE 4.4   Annual Overlapping Projection for 35 Years

```
TURKEY 'B'  POSITIVE POPULATION POLICY  (POP IN THOUSANDS) (PART A)                                    (POP IN THOUSANDS) (PART B)
POPULATION PROJECTION FOR FIFTEEN YEARS

                                                   M A L E S                                                        M A L E S
AGE    1970   1971   1972   1973   1974   1975   1976   1977   1978   1979   1980   1981   1982   1983   1984 | 1985   1986   1987
  0    2777.  2861.  2918.  2956.  2976.  2983.  3025.  3063.  3081.  3074.  3037.  3043.  3040.  3010.  2945. | 2858.  2847.  2839.
  5    2441.  2482.  2532.  2588.  2643.  2690.  2719.  2765.  2819.  2868.  2907.  2906.  2922.  2950.  2977. | 2981.  2938.  2911.
 10    2209.  2262.  2334.  2342.  2380.  2422.  2470.  2520.  2571.  2621.  2672.  2722.  2771.  2816.  2854. | 2890.  2921.  2947.
 15    1866.  1935.  2005.  2073.  2135.  2191.  2240.  2283.  2321.  2360.  2404.  2450.  2498.  2550.  2602. | 2653.  2702.  2750.
 20    1510.  1577.  1642.  1705.  1768.  1834.  1901.  1970.  2037.  2100.  2157.  2207.  2249.  2288.  2327. | 2372.  2418.  2468.
 25    1148.  1189.  1244.  1308.  1376.  1443.  1506.  1568.  1631.  1697.  1765.  1834.  1904.  1972.  2037. | 2095.  2146.  2190.
 30     986.   960.   956.   970.   998.  1034.  1078.  1132.  1195.  1260.  1326.  1395.  1464.  1531.  1598. | 1665.  1738.  1812.
 35    1134.  1108.  1053.   983.   920.   878.   857.   855.   868.   893.   926.   973.  1031.  1097.  1166. | 1234.  1305.  1376.
 40     901.   944.   994.  1040.  1067.  1065.  1038.   983.   915.   855.   816.   794.   792.   806.   835. |  873.   920.   978.
 45     694.   733.   763.   789.   818.   854.   895.   944.   989.  1015.  1014.   987.   935.   870.   814. |  777.   759.   758.
 50     473.   483.   516.   565.   614.   655.   691.   720.   745.   774.   809.   849.   896.   940.   966. |  966.   940.   891.
 55     610.   587.   543.   490.   451.   438.   448.   479.   524.   570.   609.   642.   668.   692.   720. |  754.   793.   837.
 60     463.   472.   500.   532.   550.   546.   523.   480.   435.   403.   394.   405.   435.   476.   514. |  548.   578.   603.
 65     377.   368.   355.   351.   363.   392.   418.   452.   477.   481.   464.   427.   381.   345.   330. |  335.   355.   384.
 70     221.   263.   294.   307.   304.   290.   243.   217.   221.   251.   303.   326.   356.   356.   372. |  360.   318.   279.
75+     137.   151.   163.   176.   191.   205.   221.   236.   252.   267.   282.   294.   305.   314.   321. |  326.   339.   353.
TOTAL 17950. 18371. 18781. 19176. 19555. 19922. 20272. 20667. 21081. 21491. 21883. 22224. 22618. 23013. 23377. |23689. 24019. 24376.

SELECTED AGE GROUPS (POPULATION AND PER CENT OF TOTAL)                                                          ENT OF TOTAL)
AGE    1970   1971   1972   1973   1974   1975   1976   1977   1978   1979   1980   1981   1982   1983   1984 | 1985   1986   1987

0-14   7428.  7603.  7754.  7885.  7999.  8095.  8214.  8347.  8471.  8562.  8615.  8670.  8733.  8776.  8776. | 8729.  8705.  8697.
  %   41.38  41.38  41.29  41.12  40.90  40.64  40.52  40.39  40.18  39.84  39.37  39.01  38.61  38.13  37.54 |36.85  36.24  35.68

15-64  9786.  9988. 10216. 10455. 10698. 10939. 11177. 11414. 11661. 11929. 12220. 12535. 12872. 13223. 13579. |13939. 14300. 14663.
  %   54.52  54.37  54.39  54.52  54.71  54.91  55.13  55.23  55.32  55.51  55.84  56.40  56.91  57.46  58.09 |58.84  59.54  60.15

65-75   736.   781.   811.   835.   858.   887.   882.   906.   914.   949.   999.  1048.  1019.  1012.  1015.  1022. |1021.  1013.  1016.
  %    4.10   4.25   4.32   4.35   4.39   4.45   4.35   4.38   4.50   4.65   4.79   4.58   4.48   4.41   4.37 | 4.31   4.22   4.17

7-11   2354.  2393.  2434.  2478.  2529.  2582.  2633.  2678.  2727.  2779.  2825.  2865.  2894.  2916.  2945. | 2969.  2978.  2973.
  %   13.12  13.02  12.96  12.92  12.93  12.96  12.99  12.96  12.94  12.93  12.91  12.89  12.79  12.67  12.60 |12.53  12.40  12.20

12-14  1293.  1329.  1358.  1381.  1402.  1423.  1448.  1478.  1510.  1541.  1571.  1600.  1631.  1662.  1690. | 1712.  1734.  1753.
  %    7.20   7.23   7.23   7.20   7.17   7.15   7.14   7.15   7.16   7.17   7.18   7.20   7.21   7.22   7.23 | 7.23   7.22   7.19

15-17  1163.  1205.  1248.  1287.  1322.  1350.  1374.  1395.  1417.  1442.  1471.  1502.  1533.  1564.  1594. | 1625.  1654.  1681.
  %    6.48   6.56   6.64   6.71   6.76   6.78   6.78   6.75   6.72   6.71   6.72   6.76   6.78   6.79   6.82 | 6.86   6.89   6.90

18-21  1352.  1404.  1457.  1510.  1565.  1620.  1674.  1723.  1765.  1801.  1831.  1860.  1892.  1928.  1968. | 2010.  2051.  2092.
  %    7.53   7.64   7.76   7.88   8.00   8.13   8.26   8.34   8.37   8.38   8.37   8.37   8.37   8.38   8.42 | 8.49   8.54   8.58

20-44  5679.  5779.  5889.  6007.  6129.  6254.  6380.  6508.  6647.  6806.  6991.  7203.  7439.  7695.  7963. | 8240.  8528.  8824.
  %   31.64  31.45  31.35  31.32  31.34  31.39  31.47  31.49  31.53  31.67  31.94  32.41  32.89  33.44  34.07 |34.78  35.51  36.20
```

FIGURE 4.5   Excerpt from Single-Year Output

			Years			
Mean ages →		0	1	2	3	4
		0.5	*1.5*	*2.5*	*3.5*	*4.5*
Exact ranges →	18 *18-19*	417	422	429	438	447
Age	19 *19-20*	411	415	420	428	437
	20 *20-21*	404	409	414	419	426
	21 *21-22*	399	403	407	412	412

POP IN THOUSANDS) (PART C)   PAGE 6

M A L E S

1988	1989	1990	1991	1992	1993	1994	1995	1996	1997	1998	1999	2000	2001	2002	2003	2004	2005
2828.	2815.	2802.	2820.	2843.	2863.	2876.	2886.	2922.	2971.	3024.	3077.	3123.	3163.	3202.	3234.	3252.	3252.
2888.	2858.	2823.	2779.	2760.	2761.	2771.	2778.	2777.	2789.	2808.	2833.	2864.	2902.	2947.	2997.	3052.	3103.
2964.	2971.	2966.	2950.	2922.	2883.	2842.	2811.	2789.	2776.	2769.	2766.	2767.	2773.	2785.	2801.	2823.	2854.
2795.	2836.	2872.	2903.	2929.	2948.	2956.	2950.	2932.	2901.	2863.	2826.	2797.	2775.	2761.	2754.	2752.	2755.
2520.	2572.	2623.	2673.	2722.	2767.	2809.	2845.	2876.	2903.	2922.	2930.	2925.	2907.	2876.	2839.	2803.	2775.
2231.	2273.	2319.	2369.	2420.	2474.	2527.	2580.	2630.	2678.	2723.	2765.	2802.	2834.	2860.	2879.	2888.	2884.
1885.	1952.	2013.	2070.	2119.	2164.	2209.	2257.	2307.	2359.	2413.	2466.	2517.	2568.	2618.	2664.	2705.	2740.
1446.	1516.	1589.	1664.	1741.	1817.	1889.	1953.	2010.	2060.	2105.	2149.	2196.	2246.	2299.	2353.	2406.	2457.
1045.	1115.	1186.	1257.	1326.	1396.	1469.	1546.	1621.	1697.	1773.	1843.	1907.	1963.	2011.	2056.	2101.	2149.
774.	802.	839.	885.	943.	1009.	1079.	1150.	1220.	1290.	1359.	1430.	1503.	1577.	1652.	1727.	1796.	1860.
830.	776.	742.	724.	724.	740.	767.	804.	849.	906.	970.	1037.	1105.	1173.	1240.	1308.	1377.	1449.
880.	904.	903.	879.	832.	775.	726.	695.	680.	681.	696.	722.	756.	799.	852.	913.	977.	1042.
625.	650.	681.	717.	759.	798.	819.	818.	794.	750.	700.	658.	632.	621.	623.	636.	658.	690.
414.	443.	469.	489.	505.	524.	551.	585.	627.	675.	710.	721.	706.	672.	629.	590.	563.	549.
255.	250.	262.	276.	301.	329.	354.	369.	346.	338.	355.	398.	464.	466.	501.	539.	564.	564.
367.	378.	387.	387.	384.	376.	365.	350.	357.	366.	379.	394.	412.	428.	446.	465.	487.	510.
24744.	25112.	25477.	25841.	26230.	26624.	27009.	27376.	27739.	28139.	28567.	29016.	29476.	29867.	30301.	30754.	31203.	31633.

ENT OF TOTAL)

1988	1989	1990	1991	1992	1993	1994	1995	1996	1997	1998	1999	2000	2001	2002	2003	2004	2005
8680.	8644.	8592.	8550.	8525.	8507.	8490.	8475.	8489.	8535.	8601.	8676.	8754.	8839.	8934.	9032.	9126.	9210.
35.08	34.42	33.72	33.09	32.50	31.95	31.43	30.96	30.60	30.33	30.11	29.90	29.70	29.59	29.48	29.37	29.25	29.11
15029.	15397.	15767.	16140.	16516.	16888.	17250.	17597.	17920.	18224.	18522.	18827.	19140.	19462.	19792.	20127.	20464.	20800.
60.74	61.31	61.89	62.46	62.96	63.43	63.87	64.28	64.60	64.77	64.84	64.88	64.94	65.16	65.32	65.45	65.58	65.75
1036.	1071.	1118.	1152.	1189.	1229.	1269.	1304.	1330.	1379.	1444.	1513.	1582.	1566.	1575.	1594.	1614.	1623.
4.19	4.27	4.39	4.46	4.53	4.62	4.70	4.76	4.79	4.90	5.05	5.21	5.37	5.24	5.20	5.18	5.17	5.13
2953.	2928.	2891.	2853.	2816.	2786.	2775.	2775.	2773.	2772.	2778.	2791.	2809.	2831.	2859.	2899.	2947.	3000.
11.94	11.66	11.35	11.04	10.74	10.46	10.27	10.13	10.00	9.85	9.72	9.62	9.53	9.48	9.43	9.83	9.84	9.48
1769.	1780.	1788.	1787.	1772.	1753.	1727.	1700.	1680.	1668.	1663.	1659.	1656.	1656.	1660.	1668.	1677.	1688.
7.15	7.09	7.02	6.91	6.76	6.58	6.40	6.21	6.06	5.93	5.82	5.72	5.62	5.55	5.48	5.42	5.37	5.33
1706.	1728.	1747.	1761.	1774.	1781.	1781.	1768.	1745.	1719.	1695.	1675.	1663.	1657.	1653.	1651.	1652.	1656.
6.90	6.88	6.86	6.82	6.76	6.69	6.59	6.46	6.29	6.11	5.93	5.77	5.64	5.55	5.46	5.37	5.30	5.24
2132.	2172.	2210.	2245.	2276.	2303.	2325.	2344.	2357.	2360.	2351.	2329.	2298.	2266.	2238.	2217.	2204.	2198.
8.62	8.65	8.67	8.69	8.68	8.65	8.61	8.56	8.50	8.39	8.23	8.03	7.80	7.59	7.38	7.21	7.06	6.95
9125.	9429.	9731.	10032.	10328.	10619.	10903.	11181.	11444.	11697.	11935.	12153.	12347.	12518.	12664.	12790.	12902.	13005.
36.88	37.55	38.19	38.82	39.38	39.88	40.37	40.84	41.26	41.57	41.78	41.88	41.89	41.91	41.79	41.59	41.35	41.11

CHAPTER FIVE: URBAN POPULATION AND MIGRATION ———————

Up to this point, all examples have referred to national populations. The populations of cities also can be projected by the modified cohort-component method. The differences between national and urban projections, when made by the same method, are practical ones related to the formulation of assumptions about the initial age and sex structure of the population and about fertility, mortality, and migration. The plan of this chapter, therefore, is to suggest ways of meeting the more common practical problems that are encountered when making urban projections. Particular attention will be given to migration, because population change in urban areas is especially affected by migration.

DEFINITION OF THE URBAN POPULATION

Populations must be bounded by precise definition so that it is clear to what particular population a projection refers. Urban populations change not only by natural increase and by migration but also by reclassification of population previously enumerated as rural. As the spatial boundaries of cities are moved outward over time, people are added to the city population by boundary movement rather than by movement of the people themselves. Urban population defined as an aggregate of more than one city also grows when reclassification of communities transfers them from the rural to the

urban category due to growth, if the criterion is size, or due to administrative change, if the criterion of urban is administrative status. Both types of
urban population change, one due to spatial boundary changes and the
other due to reclassification, are components of urban population change
that may be included in population projections or not, according to the
analyst's decision.

If boundary changes and reclassification are included in projections,
these components are most conveniently treated as a part of net migration,
which then consists of real movements of persons plus transfers of persons
by boundary change and reclassification. The assumptions about migration
should then be based on an analysis of past changes in population due to all
of these causes combined. Projections of migration into the future must
refer to this collective component of population change. If the analyst
chooses to hold boundaries constant and to retain a fixed list of urban
communities, past change and assumptions about future migration must be
defined in the same way. It usually involves less adjustment of data to use
the former rather than the latter approach. The former also corresponds
well with planning categories since administrative areas defined as urban do
change over time.

Urban population may be defined as a single population aggregate to
which all persons belong, or new migrant population may be treated as a
separate subdivision of the urban population. When the second approach is
followed there are two urban populations and two projections: One refers
to the initial population with assumptions about its mortality, fertility, and
losses through out-migration. The other refers to in-migrants and their
mortality and fertility, which may be assumed to have different values. The
second projection starts from a zero population. The two projections are
added together to obtain urban estimates for future dates.

FIVFIV can accommodate either approach. An initial population of zero
can be given on the INIT.POP cards as required when a separate population
of new migrants is defined. The INIT.POP cards are all included, but the
numeric data fields are left empty.

Normally, separate projections for the migration cohorts will not be
worthwhile, or may even be logically inconsistent. The initial population of
an urban area includes in-born and out-born population. Measures of past
trends and levels of fertility and mortality for that urban population are
likely to be average measures for migrant and nonmigrant population
combined. Consequently, projections of the future urban population as a
single population may be the most expedient way to retain consistency with
past measurements that are used as a basis for assumptions about the future.

ADJUSTMENTS FOR AGE MISREPORTING

If age misreporting requires adjustment of the reported national population,
it is probably serious enough to require adjustment of the reported urban
population as well. Earlier discussions referred to methods of adjusting
national age distributions.[13] In each instance, the method was valid only if
the national population was actually closed against migration, or the quanti-

---

[13] See Demeny and Shorter, *Estimating Turkish Mortality, Fertility and Age Structure*, pp. 29–37 and Chapter Three of this manual.

ties of migration by age and sex were known with sufficient accuracy to permit a simulation of closure. This condition cannot be met for most urban populations, and consequently age misreporting cannot be estimated for them by the methods already mentioned.

The analysis of age misreporting in the national population provides, however, a first approximation for age misreporting in the urban population of the same country. The possibilities for approximation can be seen in the examples for Turkey and Iran. If the national age distributions by sex are taken in their adjusted form and are divided by the reported distributions of the same dates, age- and sex-specific adjustment factors for age misreporting can be found. Precisely, the adjustment factors ($k_{s,i}$, where s refers to sex and i to age group) are given by:

$$k_{s,i} = (P^a_{s,i} / P^r_{s,i}) - 1$$

where P refers to the population as reported (P^r) or as adjusted (P^a).

To illustrate the computation of adjustment factors, the Iranian population of 1966 is used, and the details are shown in Table 5.1. The adjustment factors ($k_{s,i}$) stand for differences between reported and adjusted populations, differences that can be seen by plotting the model population for Iran (adjusted) against the census population (reported) as done in Figure 3.3.

The Iranian example illustrates not only an adjustment for age misreporting, but also one for sex misreporting (see column totals separately by sex in Table 5.1). As mentioned earlier, the estimation of sex misreporting is less reliable than that for age misreporting. This limitation applies

TABLE 5.1 National Adjustment Factors for Age Misreporting in Iran, 1966 (population in thousands)

Age group	Males			Females		
	Reported	Adjusted	Adjustment factor	Reported	Adjusted	Adjustment factor
	(P^r)	(P^a)	(k)	(P^r)	(P^a)	(k)
0–4	2307.7	2329.4	.009	2129.2	2220.4	.043
5–9	2127.7	1900.0	−.107	1978.5	1804.8	−.088
10–14	1593.8	1555.8	−.024	1423.4	1477.4	.038
15–19	1060.0	1248.5	.179	1069.0	1181.2	.105
20–24	792.9	1049.9	.324	889.3	985.3	.108
25–29	801.7	890.5	.111	848.0	829.0	−.022
30–34	863.3	782.5	−.094	804.7	720.9	−.104
35–39	763.9	688.5	−.099	654.4	629.8	−.038
40–44	737.8	595.8	−.192	583.2	544.1	−.067
45–49	479.4	504.5	.052	364.2	463.9	.274
50–54	370.5	414.9	.120	370.4	388.3	.048
55–59	223.5	328.2	.468	204.4	316.3	.547
60–64	344.2	245.7	−.286	325.7	246.6	−.243
65–69	188.9	169.7	−.102	157.1	179.0	.139
70–75	177.9	104.2	−.414	162.8	115.9	−.288
75+	148.4	76.3	−.486	133.0	91.3	−.314
Total	**12981.7**	**12884.4**	**−.007**	**12097.3**	**12194.5**	**.008**

with even greater force to urban populations. If sex adjustments are not planned for the urban population, the adjusted national population in Table 5.1 should be scaled to bring the totals by sex into agreement with the reported population by sex before the adjustment factors are calculated. The controlling totals for each sex are then the reported totals by sex.

The national adjustment factors are only a first approximation for application to urban populations. In Iran, as in other countries, age misreporting has a different intensity in urban than rural areas. A way of allowing for the difference in intensity is to estimate a constant, w, that can be used as a multiplying factor to inflate or deflate the national adjustment factors ($k_{s,i}$) to reflect the difference between misreporting in the urban population and in the national population. In a study of over 200 cities in Turkey, values of w have been estimated that range from near zero in the more-developed western cities to as high as 2.0 in the less-developed eastern parts of the country.[14] Urban populations generally have better age reporting than rural populations, but city populations in regions where misreporting is generally severe reflect the same lack of knowledge of age as their hinterlands. On the basis of this study, it is evident that national adjustment factors are, indeed, only a first approximation and should be inflated or deflated accordingly if there is any available basis upon which to estimate values of w.

The assumption that justifies the use of an estimate of w to scale values of $k_{s,i}$ is that differences between urban and general age misreporting are proportional over all age groups. This assumption also allows estimates of w that are made by an analysis of one part of the age distribution to be generalized for the entire age distribution. In many countries, a comparison of reported age distributions for the urban and national populations above about age 45 will provide clues concerning the relative intensity of age misreporting in the two populations and permit w to be estimated. A procedure for making such estimates of w will be described next, followed by a discussion of the conditions under which this approach is valid.

Estimation of (w)

The example refers to the urban population of Turkey in 1965. The procedure for estimating w is to examine ratios of the urban to the national population when the urban population is adjusted using alternative (trial) values of w, and the national population is the adjusted national population, using its one and only set of national adjustment factors. The basic equation for calculation of the trial urban population is:

$$P^a_{s,i} = P^r_{s,i}\,(1 + k_{s,i} \cdot w_s)$$

When $w = 0$, the trial urban population is the reported urban population. Hence, $w = 0$ stands for a situation with no urban age misreporting. When $w = 1$, urban age misreporting is assumed to be the same as national misreporting. Values smaller or larger than $w = 1$ indicate lesser or greater intensity of urban age misreporting, respectively.

The computation of ratios of urban to national population for the age range 45–64 is shown in Table 5.2 for females. The given values for the

---

[14] Belgin Tekçe, "Urbanization and Migration in Turkey," Ph.D. dissertation (sociology), Princeton University, 1974, Chapter 2.

TABLE 5.2 Adjustment of Urban Population for Age Misreporting with National Adjustment Factors (k) and Trial Values of (w): Turkey, Females, 1965

| Age group | National adjustment factors (k) | Urban population (thousands) | | | |
| | | Reported w = 0.0 | Adjusted population: Trials | | |
			w = 1.0	w = 0.5	w = 0.6
(1)	(2)	(3)	(4)	(5)	(6)
45-49	.178	136.2	160.4	148.3	150.7
50-54	−.047	167.4	159.5	163.5	162.7
55-59	.251	133.2	166.6	149.9	153.3
60-64	−.164	133.2	111.4	122.3	120.1

| Age group | Adjusted national population (thousands) | Ratio of urban to national population (ratios x 10^3) | | | |
		w = 0.0	w = 1.0	w = 0.5	w = 0.6
(7)	(8)	(9)	(10)	(11)	(12)
45-49	506.3	269	317	293	298
50-54	563.3	297	283	290	289
55-59	519.9	256	320	288	295
60-64	419.3	318	266	292	286

Note: The adjusted populations shown in columns 4-6 are obtained by multiplying the reported population in column 3 by $(1 + kw)$. The numerators for the ratios shown in columns 9-12 are from columns 3-6, respectively, and the denominators are from column 8.

computations are the national adjustment factors (k) in column 2, the reported urban population in column 3, and the adjusted national population in column 8. The rest of the columns are found by internal computation. It begins with the computation of the ratios for $w = 0$ shown in column 9. They are plotted immediately on graph paper as in Figure 5.3. To facilitate plotting, values of the ratio are raised to a power of 10 (any suitable power) that will give three digits. In order to follow this example, the reader should imagine that only females are charted and that the curves are drawn one by one as the analysis proceeds.

In this example, when $w = 0$, a characteristic zigzag is seen. It indicates the presence of urban age misreporting. Further trials are necessary. Next, a value for w of 1.0 was used. The result is shown in the chart, and it can be seen that the correction was too strong. It appears that the correct value of w lies between 0 and 1.0. The next trial is 0.5, which still leaves some irregularity and suggests that the solution lies on the upper side of 0.5. A trial of 0.6 fails to improve the situation. Hence, the former value of 0.5 is selected.

The implicit criterion for selection was that variance around a fitted straight line should be minimized. Graphical methods are generally sufficient to apply such a criterion and to make a selection to the nearest 0.1 units of w. More precise computation is not warranted. Numerical, rather than graphical, methods can also be used, as in the study of over 200 Turkish cities mentioned above. The rule is to find a value of w that minimizes the

FIGURE 5.3 Ratios of Urban to National Population with Alternative Trial Values of (w): Turkey, 1965.

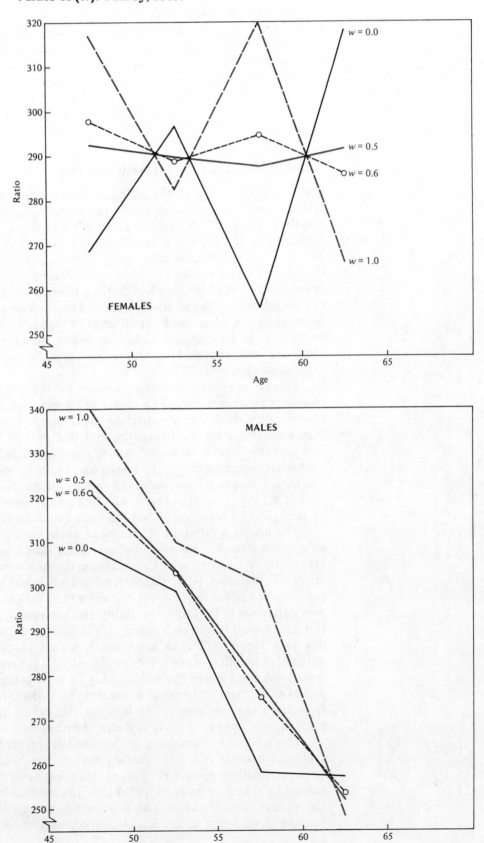

sum of the squares of the deviation from a straight line fitted by the method of least squares.

The age distribution for urban males was examined also, and the graphical results are shown in the lower panel of Figure 5.3. Exactly the same principles were applied. It is not necessary that the selected values of w should be the same for each sex, since differentials between urban and national knowledge of age may differ by sex. However, values different by more than 0.3 by sex would be surprising and reason for further study of the underlying data. In the Turkish example for 1965, the selected values of w turned out to be 0.5 for males as well as females.

Conditions for Valid Estimation of (w)

The downward slope of the ratios of national to urban population in the male population is noticeably different from the relatively flat slope in the female population. The difference is due to different histories of internal migration in the male and female populations. A downward slope in the ratios can arise when the urban population is growing rapidly due to migration that is concentrated at young ages. The effect on the age distribution is similar to that of births when fertility is high, except that the peak in the age distribution from which the curve extends downward is at the age of heavy selective migration rather than at birth. Male rural to urban migration in Turkey is strongly age selective below about age 25 and has been prevalent long enough to create a downward slope in the ratio of urban to national above age 45.

Female migration is less age selective than male. Hence, the urban female population tends to be closer in its age distribution to the national female population. Female rural to urban migration was also less strong than male migration until recently, and that part of female migration that was age selective at younger ages has not yet aged enough to impart a downward slope to the ratios above age 45 in Figure 5.3. A difference in downward slopes of the male and female urban populations can also be seen in the lower panel of Figure 5.5. To a small extent, mortality differences by sex could be responsible, but the main factor is migration.

The use of a criterion of minimum deviation for the ratios in relation to a fitted straight line over the age range 45-64 permits the method of estimating w to work well even though the two sexes have different histories of migration with different effects on urban age distribution. The presence of undersized or oversized cohorts in the general population due to past variations in fertility or mortality also are managed well by the method. Note, for example, the undersized cohort aged 45–50 in the national population (see Figure 5.5). The same notch occurs in all subdivisions of the national population, since it was produced by a general experience of heavy infant and child mortality, and possibly by a reduction of fertility, during a period of war and widespread dislocation in Turkey. No spurious deviations from the linear criterion arise because the urban age distribution is expressed as a ratio to the national age distribution.

The method of estimating w that has been described is generally satisfactory when the age misreporting that occurs between ages 45 and 64 (or over another age range if used as a basis) is dominated by zigzags caused by rounding on preferred digits. The method is designed to evaluate the relative intensity of such alternating movements independently of other sources of variation in the rural to national ratios. Strength is gained from the use of a sequence of ratios of urban to national population, rather than only one or two, because variations from a linear relationship that are caused by factors other than systematic age misreporting are likely to offset each other.

The method is less reliable whenever irregularities in the sequence of ratios from age 45 to 64 arise due to actual demographic events or mis-enumeration that falls outside the range of systematic response biases that have been evaluated by analysis at the national level. A potential source of trouble is fluctuations in past migration quantities that were not normally distributed around an average rate of change in population due to migration. If, in addition, the past migration was highly age selective, the sequence of cohorts aging into the range 45–64 will be irregular. The use of four ratios for the evaluation of w provides insulation against errors of estimate due to the irregularities. However, the analyst should use judgment to decide whether the selected value of w has been biased by one or two spurious fluctuations that were not balanced by opposite movements.

Any errors of tabulation in the age range 45–64, or misreporting that is nonsystematic and therefore not included within the scope of the national pattern of adjustment factors, can also cause an erroneous w to be estimated. If there is doubt about the validity of an estimate of w, a value may be borrowed from a census at a different date for the same population, from the opposite sex in the same census, or from another urban population in the same country believed to have similar conditions relating to the need for knowledge of age, and origins of the migrant part of the population, both of which appear to influence the intensity of misreporting.

Initial Population for the Urban Projection

Once a value of w has been selected for each sex, an adjusted urban population can be computed as in Table 5.4. There are two steps: First, the adjustment factors, weighted by w, are applied (see equation on page 77). Next, the adjusted population is totalled by sex and the column total is compared with the reported total (or with a reported total adjusted for sex misreporting, if that factor is included). Usually, a minor disagreement is noted, which is due to multiplying different population structures by the same set of factors. The adjusted population in column 4 is scaled by a multiplier (4328.5/4329.7) to obtain the final results shown in column 5. The latter may be used as the INIT.POP for urban Turkey for 1965.

A recapitulation of the results of the age adjustments is shown in Figure 5.5. The figure has been drawn with a "deflated" scale for the national population, so that the slopes in the national and the urban population can be compared visually. The deflator was the proportion urban in the national population. The chart shows that the urban adjustment preserved two major hollows in the age distributions. The hollows move out (rightward) in each successive national census and are, therefore, actual hollows, not effects of age misreporting of the type seen in the Iranian example. In addition, the adjustment procedure has retained other irregularities in the urban age distribution that are actual characteristics and peculiar to the urban population.

There is, for example, an extraordinary peak in the male age distribution at the age interval 20–25. It is due to universal military service that is concentrated on that age range and brings males to large military installations. If the military installations were distributed between rural and urban

TABLE 5.4   **Application of Values (k) and (w) to Obtain Urban Population Adjusted for Age Misreporting: Turkey, Females, 1965 (population in thousands)**

Age group	Reported population	National adjustment factors(k)	Population adjusted with w = 0.5	Adjusted population scaled
(1)	(2)	(3)	(4)	(5)
0-4	531.9	.100	558.5	558.3
5-9	563.2	−.005	547.7	547.6
10-14	485.2	−.006	483.7	483.6
15-19	420.1	.071	435.0	434.9
20-24	350.9	−.021	347.2	347.1
25-29	345.7	−.074	332.9	332.8
30-34	331.6	−.064	321.0	320.9
35-39	301.9	−.039	296.0	295.9
40-44	207.3	−.044	202.7	202.7
45-49	136.2	.178	148.3	148.3
50-54	167.4	−.047	163.5	163.4
55-59	133.2	.251	149.9	149.9
60-64	133.2	−.164	122.3	122.2
65-69	88.0	.215	97.5	97.4
70-74	62.6	−.089	59.8	59.8
75+	70.1	−.184	63.7	63.6
Total	**4328.5**	**0.0**	**4329.7**	**4328.5**

Note: Small inconsistencies of multiplication and addition are due to rounding from original computations that were made at a higher level of precision than shown.

in the same proportions as population there would be no peaking, but the whole population is less urbanized than the military population. Many men who serve in the armed forces do not remain in the cities. If they did, cohorts that served throughout the decades before 1965 would still be in the urban population at higher ages than 20–25 and would greatly elevate the male urban distribution above age 25. Such elevation is not seen in Figure 5.5.

The importance of preparing age distributions as carefully as possible is stressed because population projections for short and medium durations into the future are strongly influenced by the initial population structure. This justifies major attention to this subject.

MIGRATION: COMPOSITION BY AGE AND SEX

Assumptions for urban projections typically involve a major migration component. Consequently, the age and sex composition of migration is an important parameter for such projections and requires special attention. The structure of past migration can be learned by a number of different approaches, depending upon the types of data available. An approach that relies on a minimum amount of data and is, therefore, likely to be applicable in a wide range of situations will now be illustrated.

FIGURE 5.5   National and Urban Populations Adjusted for Age Misreporting: Turkey, 1965

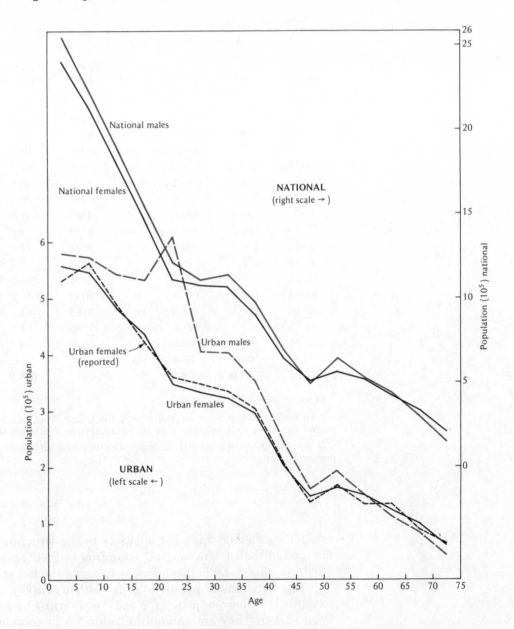

The illustration refers to the urban sector of Turkey, defined as communities of 10,000 and over. Net migration will be estimated inclusive of population change due to boundary expansion and reclassification of communities from rural to urban. The use of this definition of migration is justified when the population projection refers to an urban sector that grows by such spatial expansion as well as by genuine migration. The method to be described is equally applicable to urban populations defined by boundaries and lists of communities that are fixed over time.

The method of estimation is a classical survival procedure that uses two successive censuses of the population. As normally implemented, age at the time of migration is not made especially clear; yet, it must be unambiguous for use in population projections. The modified cohort-

TABLE 5.6   Computation of the Age Distribution of Population Change Due to Migration: Turkey, Females, 1960-1965 (population in thousands)

Age in census	Population at two dates — Adjusted population		Survival estimate of migration			Distribution by age	
	1960	1965	Cohort	Survival rate	Net migration	Age at migration	Net migrants
(1)	(2)	(3)	(4)	(5)	(6)	(7)	(8)
0-4	442.1	558.3	1	.9562	127.6	0-4	102.0[b]
5-9	402.6	547.6	2	.9900	85.4	5-9	106.5
10-14	340.6	483.6	3	.9905	97.9	10-14	91.7
15-19	290.1	434.9	4	.9869	61.2	15-19	79.6
20-24	291.0	347.1	5	.9838	46.9	20-24	54.1
25-29	284.4	332.8	6	.9812	42.3	25-29	44.6
30-34	254.0	320.9	7	.9782	47.9	30-34	45.1
35-39	198.6	295.9	8	.9749	9.2	35-39	28.6
40-44	134.3	202.7	9	.9688	18.4	40-44	13.8
45-49	158.2	148.3	10	.9583	12.1	×.5 → 45-49	15.3
50-54	139.5	163.4	11	.9401	19.3	×.5 → 50-54	15.7
55-59	123.2	149.9	12	.9093	10.7	55-59	15.0
60-64	101.2	122.2	13	.8581	11.5	60-64	11.1
65-69	72.0	97.4	14	.7786	4.2	65-69	7.9
70-74	97.1[a]	59.8	15	.5523	14.1	70+	16.2
75+	—	63.6	—	—	—	—	—
Total	3329.0	4328.6			609.0		647.2[b]

[a] Combined for age 70 and over.

[b] An estimate of 38.2 net migrants from the cohort born during the five-year migration period has been included. See text for computation of this element of net migration.

Note: Minor inconsistencies in multiplication and addition are due to rounding for presentation.

component method adds net migrants to the structure of the population at the time of their migration and according to their ages at that time. Special attention, therefore, is given below to aging the net migrants.

The two census populations for urban Turkey that are used in the example have been adjusted for age misreporting by using the methods outlined earlier. They are entered in Table 5.6 in columns 2 and 3. Since the adjustments for age misreporting were themselves estimated from the graduation of survival rates in model life tables, life-table survival rates are the appropriate ones to use for the migration estimates. The survival rates shown in column 5 are from an 'East' model life table assumed to represent urban mortality prevailing in 1960–1965.

In the standard survival procedure, adjustments for age misreporting are not made, and the survival rates are calculated from the reported national census. The justification for this approach depends on the assumption that the intensity of age misreporting and mortality are the same in the urban area and in the country as a whole. Sometimes allowance is made for an urban mortality differential by raising the survival rates computed from the census. Once age adjustments are introduced, however, survival rates from the national census must be replaced by life-table survival rates, because the former incorporate an unwanted adjustment for age misreporting at the national level of intensity.

Analysts faced with less information than that available in Turkey may find it necessary to assume that age misreporting and mortality are the same in urban areas as in the rest of the national population. If so, the simplest procedure is to use reported, not adjusted, urban populations, and survival rates calculated from the reported, not adjusted, national population. If there is significant international migration, one of the pair of national censuses must be modified so that the two censuses, taken together, simulate change due to fertility and mortality alone in a closed national population. In other respects, the estimation of urban population change due to migration would proceed in the same way as below.

The estimates of net migration are made by five-year cohorts, with the cohorts defined as follows:

Cohort	Initial age	Terminal age
0	Born	0-4
1	0-4	5-9
2	5-9	10-14
..		
15	70+	75+

The basic equation for net migration combines forward and reverse projection to obtain an unbiased estimate of the number of net migrants. It is unbiased in that migration events and deaths occurring to persons after migration are assumed to be distributed evenly over the migration period.

$$M_c = .5[P_c^{1965} - S_c P_c^{1960} + P_c^{1965}/S_c - P_c^{1960}] \quad \text{for } c = 1, 15$$

where M is net migration for a single cohort, c; P is the population of a cohort at the dates indicated; and the survival rates are S. The computation is illustrated by cohort 10 from Table 5.6 as follows:

$$M = .5[163.4 - (.9583 \times 158.2) + (163.4/.9583) - 158.2] = 12.1$$

The number of migrants in the cohort that was born during the interval can be estimated roughly on the assumption that migrant women are accompanied by young children in the same numbers as women resident in the urban area. The relationship of children aged 0–4 to females aged 20–49 at the terminal date, 1965, is used:

(1) Children aged 0–4:
   Males 579.4
   Females 558.3   1137.7

(2) Females aged 20–49   1647.7

(3) Ratio of young children
   to females aged 20–49   .690

The number of children who accompanied female migrants can be estimated as the number of female migrants in cohorts 4 to 9 multiplied by the child-woman ratio: $225.9 \times .690 = 155.9$. Since the women are assumed to migrate at dates spread evenly over the period, half of the children were alive before migration and half were born afterwards. This rough assumption gives the answer that one-half of 155.9 were net migrants, namely 77.94. Children aged 0–4 have a masculinity ratio of 579.4/558.3, namely 103.8 males per hundred females. Hence, net migrants in the cohort born during the interval were:

Males $77.94 \times (103.8/203.8) = 39.7$

Females $77.94 - 39.7 \qquad = 38.2$

The female migrants of cohort, $c = 0$, are included in the first entry of the last column of Table 5.4 when net migrants are shown by age at migration.

Net migrants by cohort are distributed according to age at migration by taking into consideration the full range of ages experienced by the cohort during the migration period. A five-year cohort ages five years over a five-year migration period, and contains members who could have migrated at ages distributed over a ten-year age range. For example, the cohort that ages from 45–49 to 50–54 includes persons who migrated at ages from 45 to 54 (up to exact age 55). In order to show their ages at migration, they may be distributed one-half to the age group 45–49 and one-half to ages 50–54. Carrying through with this reasoning results in the following distribution plan:

| Cohort | Initial age | Terminal age | Cohort midpoint | Distribution by age at migration | |
				Lower (.5)	Upper (.5)
0	Born	0-4	—	0-4	0-4
1	0-4	5-9	5	0-4	5-9
2	5-9	10-14	10	5-9	10-14
..					
14	65-69	70-74	70	65-69	70+
15	70-74	75+	—	70+	70+

This plan was used to distribute net migrants by age at migration in Table 5.4.

When the analysis must be done for a ten-year migration period, the same reasoning may be applied. The age range for five-year cohorts living through a ten-year migration period is 15 years. The distribution of migrants from the cohort over the 15-year range is pyramidal, with more migration events likely in the middle five-year range than at the extremities. Hence a rough rule is to assign 50 percent to the middle period, and 25 percent to the outer two periods as follows:

| Cohort | Initial age | Terminal age | Cohort midpoint | Distribution by age at migration | | |
				Lower (.25)	Middle (.50)	Upper (.25)
1	0-4	10-14	7.5	0-4	5-9	10-14
2	5-9	15-19	12.5	5-9	10-14	15-19
..						
12	55-59	65-69	62.5	55-59	60-64	65+
13	60-64	70-74	67.5	60-64	65+	65+
14	65+	75+	—	65+	65+	65+

The migration estimates by age are made for both sexes (details for males not shown). The results for the urban population of Turkey show 697.0 thousand males and 647.2 thousand females. The sex ratio of net migrants is, therefore, 107.7 males per hundred females.

The total quantity of net migrants can be evaluated as the sum of males and females, namely 1,344 thousand, during the period 1960–1965. The contribution of reclassification of communities can be eliminated by noting that the net change in number of cities over the period was 39. Since the size criterion was 10,000 persons to bring a city into the urban population, 39×10,000, namely 390,000 persons, were reclassified from rural to urban, not genuine migrants. Boundary changes of individual cities made a minor contribution, which cannot be estimated. As a consequence, it can be estimated that 945,000 persons (1,344 − 390 = 945) were added to the urban population by actual migration during 1960–1965.

When the age and sex patterns of migration shown in Figure 5.7 are examined, it should be understood that they include population changes due to boundary expansion and reclassification. Altogether 29 percent (390/1,344) of the change in population due to the so-called migration component was from this source. Since the age and sex distribution of the nonmovers is closer to the structure of the national population than that of actual migrants, the redistribution rates shown in the lower half of the figure tend to form a

FIGURE 5.7   Urban Population Change Due to "Migration": Turkey, 1960–1965

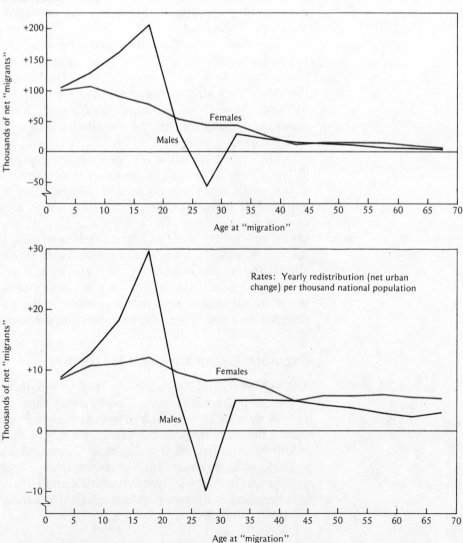

flatter curve than would otherwise appear. Even so, considerable age and sex selectivity remain.

Urban net migration is selectively more youthful in Turkey than the structure of the general population. Heavy infusions of males into the cities occur early in life, with losses later in the life cycle (in the twenties) that are not as large. The losses are mainly explained by returns to rural communities after military service. During the 1960s an additional reason for losses was movements from the Turkish urban population to join the growing stock of Turkish workers in Western Europe, particularly in West Germany. These net out-migrations from the urban population occur among males principally in their late twenties and early thirties. It is necessary to take these characteristics of age and sex structure into consideration when making urban population projections.

INDIRECT PROJECTIONS USING FINDMIGRATION

Projections of urban population can proceed in two ways with respect to the handling of the migration component: One is to prepare assumptions about the quantity or rate of population change due to migration for future projection periods. If this approach is followed, a straightforward cohort-component projection is made. For the migration component, the subject MIGRATION is used.

The other way of treating migration is to regard the total quantity of net migration as an unknown. Assumptions are prepared about the total urban population size that is to be reached at time $t+5$, $t+10$, and so on (duration is as long as the projection desired). The computer can find the unknown quantity of net migration for each five-year period provided it is given the age and sex structure of that migration. The subject FINDMIGRATION is used.

The first approach is preferable if the analyst knows enough about the determinants of net migration flows to develop a forecast of quantity consistent with other economic and demographic assumptions. The second approach is more appealing in the absence of an adequate model for forecasting net migration. The analyst can fix future population targets for the urban area on the basis of extrapolations of past trends, modified by information thought to be relevant but difficult to evaluate explicitly. Neither alternative is fully satisfactory and usually leaves a great deal of possibility for error. Inherent limitations on the validity of migration assumptions are the principal reason for regarding urban projections as estimates of rapidly diminishing reliability as the time duration increases.

Example: Urban Turkey, 1965-1970

The FINDMIGRATION approach may be illustrated by considering a population projection for urban Turkey from the census date in 1965 to the census date in 1970, which is a duration of five years (censuses are held during the same week of the year). The size of the urban population in 1970 is known from lists of cities by size. Census tabulations by age and sex are not available, however, for the entire urban population. This gap in information can be filled temporarily until complete 1970 data become available by projecting the urban population of 1965 forward to 1970 with the aid of FINDMIGRATION.

Instructions for this projection were prepared as shown in Example 5.8. The initial urban age distribution for 1965 is the one prepared earlier as an illustration of age-adjustment procedures (see Table 5.6). The target population for 1970 is from the 1970 census (12,862 thousand persons), and the sex ratio of net migrants is the one found immediately above by analysis of the structure of migration for 1960–1965. The age structure was similarly found. One small detail is that the estimated age structure has an open age interval at 70+ that is punched in the numeric data field for 70–74. The remaining data field is left empty.

The user need not go to the trouble of converting the figures on migration structure into a standard form such as percentages of total, but can punch them as they are (see Table 5.6) and the computer will do the conversion. Assumptions for fertility and mortality were made that correspond with national intercensal characteristics, modified to reflect the urban differential.The MIGR and FERDIST cards are punched to refer to seven five-year periods even though the meaningful part of the projection is only the first five years. This is done to fulfill the FIVFIV requirement that assumptions be provided for the full seven periods on these types of instruction cards.

A result of the urban projection for 1965–1970 is an estimate of the quantity of migration that is implied by the target size of population assumed for 1970. It is found on page 2 of the printed output, spread by age and sex

EXAMPLE 5.8   Instructions for a Projection with FINDMIGRATION

```
0         1         2         3         4         5         6         7         8
1234567890123456789012345678901234567890123456789012345678901234567890123456789 0

YEAR.TITLE
YR.1965.URBAN TURKEY FROM CENSUS DATE 1965 TO CENSUS DATE 1970 ONLY   (THOUSANDS)
INIT.POP
INIT.F.A      558.3     547.6     483.6     434.9     347.1     332.8     320.9
INIT.F.B      295.9     202.7     148.3     163.4     149.9     122.2      97.4
INIT.F.C      123.5
INIT.M.A      579.4     572.3     541.6     580.5     609.7     403.2     402.8
INIT.M.B      350.1     246.7     159.7     193.6     146.6     110.4      80.5
INIT.M.C       77.3
FINDMIGRATION
TARGETPOP   12862.
MPERHUNDF     107.7
MIGRM1.7.A    106.6     129.3     163.2     206.5      35.7     -57.1      26.9
MIGRM1.7.B     22.1      15.7      13.4      11.7       7.7       5.4       3.9
MIGRM1.7.C      3.0       3.0
MIGRF1.7.A    102.0     106.5      91.7      79.6      54.1      44.6      45.1
MIGRF1.7.B     28.6      13.8      15.3      15.7      15.0      11.1       7.9
MIGRF1.7.C      7.0       9.2
MEND
MORT.SPLIT
CHILD.LV.F     17.6
CHILD.LV.M     18.6
ADULT.LV.F     19.6
ADULT.LV.M     20.6
FERTILITY
TOTAL.FERT      4.2
FERDIST1.7      .017      .056      .053      .038      .024      .008      .004
FEND
END PROJECTION

1234567890123456789012345678901234567890123456789012345678901234567890123456789 0
```

according to the structure that was assumed (Example 5.9). In this particular example, the net migration for 1965–1970 was found to be 2,298 thousand persons. Allowing for the inclusion of 69 more cities in 1970 than in 1965 (this fact is known independently), the estimate of genuine net migration is as follows (in thousands): $2{,}298 - (69 \times 10) = 1{,}608$. Recall that genuine net migration in the preceding five-year period was 954 thousand; hence a substantial increase in urbanward migration has been experienced by Turkey during the 1960s.

A further result of the projection is an estimate of urban age and sex structure in 1970 consistent with all the information available at the time. The portions of the FIVFIV projection that refer to dates later than 1970 are crossed out in Example 5.9 because they are entirely the result of default assumptions by FIVFIV.

EXAMPLE 5.9   Urban Projection with FINDMIGRATION

URBAN TURKEY FROM CENSUS DATE 1965 TO CENSUS DATE 1970 ONLY   (THOUSANDS)   PAGE   1

THE INPUT POPULATION IS DATED 1965

FERTILITY ASSUMPTIONS

     SEX RATIO AT BIRTH: 105.0 MALES PER 100 FEMALES.

        DISTRIBUTION BY AGE OF ONE UNIT OF TOTAL FERTILITY

AGE	1965	1970	1975	1980	1985	1990	1995	2000
15	0.017	0.017	0.017	0.017	0.017	0.017	0.017	
20	0.056	0.056	0.056	0.056	0.056	0.056	0.056	
25	0.053	0.053	0.053	0.053	0.053	0.053	0.053	
30	0.038	0.038	0.038	0.038	0.038	0.038	0.038	
35	0.024	0.024	0.024	0.024	0.024	0.024	0.024	
40	0.008	0.008	0.008	0.008	0.008	0.008	0.008	
45	0.004	0.004	0.004	0.004	0.004	0.004	0.004	
5*TOT=TF	1.000	1.000	1.000	1.000	1.000	1.000	1.000	

        AGE SPECIFIC FERTILITY SCHEDULE

AGE	1965	1970	1975	1980	1985	1990	1995	2000
15	0.071	0.071	0.071	0.071	0.071	0.071	0.071	
20	0.235	0.235	0.235	0.235	0.235	0.235	0.235	
25	0.223	0.223	0.223	0.223	0.223	0.223	0.223	
30	0.160	0.160	0.160	0.160	0.160	0.160	0.160	
35	0.101	0.101	0.101	0.101	0.101	0.101	0.101	
40	0.034	0.034	0.034	0.034	0.034	0.034	0.034	
45	0.017	0.017	0.017	0.017	0.017	0.017	0.017	
5*TOT=TF	4.200	4.200	4.200	4.200	4.200	4.200	4.200	
GRR	2.049	2.049	2.049	2.049	2.049	2.049	2.049	
NRR	1.776	1.776	1.776	1.776	1.776	1.776	1.776	
MEAN AGE	28.400	28.400	28.400	28.400	28.400	28.400	28.400	

MORTALITY ASSUMPTIONS

		1965	1970	1975	1980	1985	1990	1995	2000
		MODEL LEVELS FROM 'EAST' FAMILY LIFE TABLES							
* UNDER 5	FEMALES	17.60	17.60	17.60	17.60	17.60	17.60	17.60	17.60
* UNDER 5	MALES	18.60	18.60	18.60	18.60	18.60	18.60	18.60	18.60
* OVER 5	FEMALES	19.60	19.60	19.60	19.60	19.60	19.60	19.60	19.60
* OVER 5	MALES	20.60	20.60	20.60	20.60	20.60	20.60	20.60	20.60
E(0)	FEMALES	63.96	63.96	63.96	63.96	63.96	63.96	63.96	63.96
E(0)	MALES	61.80	61.80	61.80	61.80	61.80	61.80	61.80	61.80
INF MORT	FEMALES	81.71	81.71	81.71	81.71	81.71	81.71	81.71	81.71
INF MORT	MALES	84.61	84.61	84.61	84.61	84.61	84.61	84.61	84.61
E(5)	FEMALES	66.50	66.50	66.50	66.50	66.50	66.50	66.50	66.50
E(5)	MALES	63.93	63.93	63.93	63.93	63.93	63.93	63.93	63.93

* TYPE OF MORTALITY INPUT

URBAN TURKEY FROM CENSUS DATE 1965 TO CENSUS DATE 1970 ONLY   (THOUSANDS)   PAGE   2

MIGRATION COMPUTED BY 'FINDMIGRATION'

YEARLY VALUES DURING FIVE-YEAR PERIODS

FEMALES

AGE	1965	1970	1975	1980	1985	1990	1995	2000
0	34.9	-21.1	-21.2	-20.1	-18.3	-16.8	-16.8
5	36.4	-22.1	-22.1	-21.0	-19.2	-17.5	-16.7
10	31.4	-19.0	-19.0	-18.1	-16.5	-15.1	-14.4
15	27.2	-16.5	-16.5	-15.7	-14.3	-13.1	-12.5
20	18.5	-11.2	-11.2	-10.7	-9.7	-8.9	-8.5
25	15.2	-9.2	-9.3	-8.8	-8.0	-7.3	-7.0
30	15.4	-9.3	-9.4	-8.9	-8.1	-7.4	-7.1
35	9.8	-5.9	-5.9	-5.6	-5.1	-4.7	-4.5
40	4.7	-2.9	-2.9	-2.7	-2.5	-2.3	-2.2
45	5.2	-3.2	-3.2	-3.0	-2.8	-2.5	-2.4
50	5.4	-3.3	-3.3	-3.1	-2.8	-2.6	-2.5
55	5.1	-3.1	-3.1	-3.0	-2.7	-2.5	-2.4
60	3.8	-2.3	-2.3	-2.2	-2.0	-1.8	-1.7
65	2.7	-1.6	-1.6	-1.6	-1.4	-1.3	-1.2
70	2.4	-1.5	-1.5	-1.4	-1.3	-1.2	-1.1
75+	3.1	-1.9	-1.9	-1.8	-1.7	-1.5	-1.4
TOT	1106.5	-670.7	-671.8	-639.2	-581.9	-532.7	-507.3

MALES

AGE	1965	1970	1975	1980	1985	1990	1995	2000
0	36.4	-22.1	-22.1	-21.1	-19.2	-17.6	-16.7
5	44.2	-26.8	-26.9	-25.6	-23.3	-21.3	-20.3
10	55.8	-33.8	-33.9	-32.3	-29.4	-26.9	-25.6
15	70.6	-42.8	-42.9	-40.8	-37.2	-34.0	-32.4
20	12.2	-7.4	-7.4	-7.1	-6.4	-5.9	-5.6
25	-19.5	11.8	11.9	11.3	10.3	9.4	9.0
30	9.2	-5.6	-5.6	-5.3	-4.8	-4.4	-4.2
35	7.6	-4.6	-4.6	-4.4	-4.0	-3.6	-3.5
40	5.4	-3.3	-3.3	-3.1	-2.8	-2.6	-2.5
45	4.6	-2.8	-2.8	-2.6	-2.4	-2.2	-2.1
50	4.0	-2.4	-2.4	-2.3	-2.1	-1.9	-1.8
55	2.6	-1.6	-1.6	-1.5	-1.4	-1.3	-1.2
60	1.8	-1.1	-1.1	-1.1	-1.0	-0.9	-0.8
65	1.3	-0.8	-0.8	-0.8	-0.7	-0.6	-0.6
70	1.0	-0.6	-0.6	-0.6	-0.5	-0.5	-0.5
75+	1.0	-0.6	-0.6	-0.6	-0.5	-0.5	-0.5
TOT	1191.3	-722.7	-723.9	-688.8	-627.1	-574.1	-546.7

| GRAND TOTAL | 2297.7 | -1393.4 | -1395.8 | -1328.0 | -1209.0 | -1106.8 | -1054.8 |

URBAN TURKEY FROM CENSUS DATE 1965 TO CENSUS DATE 1970 ONLY   (THOUSANDS)   PAGE   3
POPULATION PROJECTION

FEMALES

AGE	1965	1970	1975	1980	1985	1990	1995	2000
0	558.3	809.3	817.4	830.7	813.6	775.2	747.1	704.3
5	547.6	723.4	686.0	693.8	712.0	704.3	674.6	651.1
10	483.6	714.3	617.9	580.4	593.1	620.1	619.9	594.2
15	434.9	627.5	622.5	526.3	493.4	513.6	546.9	550.1
20	347.1	545.9	554.2	549.2	457.0	430.2	455.3	491.0
25	332.8	428.2	490.4	498.6	496.0	409.0	386.1	413.0
30	320.9	405.8	377.8	439.3	449.6	451.0	368.2	347.4
35	295.9	379.7	363.0	335.2	397.8	411.3	415.5	335.1
40	202.7	327.4	352.1	335.6	309.3	372.8	387.7	392.6
45	148.3	223.1	305.7	329.9	314.5	290.0	353.3	368.4
50	163.4	170.0	200.7	280.8	305.0	291.5	268.9	330.9
55	149.9	181.9	147.0	176.4	253.7	278.2	266.3	245.3
60	122.2	161.2	156.5	123.9	151.9	225.1	248.9	238.3
65	97.4	124.0	134.1	129.8	101.3	127.0	192.7	214.3
70	60.7	91.2	94.4	102.6	99.4	76.8	98.2	152.3
75+	80.4	98.0	99.5	102.5	110.2	112.5	98.2	107.2
TOT	4328.5	6011.0	6019.1	6034.9	6057.9	6088.4	6127.8	6175.5

(continued)

```
              MALES
              AGE      1965      1970      1975      1980      1985      1990      1995      2000
               0       579.4     849.2     858.3     872.3     854.2     814.0     784.5     781.5
               5       572.3     769.3     713.3     722.1     741.7     734.3     703.6     679.2
              10       541.6     819.4     614.8     558.8     574.8     607.3     611.1     586.2
              15       580.5     853.7     623.7     459.9     373.5     405.8     452.2     463.1
              20       609.7     781.5     721.2     493.1     297.1     261.8     303.0     353.6
              25       403.2     585.2     784.4     724.8     498.5     303.6     267.8     308.2
              30       402.8     373.1     594.3     791.4     731.7     506.5     312.6     276.7
              35       350.1     439.2     343.0     561.3     757.1     780.3     479.9     289.5
              40       246.7     376.1     412.1     317.6     533.1     727.1     672.7     456.9
              45       159.7     264.9     351.4     386.6     295.2     506.4     696.5     644.0
              50       193.6     174.1     241.2     324.2     358.5     272.0     475.4     658.2
              55       146.6     197.1     153.2     215.9     294.0     326.9     246.7     437.3
              60       110.4     142.9     171.4     131.9     188.6     259.7     289.9     217.7
              65        80.5     101.7     117.6     142.0     108.3     157.3     218.3     244.2
              70        41.2      68.1      76.2      86.7     107.8      81.8     120.3     168.0
             75+        49.5      55.6      66.6      76.8      89.9     108.9      99.8     122.0
             TOT      5054.4    6851.0    6842.9    6827.1    6804.1    6773.6    6734.2    6686.5

    GRAND TOTAL      9382.9   12862.0   12862.0   12862.0   12862.0   12862.0   12862.0   12862.0

                    MIDPERIOD INDICES FOR FIVE-YEAR TIME PERIODS
  POPULATION SIZE    10985.6   12862.0   12862.0   12862.0   12862.0   12862.0   12862.0
  YEARLY BIRTHS        326.8     391.7     397.8     388.9     369.6     355.2     353.1
  YEARLY DEATHS         90.5     113.0     118.6     123.3     127.8     133.9     142.3
  NET YEARLY MIGRANTS  459.5    -278.7    -279.2    -265.6    -241.8    -221.4    -210.8

                    YEARLY RATES PER THOUSAND POPULATION
  GFR=BIRTHS/FEM(15-44) 142.8   143.2     146.3     147.3     142.6     138.2     138.9

  BIRTH RATE            29.7      30.5      30.9      30.2      28.7      27.6      27.5
  DEATH RATE             8.2       8.8       9.2       9.6       9.9      10.4      11.1
  NATURAL INCREASE      21.5      21.7      21.7      20.7      18.8      17.2      16.4
  NET MIGRATION         41.8     -21.7     -21.7     -20.6     -18.8     -17.2     -16.4
  POP INCREASE          63.3      -0.0      -0.0       0.0      -0.0       0.0       0.0
```

URBAN TURKEY FROM CENSUS DATE 1965 TO CENSUS DATE 1970 ONLY   (THOUSANDS)   PAGE   4
POPULATION PROJECTION, PERCENTAGES

```
          FEMALES     1965      1970      1975      1980      1985      1990      1995      2000
               0      12.90     13.46     13.58     13.77     13.43     12.73     12.19     12.05
               5      12.65     12.04     11.40     11.50     11.75     11.57     11.01     10.54
              10      11.17     11.88     10.36      9.62      9.79     10.18     10.12      9.62
              15      10.05     10.44     10.34      8.72      8.14      8.44      8.92      8.91
              20       8.02      9.08      9.21      9.10      7.54      7.07      7.43      7.95
              25       7.69      7.12      8.15      8.26      8.19      6.72      6.30      6.69
              30       7.41      6.75      6.28      7.28      7.42      7.41      6.01      5.62
              35       6.84      6.32      6.03      5.55      6.57      6.76      6.78      5.43
              40       4.68      5.45      5.85      5.56      5.11      6.12      6.33      6.36
              45       3.43      3.71      5.08      5.47      5.19      4.76      5.77      5.97
              50       3.77      2.83      3.33      4.65      5.04      4.79      4.39      5.36
              55       3.46      3.03      2.44      2.92      4.19      4.57      4.35      3.97
              60       2.82      2.68      2.60      2.05      2.51      3.70      4.06      3.86
              65       2.25      2.06      2.23      2.15      1.67      2.09      3.15      3.47
              70       1.40      1.52      1.57      1.70      1.64      1.26      1.60      2.47
             75+       1.86      1.63      1.65      1.70      1.82      1.85      1.60      1.74
             TOT     100.00    100.00    100.00    100.00    100.00    100.00    100.00    100.00

            MALES     1965      1970      1975      1980      1985      1990      1995      2000
               0      11.46     12.39     12.54     12.78     12.55     12.02     11.65     11.69
               5      11.32     11.23     10.42     10.58     10.90     10.84     10.45     10.16
              10      10.72     11.96      8.98      8.18      8.45      8.97      9.07      8.77
              15      11.49     12.46      9.12      6.15      5.49      5.99      6.71      6.93
              20      12.06     11.41     10.54      7.22      4.37      3.86      4.50      5.29
              25       7.98      8.54     11.46     10.62      7.33      4.48      3.98      4.61
              30       7.97      5.45      8.69     11.59     10.75      7.48      4.64      4.14
              35       6.93      6.41      5.01      8.22     11.13     10.34      7.13      4.33
              40       4.88      5.49      6.02      4.65      7.83     10.73      9.99      6.83
              45       3.16      3.87      5.14      5.66      4.34      7.48     10.34      9.63
              50       3.83      2.54      3.53      4.75      5.27      4.02      7.06      9.84
              55       2.90      2.88      2.24      3.16      4.32      4.83      3.66      6.54
              60       2.18      2.09      2.51      1.93      2.77      3.83      4.30      3.26
              65       1.59      1.48      1.72      2.08      1.59      2.32      3.24      3.65
              70       0.82      0.99      1.11      1.30      1.58      1.21      1.79      2.51
             75+       0.98      0.81      0.97      1.13      1.32      1.61      1.48      1.83
             TOT     100.00    100.00    100.00    100.00    100.00    100.00    100.00    100.00

            AGE       1965      1970      1975      1980      1985      1990      1995      2000
 FEMALES   0-14      36.72     37.38     35.24     34.88     34.97     34.49     33.32     32.22
          15-64      58.17     57.41     59.31     59.57     59.89     60.32     60.33     60.11
            65+       5.51      5.21      5.45      5.55      5.13      5.19      6.36      7.67

 MALES     0-14      33.50     35.58     31.95     31.54     31.90     31.82     31.17     30.61
          15-64      63.38     61.13     64.24     63.96     63.60     63.04     62.32     61.40
            65+       3.39      3.29      3.81      4.50      4.50      5.14      6.51      7.99

 TOTAL     0-14      34.99     36.42     33.49     33.11     33.35     33.08     32.19     31.38
          15-64      60.98     59.39     61.93     61.90     61.85     61.75     61.37     60.78
            65+       4.37      4.19      4.57      4.99      4.80      5.16      6.43      7.84

 MALES/FEMALES       1.168     1.140     1.137     1.131     1.123     1.113     1.099     1.083
```

Assumptions about Future Population Size

The closer one comes to specific situations, the more difficult it is to rely on general rules for projecting urban population size. When the urban population is the entire urban sector, some observations about rates of urbanization in developing countries may be useful nevertheless. The proportion urban in the national population provides an easily understood measure of the extent of urbanization in demographic terms. Definitions of urban differ widely among countries, but if the accepted statistical criteria of a country are used, and held fixed over time, changes in the proportion urban will provide a measure of the rate of urbanization. This measure of urbanization is preferable to the rate of increase in urban population, which tells nothing about the distribution of population between rural and urban communities. Changes in the proportion urban show genuine redistribution in a structural sense. Numerically, the percentage urban will represent the achieved level of urbanization, and the yearly change in the percentage will represent the rate of urbanization.

Since the proportion urban is restricted to a range between zero and one, it is certain that the rate of urbanization cannot remain high for long. Only in populations of a few million or less, and within small habitable areas, has the proportion urban risen above about 80 percent. Among the demographically less-developed countries, defined roughly as those with annual growth rates of 1.5 percent or more, and among those national populations exceeding five million persons, the upper limit for the proportion urban is presently about 60 percent. Data compiled by Kingsley Davis show that within this category of countries during 1950–1960, rates of urbanization were all positive and ranged upward to about one percentage point per annum.[15] Instances of increases sustained over the decade of more than one point per annum were rare. The highest rates of urbanization were observed for countries that had already reached proportions urban of 25 or 30 percent, but not all countries above those levels had high rates. Only five observations were available above an achieved level of urbanization of 40 percent, and the rates of urbanization were too scattered to permit generalization. These historical data set broad limits within which an analyst can accept assumptions about urban population growth without raising serious questions.

A request was received by the author to prepare estimates of the urban labor force in Turkey between 1973 and 1982 on the assumption that the urban population would grow after 1970 at a rate of 6.5 percent per annum. The assumption was applied to the period 1970–1985 in conjunction with the laissez-faire national population projection illustrated earlier to learn what rate of urbanization was implied:

	Census October 1970	Projection midyear 1985
National population (thousand)	35,667	50,287
Urban population (thousand)	12,862	33,441
Proportion urban (percent)	36.1	66.5
Yearly rate of urbanization		2.0

---

[15] Kingsley Davis, *World Urbanization 1950–1970*, Volume 1, "Basic Data for Cities, Countries, and Regions" (Berkeley: University of California, 1969).

The implied rate of urbanization of 2.0 points per annum may be compared with the highest rate previously observed in Turkey. It occurred during 1965–1970 and was 1.2 points per annum. Rates above one point per annum are unusual in world experience, but not impossible to achieve, as demonstrated in Turkey. The frequency of such high rates may also increase as more developing countries move from 35 or 40 percent urban to 60 or 65 percent. A sustained rate of 2.0 points per annum for Turkey, however, appeared excessive on its face, so further study was undertaken, and it was finally decided to base the urban projection on a sustained urbanization rate of approximately 1.2 points per annum up to 1985.

The implications of the new urbanization assumption are shown in Table 5.10. A table of this type provides a means for thinking about the plausibility of alternative assumptions. The national population in column 2 comes from the national population projection. The proportion urban (column 3) is assumed to increase at the rates shown in column 4. The rest of the table (for 1975 and following) is computed to show the implications of

TABLE 5.10 Assumptions about Urban Population Size to Accompany Laissez-Faire Projection of National Population: Turkey

Year and date	National population (thousand)	Proportion urban (percent)	Yearly change in percentage urban	Population size		Urban growth rate (percent per annum)
				Urban (thousand)	Rural (thousand)	
(1)	(2)	(3)	(4)	(5)	(6)	(7)
October		**Historical Record of Urbanization**				
1945	18,790	18.4	—	3,466	15,324	—
1950	20,947	18.7	0.06	3,924	17,023	2.5
1955	24,065	22.5	0.76	5,425	18,640	6.5
1960	27,755	26.3	0.76	7,308	20,447	6.0
1965	31,391	29.9	0.72	9,383	22,008	5.0
1970	35,667	36.1	1.24	12,862	22,805	6.3
Midyear		**First: Assume Annual Rate of Urbanization = 1.2**[b]				
1975	39,614	42.	1.26[a]	16,638	22,976	5.5[a]
1980	44,568	48.	1.20	21,393	23,175	5.0
1985	50,287	54.	1.20	27,155	23,132	4.8
1990	56,800	60.	1.20	34,080	22,720	4.5
1995	63,781	66.	1.20	42,095	21,686	4.2
		Second: Assume High Declining Rate of Urbanization				
1975	39,614	44.	1.68[a]	17,430	22,184	6.5[a]
1980	44,568	51.	1.40	22,730	21,838	5.3
1985	50,287	57.	1.20	28,664	21,623	4.6
1990	56,800	62.	1.00	35,216	21,584	4.1
1995	63,781	66.	.80	42,095	21,686	3.6

[a] Refers to a period of less than five years, namely 4.7 years.

[b] The rate of urbanization is the yearly change in the percentage urban shown in column 4.

the given values and assumptions. The constant rate of urbanization was carried down an additional ten years to 1995, although for that date there is little possibility of producing an urban projection with any reliability. One implication that probably is realistic, however, is that the rate of increase in the urban population (column 7) will decline. This is due to the effect of an expanding base of urban population when the urbanization rate is held constant. Eventually, as the proportion urban rises, the urban growth rate must converge toward the national population growth rate, which is projected at 2.3 percent per annum for 1990–1995 in the laissez-faire projection.

Instructions and results for the example of a constant rate of urbanization are shown in Examples 5.11 and 5.12, respectively. Since results were desired for 1970–1995 only, assumptions for the last two five-year periods were allowed to assume default values.

EXAMPLE 5.11   Instructions for a Projection with a Constant Rate of Urbanization of 1.2 Percentage Points Per Annum

```
0          1          2          3          4          5          6          7          8
1234567890123456789012345678901234567890123456789012345678901234567890123456789012345678 90

YEAR.TITLE
YR.1970.URBAN TURKEY.   RATE OF URBANIZATION=1.2 POINTS PER ANNUM TO 1995
REGROUP
GROUPS.
INIT.POP
OLD.POP.1970
DATE.SHIFT
YR.1970.WEEK.43
FINDMIGRATION
TARGETPOP     16638.     21393.     27155.     34080.     42095.
MPERHUNDF     107.4      107.1      106.8      106.5      106.2
MIGRM1.7.A    106.6      129.3      163.2      206.5      35.7      -57.1      26.9
MIGRM1.7.B    22.1       15.7       13.4       11.7       7.7       5.4       3.9
MIGRM1.7.C    3.0        3.0
MIGRF1.7.A    102.0      106.5      91.7       79.6       54.1      44.6      45.1
MIGRF1.7.B    28.6       13.8       15.3       15.7       15.0      11.1       7.9
MIGRF1.7.C    7.0        9.2
MEND
MORT.SPLIT
CHILD.LV.F    17.9       18.8       19.6       20.4       21.1      21.4      21.5
CHILD.LV.M    18.8       19.5       20.1       20.7       21.3      21.4      21.5
ADULT.LV.F    19.9       20.3       20.6       20.9       21.1      21.4      21.5
ADULT.LV.M    20.8       21.0       21.1       21.2       21.3      21.4      21.5
FERTILITY
TOTAL.FERT    4.03       3.86       3.69       3.51       3.34      3.17      3.00
FERDIST1.7    .017       .056       .053       .038       .024      .008      .004
FEND
END PROJECTION

1234567890123456789012345678901234567890123456789012345678901234567890123456789012345678 90
```

EXAMPLE 5.12   Projection with Constant Urbanization Rate

URBAN TURKEY. RATE OF URBANIZATION=1.2 POINTS PER ANNUM TO 1995   PAGE 2

MIGRATION COMPUTED BY 'FINDMIGRATION'

YEARLY VALUES DURING FIVE-YEAR PERIODS

FEMALES

AGE	1970	1975	1980	1985	1990	1995	2000	2005
0		37.7	41.6	48.5	57.2	63.9	-61.9	-56.9
5		39.3	43.4	50.6	59.7	66.8	-64.7	-59.4
10		33.9	37.4	43.6	51.4	57.5	-55.7	-51.2
15		29.4	32.4	37.8	44.6	49.9	-48.3	-44.4
20		20.0	22.1	25.7	30.3	33.9	-32.9	-30.2
25		16.5	18.2	21.2	25.0	28.0	-27.1	-24.9
30		16.7	18.4	21.4	25.3	28.3	-27.4	-25.2
35		10.6	11.7	13.6	16.0	17.9	-17.4	-16.0
40		5.1	5.6	6.6	7.7	8.7	-8.4	-7.7
45		5.7	6.2	7.3	8.6	9.6	-9.3	-8.5
50		5.8	6.4	7.5	8.8	9.8	-9.5	-8.8
55		5.5	6.1	7.1	8.4	9.4	-9.1	-8.4
60		4.1	4.5	5.3	6.2	7.0	-6.7	-6.2
65		2.9	3.2	3.8	4.4	5.0	-4.8	-4.4
70		2.6	2.9	3.3	3.9	4.4	-4.3	-3.9
75+		3.4	3.7	4.4	5.2	5.8	-5.6	-5.1
TOT		1195.1	1319.0	1537.6	1813.3	2028.4	-1965.3	-1805.7

MALES

AGE	1970	1975	1980	1985	1990	1995	2000	2005
0		39.3	43.2	50.2	59.1	65.9	-63.9	-58.7
5		47.6	52.4	60.9	71.6	79.9	-77.4	-71.2
10		60.1	66.1	76.9	90.4	100.9	-97.8	-89.8
15		76.0	83.7	97.3	114.4	127.6	-123.7	-113.6
20		13.1	14.5	16.8	19.8	22.1	-21.4	-19.6
25		-21.0	-23.1	-26.9	-31.6	-35.3	34.2	31.4
30		9.9	10.9	12.7	14.9	16.6	-16.1	-14.8
35		8.1	9.0	10.4	12.2	13.7	-13.2	-12.2
40		5.8	6.4	7.4	8.7	9.7	-9.4	-8.6
45		4.9	5.4	6.3	7.4	8.3	-8.0	-7.4
50		4.3	4.7	5.5	6.5	7.2	-7.0	-6.4
55		2.8	3.1	3.6	4.3	4.8	-4.6	-4.2
60		2.0	2.2	2.5	3.0	3.3	-3.2	-3.0
65		1.4	1.6	1.8	2.2	2.4	-2.3	-2.1
70		1.1	1.2	1.4	1.7	1.9	-1.8	-1.7
75+		1.1	1.2	1.4	1.7	1.9	-1.8	-1.7
TOT		1283.2	1412.3	1641.8	1930.8	2153.9	-2087.5	-1917.9

| GRAND TOTAL | | 2478.3 | 2731.2 | 3179.5 | 3744.1 | 4182.3 | -4052.8 | -3723.6 |

URBAN TURKEY   RATE OF URBANIZATION=1.2 POINTS PER ANNUM TO 1995   PAGE 3
POPULATION PROJECTION

FEMALES

AGE	1970	1975	1980	1985	1990	1995	2000	2005
0	795.3	1037.3	1339.2	1684.8	2066.1	2480.2	2335.9	2229.9
5	708.8	971.4	1233.8	1571.1	1961.1	2379.4	2151.3	2034.0
10	703.3	888.7	1169.7	1465.1	1844.2	2266.4	2073.5	1870.5
15	614.1	858.1	1059.6	1368.9	1700.3	2107.1	2000.9	1829.7
20	534.7	733.4	989.3	1212.8	1549.7	1902.4	1896.5	1807.5
25	417.4	621.4	828.6	1100.0	1343.8	1695.8	1743.7	1750.4
30	399.9	496.0	707.3	928.5	1217.7	1475.3	1550.1	1609.0
35	374.4	463.1	565.6	787.7	1023.1	1322.6	1352.6	1436.1
40	322.4	407.9	499.8	608.6	837.5	1077.7	1244.7	1279.9
45	216.8	342.6	429.7	525.2	638.8	869.2	1017.4	1185.8
50	166.0	238.8	364.5	454.8	555.0	671.3	802.6	951.6
55	181.3	186.7	259.8	386.0	479.9	581.9	602.1	733.0
60	159.3	192.6	200.6	273.9	398.6	491.9	511.2	533.8
65	121.9	158.7	190.9	201.7	272.2	388.5	418.8	439.1
70	80.9	112.6	144.9	174.6	187.3	249.2	306.1	339.9
75+	96.2	128.2	162.7	207.3	256.2	294.0	296.2	342.9
TOT	5901.6	7837.4	10145.9	12950.9	16331.4	20252.7	20303.4	20367.1

MALES AGE	1970	1975	1980	1985	1990	1995	2000	2005
0	834.5	1086.8	1400.3	1758.1	2151.6	2581.4	2430.0	2320.2
5	753.6	1036.4	1308.9	1662.2	2067.9	2499.6	2211.8	2090.7
10	816.7	1019.3	1328.4	1648.0	2060.7	2512.0	2054.0	1802.9
15	836.7	1141.9	1387.8	1756.2	2151.0	2621.0	1944.2	1537.3
20	765.5	1051.7	1377.1	1661.0	2076.9	2507.6	2240.4	1602.2
25	575.6	738.3	1020.1	1339.2	1616.3	2025.4	2517.6	2250.5
30	363.7	541.8	700.3	974.6	1284.5	1554.5	2051.6	2536.1
35	440.9	404.0	584.7	749.5	1030.9	1345.4	1464.5	1962.5
40	377.8	468.0	435.5	619.6	789.8	1073.1	1269.1	1391.5
45	259.1	387.9	485.7	458.8	644.7	815.9	1005.5	1201.1
50	168.9	270.3	397.5	495.7	475.3	658.4	748.5	934.6
55	198.3	175.5	272.5	395.0	491.4	475.6	590.7	678.2
60	140.3	190.6	171.4	261.5	375.4	465.2	413.2	519.7
65	100.0	128.0	172.2	157.4	236.7	336.5	387.9	344.6
70	67.1	84.0	106.8	142.7	132.5	196.3	256.7	298.6
75+	54.4	76.0	98.0	124.6	162.8	174.5	201.9	257.2
TOT	6735.1	8800.6	11247.1	14204.1	17748.6	21842.3	21791.6	21727.9
GRAND TOTAL	12636.6	16638.0	21393.0	27155.0	34080.0	42095.0	42095.0	42095.0

MIDPERIOD INDICES FOR FIVE-YEAR TIME PERIODS

POPULATION SIZE		14499.9	18866.3	24102.4	30421.1	37876.1	42095.0	42095.0
YEARLY BIRTHS		424.4	547.6	684.6	832.3	994.6	1062.0	1010.3
YEARLY DEATHS		119.8	142.9	168.1	196.1	228.0	251.4	265.6
NET YEARLY MIGRANTS		495.7	546.2	635.9	748.8	836.5	-810.6	-744.7

YEARLY RATES PER THOUSAND POPULATION

GFR=BIRTHS/FFM(15-44)		137.5	134.3	129.6	122.6	116.0	109.7	103.6
BIRTH RATE		29.3	29.0	28.4	27.4	26.3	25.2	24.0
DEATH RATE		8.3	7.6	7.0	6.4	6.0	6.0	6.3
NATURAL INCREASE		21.0	21.5	21.4	20.9	20.2	19.3	17.7
NET MIGRATION		34.2	29.0	26.4	24.6	22.1	-19.3	-17.7
POP INCREASE		55.2	50.4	47.8	45.5	42.3	0.0	-0.0

DIRECT ASSUMPTIONS FOR MIGRATION

Adoption of the FINDMIGRATION approach may result in projected quantities of migration that appear implausible based on plans and expected evolution of the economy. Therefore, it is advisable to consider the migration results of FINDMIGRATION in the same way as one would view direct assumptions when using MIGRATION as the subject. An illustration of how to do this is to review the results of the projection shown in Example 5.12.

The determinative assumptions were those relating to the proportion urban. They are shown in the upper panel of Figure 5.13. The consequential quantities of urban population change due to migration are shown in the lower panel. The reader should imagine that only the assumptions and results of the "first" urban projection are plotted on the chart at this stage. In order to provide historical perspective to evaluate the projections, past records of the proportion urban and of the quantity of urban net migrants are also plotted.[16]

Demographic analysis alone cannot provide a basis for deciding whether to accept or reject the implications of the assumption of a constant rate of urbanization after 1970. Economic considerations, and particularly employment prospects in urban as compared with rural areas, require study. If, after further examination, it were decided to make another trial with a higher urbanization rate, a second projection such as the one shown in Figure 5.13 could be made. The steps would require almost no labor. Simply recalculate the target populations using the new proportions urban, follow-

---

[16] For the historical computation, see Tekçe, "Urbanization and Migration in Turkey," appendix to Chapter 1.

FIGURE 5.13   Projections of the Proportion Urban and Urban Population Change Due to "Migration" (Includes Reclassification of Communities)

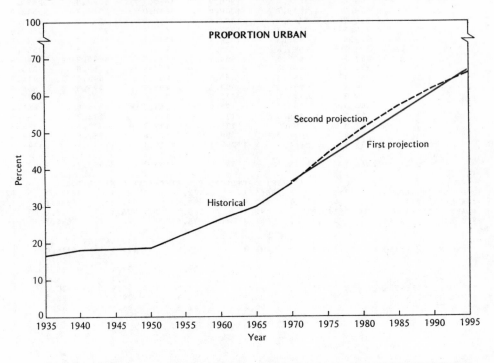

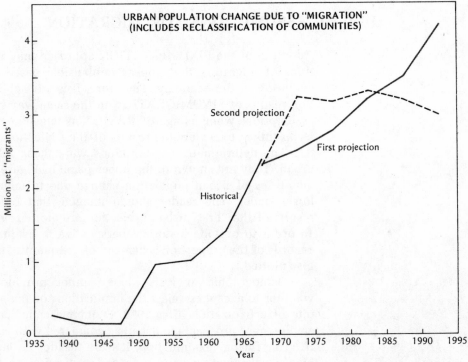

ing the plan of Table 5.10 to obtain new numbers for column 5 for 1975–1995. Then repunch one instruction card, TARGETPOP, and give a new title to the projection on the title card. The second urban projection would be ready to run immediately on FIVFIV, and the results would include new estimates of net migration as shown in the lower panel of Figure 5.13.

This example stresses the value of making more than one projection, and of using the computational methods in this book as flexible tools for exploring alternatives. The implications of alternative assumptions always should be computed, charted, and compared with historical information and prospective conditions. The process is necessarily interactive with the policy plans and projections of economists and social planners. They must evaluate the implications of each alternative population projection in terms of such variables as rates of unemployment, schooling shortages, and other factors that are consequences, in part, of the demographic projections. These consequences could produce conditions that would signal lower or higher rates of urbanization. Additional trial projections would be needed until a projection consistent with all other information and plans is found.

CHAPTER
SIX: SUBDIVIDING
POPULATIONS ⎯⎯⎯⎯⎯⎯⎯⎯

The need for population projections that refer to areas smaller than the nation arises frequently in social and economic planning. From the demographer's standpoint, projections for regions, local areas, and individual cities are often unrewarding, because lack of information forces the use of inelegant procedures that violate knowledge of the way in which human populations actually develop over time. Yet, these procedures provide statistical extrapolations from the present into the future that are more valuable than no projection at all. Hence, such projections continue to find a market, even though a critical one.

CLASSICAL RATIO METHOD

Ratio methods are the ones most commonly used for projecting subdivisions of a national or other "parent" population. The assumption of the method is that the local population shares the fertility, mortality, and international migration rates of the national population. Thus, it is subject to elements of change that are the same as those affecting the national population, and has, in this respect, a stable proportional relationship to the national population. However, the local population is also subject to unique elements of change in fertility, mortality, and migration that cause the relationship of the age and sex structure of the local population to the national population to change over time. Thus, ratios of the smaller to the larger population must be allowed to change in projections.

The procedure for making projections by the ratio method is to estimate the ratio of the local population to the national population at a recent date and to observe the past trend in the ratio. The ratio itself is then projected by direct assumption, using whatever information and judgment is available to assign a trend. The resulting ratios at each future date are then applied to the national population projection to estimate the local population at each projection date. If the ratio method is applied separately to age and sex groups, the results by age and sex are summed at each date to obtain a provisional total population. The sum is compared with a separate estimate by the ratio method of the total local population. The details by age and sex are then scaled to force agreement with the estimate of the total population. Thus, there will be no tendency for trends in age-sex specific ratios to elevate or depress the overall total, assuming that the separate projection of the total is the most reliable. The end product of this procedure is a population projection for the local area by age and sex, but without any information about births, deaths, and population change due to migration.

The principal shortcoming of the ratio method is that it extrapolates age groups over time, without in any way simulating the processes by which populations change over time. It may be likened to positivistic predictions, the test of which is the accuracy of the predictions. Cohort-component projections differ in that they are models of the actual relationships that produce change in the population. Whether their results are demonstrably better as predictions is an open question.

The ratio method is applied by using the subject SUBDIVIDE. Since the local population is a part of a national (or "parent") population, the national and local projections are made simultaneously. SUBDIVIDE is included along with other subjects in the instructions for the national projection. When SUBDIVIDE is present, REGROUP must also be present in order to bring SINSIN into operation. The actual local projection is carried out by SINSIN and is, therefore, a 15-year annual projection.

Each time a projection is made with SUBDIVIDE included, one local projection is obtained. If desired, the difference between that local population and the entire parent population can be printed as a second projection. These two projections are designated PLACEONE and PLACETWO below. If a series of local projections are wanted, each for a different place but all related to the same national population, the national projection must be repeated in one projection after the other including a different SUBDIVIDE and naming a different subdivision as PLACEONE each time. The whole series can be done in a single run on the computer because FIVFIV and SINSIN will process an unlimited number of projections.

Ratios are specified for each age-sex group and the total population of each sex by giving the parameters of a linear expression from which SINSIN will calculate a ratio for the midyear dates 0, 5, 10, and 15 for the 15-year SINSIN projection. In Figure 6.1, R is the ratio at any date a', and a is the slope of a line passing through R expressed as a change in the ratio per year. The slope a may be zero, in which event the ratio is a constant. A second and later date b' may be specified (optional), in which event a slope b is assigned to the final indefinitely long segment. The slope b may be zero. Dates are expressed in exact years with decimal fractions. Midyear is, for example, 1975.5. The dates that specify parameters for the linear segments do not have to correspond with dates of the projection. They may, for example, refer to dates of censuses that provide the assumptions.

FIGURE 6.1   Ratios and Slopes for SUBDIVIDE

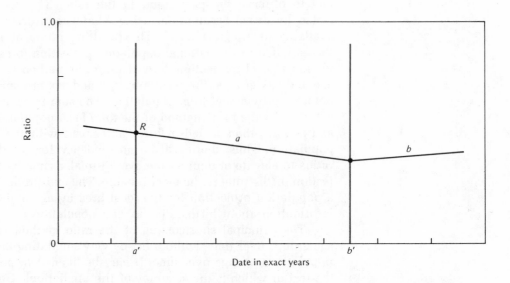

SUBDIVIDE	Optional SINSIN subject
PLACEONE.	Columns 10 to 80 for title of subdivisional projection
PLACETWO.	Title of residual if wanted; otherwise empty columns 10-80

The first two instruction cards are for titles. Normally, the user wants a projection only for a subdivision and not for the residual projection, in which event the PLACETWO card is included without any title. If a title is given on the PLACE-TWO card, the computer will respond by producing a projection for the residual population as well.

TOTALONE.F	Parameters for the total female ratios
TOTALONE.M	Same for males

Instructions are given on the TOTALONE cards to specify the ratios of the total population of each sex to the national (or parent) population. They are given in the following format:

Numeric data field	Columns	Content
1	11-20	Ratio at first date (e.g., most recent census).
2	21-30	First date. Express in exact years (e.g., June 30, 1970 is 1970.5). The date may occur earlier than the period covered by the projection or it may occur within the period.
3	31-40	Annual change in ratio. If left empty or punched zero, the initial ratio will be held constant (no change). The amount of change that is punched will be added annually to the initial ratio for forward extrapolation, and will be subtracted for backward extrapolation.

(continued)

Numeric data field	Columns	Content
4	41-50	Terminal date, if there is one, for the first linear segment. Express in exact years. Refer to a date later than that in field 2. If left empty, the annual change given in field 3 will be continued indefinitely.
5	51-60	Annual change in ratio for second linear segment, if any. This amount of change will be continued indefinitely. It will start from the date given in field 4. If no second segment, leave empty.

The TOTALONE cards provide ratios that will control the development of the total population. The results by separate age and sex groups will be scaled to agree with the totals. The remainder of the instructions refers to the ratioing of five-year age groups by sex. The same parameters are required as for total populations of each sex, but they are arranged on cards as follows:

RATIOS.F.A
RATIOS.F.B   } 16 female ratios followed by a date in field 17. Field 3 on the third card is the last one.
RATIOS.F.C

SLOPE1.F.A
SLOPE1.F.B   } Optional. Annual changes in the 16 ratios followed by terminal date, if any, for first segment.
SLOPE1.F.C

SLOPE2.F.A
SLOPE2.F.B   } Optional. Annual changes for second linear segment; 16 slopes, which may include zero (empty) fields.
SLOPE2.F.C

The initial ratios by five-year age groups are punched on the first three cards in the regular format (see INIT.POP). Ratios for 16 age groups are followed by an exact date in field 17 of the string to indicate the reference date for the ratios.

The SLOPE cards are optional. They are omitted if the ratios are to apply to all dates. However, up to two linear segments that specify change over time in the ratios may be defined. The SLOPE1 cards specify annual change for each of the 16 age-group ratios for a straight line passing through the date specified on RATIOS.F.C. These annual amounts of change will continue indefinitely unless a second set of SLOPE cards is given. If the SLOPE2 cards are used, they will define the annual change for 16 ratios in the second segment. The computer must be notified that the first segment terminates by punching the exact date of termination at the end of the first string of slopes (i.e., in field 17, which is the third numeric field on SLOPE1.F.C). Arrange the 16 ratios and slopes in the same order on both the RATIO and SLOPE cards so they will match each other. Dates always follow in field 17.

For males, instructions are prepared in the same way, except that the labels contain the symbol M instead of F.

SEND

The subject SUBDIVIDE is always closed by a SEND card.

The order of instructions is important with regard to this subject, except that males or females may come first.

```
0         1         2         3         4         5         6         7         8
1234567890123456789012345678901234567890123456789012345678901234567890123456789 0

                         EXAMPLE OF SUBDIVIDE

             *** CITY OF BURSA:    SEE TEXT BELOW FOR EXPLANATION ***

SUBDIVIDE
PLACEONE.CITY OF BURSA.    PARENT POPULATION IS URBAN TURKEY   (POP UNITS = ONE)
PLACETWO.  RESIDUAL
TOTALONE.F    .0241    1965.83     -.0003    1970.83
TOTALONE.M    .0213    1965.83     -.0001    1970.83
RATIOS.F.A    .0204    .0219       .0227     .0242     .0236     .0232     .0243
RATIOS.F.B    .0254    .0277       .0259     .0272     .0275     .0269     .0280
RATIOS.F.C    .0290    .0300     1965.83
SLOPE1.F.A   -.0001   -.0001
SLOPE1.F.B                                                       .0001     .0001
SLOPE1.F.C    .0002    .0002     1975.83
SLOPE2.F.A
SLOPE2.F.B     (NOTE EMPTY FIELDS SIGNIFY ZERO SLOPE; HENCE CONSTANT RATES)
SLOPE2.F.C
RATIOS.M.A    .0202    .0223       .0223     .0207     .0129     .0195     .0206
RATIOS.M.B    .0219    .0264       .0259     .0262     .0275     .0262     .0280
RATIOS.M.C    .0290    .0300     1965.83
SLOPE1.M.A   -.0001   -.0001                           .0002     .0003     .0003
SLOPE1.M.B    .0003    .0003       .0002                         .0001     .0001
SLOPE1.M.C    .0002    .0002     1975.83
SLOPE2.M.A
SLOPE2.M.B
SLOPE2.M.C
SEND

1234567890123456789012345678901234567890123456789012345678901234567890123456789 0
```

In the example SUBDIVIDE, the size of the local population is so much smaller than the national population that considerable precision would be lost if it were expressed in the same units. When population quantities are printed by SINSIN, either one digit or no digits are given after the decimal point, depending upon the table. In this instance, the parent population is in units of a thousand, and the city population should be expressed in units of one to provide adequate detail. In order to shift the decimal point for the local population to the right three places, every ratio and every slope planned for the TOTALONE, RATIO, and SLOPE cards is multiplied by a factor of 10^x, where x is the number of places the decimal point is to be shifted to the right in the population projection for the subdivision.

There are certain rules about the size, sign, and precision of numbers that are acceptable as ratios and slopes.

Type of number	Absolute size	Sign	Precision to right of decimal
Ratios	0.0 to 1.0	+	6 places
Slopes	0.0 to k	+ or −	6 places

The k (slope) should not be so large that it causes the ratio to become >1.0 within the time range of the 15-year projection.

It may be useful to explain in more detail the planning of projections such as the Bursa example that follows SUBDIVIDE. The parent population is the urban population of Turkey, rather than the entire national population. Thus, the example illustrates the choice of a parent population whose age structure is more likely to change over time in a manner similar to that of a city.

The most recent observations of ratios for Bursa were given by the 1965 census, so the exact date of the census was specified on the RATIOS cards and for the total population of Bursa on the TOTALONE cards. Usually, historical trends in ratios are extrapolated, but the upward or downward slopes of the ratios are forced toward zero. After that, the ratios are held constant on the assumption that stable relationships between the subdivisional and parent populations will prevail. This line of reasoning is illustrated in the example by specifying a zero slope for the ratio of the total city population after 1970.83 (note the empty fifth field on the TOTALONE cards). The ratios by age and sex were allowed to continue changing up to 1975.83 but after that are also held constant (note that the SLOPE2 cards are empty; blank spaces signify zero slopes for all the age-group ratios). The continuing change in the ratios for the individual age groups after 1970.83 affects the values of the ratios relative to each other but not as a whole, because the ratio for the total population by sex is controlling and is held constant after 1970.83.

The dates for the assumptions about ratios and slopes may be the same or different from those that position the parent projection. In the present example, the parent projection starts from midyear 1970 (see Example 5.11). Therefore, SINSIN will calculate ratios from the SUBDIVIDE instructions that apply to midyear 1970, 1975, 1980, and 1985. The resulting ratios will be applied to the FIVFIV projection to calculate a Bursa population projection at five-year intervals for 15 years, 1970 to 1985. After that is done, SINSIN will calculate the annual projection, special age groups, and any other tables that were requested.

If it happens that the parent projection is not positioned on midyear dates, SINSIN will establish a wrong correspondence between ratio dates and projection dates because SINSIN computes the ratios at midyear. To avoid this error, position the parent population on midyear (see DATE. SHIFT) or introduce a compensating error in the following way: Position the assumptions about ratios and slopes on the same date of the year as the parent population projection. Then specify year dates for the ratios and slopes as if they were exact midyear dates. SINSIN can then establish correct correspondence between the projection dates and the ratio and slope dates.

As described, the ratio method may appear less laborious to apply than in fact it is. Since the ratios should be applied by SINSIN to a parent population projection that is free of age misreporting, the observation of historical ratios also should be carried out on parent and subdivisional populations that are free of age misreporting. This was done for the Bursa example, but not without considerable labor to adjust the relevant age distributions. If one does not make the age adjustments when estimating historical ratios, there is an implicit assumption that the same pattern and relative amount of age reporting error prevail in the censuses of the subdivisional and parent populations.

The output from SUBDIVIDE is similar to other SINSIN output. It includes age-group estimates, but not births, deaths, and migrations. Whenever SUBDIVIDE is used, REGROUP must also be used. Other SINSIN subjects, such as the one described in the next chapter, can be given at the same time.

Consistency Between Parts and the Whole

When SUBDIVIDE is used to divide a national projection into a number of regional projections (or to divide in some other way), the sum of the regional projections is a national projection that may not at first agree exactly with the original national projection. In order to assure a reasonable degree of consistency, the assumptions about the ratios of total population by sex should be planned with an eye to the adding-up problem. Table 6.2 is a worksheet for one sex for the TOTALONE cards. The cards would be used for a series of five successive projections for five regions. If the first ratios sum to 1.0, if the slopes sum to zero, and if the dates are the same for all regions, the sum of the parts will exactly equal the whole, so far as total population is concerned, at dates 0, 5, 10, and 15. Only minor differences will be found at intermediate dates within the 15-year SINSIN projection.

At the level of individual age-sex groups, it is not possible to specify wholly consistent ratios and slopes unless one knows the age distribution of the national population at each date beforehand and is prepared to engage in the scaling computations necessary to make the ratios at each projection date consistent with the controlling ratios for the total population by sex. A satisfactory approach usually is to specify ratios for age-sex groups from past observations, and slopes on the basis of trends and judgment about prospective developments. Consistent totals by sex will keep inconsistencies in the age groups within reasonable bounds.

At the final stages of the work, elegance can be achieved by prorating differences by age groups, although the gain in precision will be small and the result of arbitrary allocation. The national projection should remain the controlling one. If one wants to do prorating on the computer, SINSIN can be ordered to produce the single-year arrays in machine-readable form by including the subject PUNCH.SINGLE.

COHORT-COMPONENT PROJECTIONS

An alternative to the ratio method of subdividing populations is to make separate cohort-component projections for each subdivision. The cohort-component approach requires assumptions for all the components of population change at the local level. If successful, the extra effort of producing mutually consistent assumptions at the local level is rewarded by projections that simulate the entire process of local population change, including migration, births, and deaths.

Since the sum of a set of subdivisional projections is the national (or parent) projection, an acceptable starting point is to make a series of separate subdivisional projections using preliminary assumptions about fertility, mortality, and migration for each one. Information on which to base assumptions is usually strongest at the national (or parent) level, so a national projection should be made as well. It is then treated as a controlling projection against which to check the consistency of assumptions for the individual subdivisions. A rapid means of checking is to use a worksheet such as that shown in Table 6.3. The FIVFIV projections show midperiod indices

TABLE 6.2   Assumptions for TOTALONE Cards for Five Regional Projections: Only One Sex Shown

Region	First ratio	First date	First slope	Second date	Second slope
1	.202	1976.5	.0004	1981.5	.0001
2	.305	1976.5	.0015	1981.5	.0005
3	.100	1976.5	.0	1981.5	.0
4	.159	1976.5	−.0020	1981.5	−.0006
5	.234	1976.5	.0001	1981.5	.0
Total	**1.000**	—	**.0**	—	**.0**

TABLE 6.3   Reconciliation of Parent and Subdivisional Projections

Period and subdivision	Midperiod indices for five-year periods			
	Population size	Yearly births	Yearly deaths	Net yearly migrants
First Period				
Subdivision 1				
Subdivision 2				
Subdivision 3				
Subdivision 4				
Total				
Parent				
Difference				
Second Period				
Subdivision 1				
Subdivision 2				
Subdivision 3				
Subdivision 4				
Total				
Parent				
Difference				
Third Period				
Subdivision 1				
Subdivision 2				
Subdivision 3				
Subdivision 4				
Total				
Parent				
Difference				

of population size, births, deaths, and net migrants near the bottom of page 3 (or page 2 if there is no migration). Sums of these variables across the subdivisions, when compared with the same variables in the parent projection, indicate the direction of change in subdivisional assumptions that is necessary to obtain consistency between the parts and the whole.

The amount of change that is needed in order to approach consistency can be learned by making more than one set of subdivisional projections during a run. Let each extra set of projections involve a variation in only one component: mortality level (or other index), total fertility, or migration level (quantity or rates). There is one base set plus three more sets in the run. Then, by linear interpolation, an approximation of the partial effect on all four midperiod indices of varying one component can be learned. These partial coefficients are used to adjust assumptions for one or more subdivisions to make the next run. Attention should be concentrated on the first projection period, then the second, and so on. Each time a revised set of subdivisional projections is made, extra sets should be included to reestimate the partial effects of changing the component assumptions.

After an acceptable degree of consistency has been attained, the controlling parent projection can be abandoned and replaced by the exact sum of the subdivisional projections. When the subdivisional projections are summed by age and sex, the midperiod population, births, deaths, and net migrants should be summed also. Crude birth, death, and migration rates are calculated for the parent projection by using the sum of the midperiod populations as the denominator. If one prefers to do this work on the computer, include PUNCH.FIVE in each of the final subdivisional projections. Machine-readable output will be produced that includes the complete FIVFIV projection arrays and the midperiod values for population size, births, deaths, and net migrants.

Mutually consistent subdivisional projections should be made first on FIVFIV. After they have been checked and found to be satisfactory, SINSIN subjects such as REGROUP and AGESEXSPEC (see next chapter) may be given for each subdivision. SINSIN output also must be summed across subdivisions to obtain exact consistency at the parent projection level. PUNCH.SINGLE can be used to obtain SINSIN output in machine-readable form for each subdivision.

Migration in Subdivisional Projections

Redistribution of population by migration is often a major factor in local projections. If detailed studies of each subdivision are not available on which to base assumptions, standard age-sex distributions for migrants may be prepared and used for all subdivisions. These distributions are punched on the MIGR cards whether using MIGRATION (quantity alternative) or FINDMIGRATION. One computational convenience of a standard distribution is that the sum of quantities of migration by age and sex across all subdivisions will be zero if net migration for the parent projection is zero. If the parent projection has a positive or negative balance of external migration and the standard age and sex distribution prevails, external migration can be assigned to the subdivisions without any loss in consistency at the detailed level of age-sex groups.

In the worksheet shown as Table 6.4, there is no net external migration in period 1, but there is in period 2. Completion of such a worksheet assures that migration assumptions will be consistent at the level of total population by sex, and also by age groups if a standard distribution by age is used.

TABLE 6.4 Migration Assumptions by Subdivision for MIGLEVEL Information Cards

Sex and subdivision	Projection period						
	1	2	3	4	5	6	7
MIGLEVEL.F							
Subdivision 1	−50	−50					
Subdivision 2	−30	−45					
Subdivision 3	+80	+85					
Total = Parent	—	−10					
MIGLEVEL.M							
Subdivision 1	−75	−75					
Subdivision 2	−40	−65					
Subdivision 3	+115	+120					
Total = Parent	—	−20					

The actual quantities of migration do not need to be assumed in advance if the analyst is more confident with assumptions about the future size of each subdivisional population. FINDMIGRATION may be used instead of MIGRATION. The TARGETPOP assumptions of FINDMIGRATION must be selected so that they sum to the projected parent population total at dates 5, 10, . . . 35.

The steps when using FINDMIGRATION are first, to make the parent projection and to copy the total population (both sexes) on the bottom line of the worksheet shown in Table 6.5. TARGETPOP assumptions are next developed for each of the subdivisions within the constraint that they must sum to the parent total at each projection date. Finally, sex and age distributions for migrants are specified on the MPERHUNDF and MIGR cards. If the same standard distribution is used for all subdivisions and for the parent population projection (external migration), the migration projections will become consistent when consistency is achieved in other respects as well.

FINDMIGRATION forces consistency of population size. Consequently, any failure of births or deaths to sum by subdivisions to the parent totals will be offset by errors in the FINDMIGRATION estimate of migration in the opposite direction. This problem will disappear when the assumptions about mortality and fertility are made consistent.

TABLE 6.5 TARGETPOP Assumptions by Subdivision

Subdivision	Projection year						
	5	10	15	20	25	30	35
Region A	1247.	1300.					
Region B	3432.	3844.					
Region C	565.	750.					
Total = Parent	5244.	5894.					

Adjustment Sequence for Fertility and Mortality

The quantity of births can be adjusted either by changing the fertility schedule, FERDIST, so as to affect the mean age of childbearing, or by altering total fertility, TOTAL.FERT. The latter is recommended in the absence of special information. An approximate estimate of how much change in total fertility, $\triangle$TF, is needed to achieve a specified change in the number of births, $\triangle$B, is given by the following:

$$\triangle TF = \left(\frac{TF}{B} \right) \times (\triangle B)$$

where TF and B are taken from the projection (find TF on the first page of output). This adjustment is made for each period of the projection.

Differentials in total fertility among the subdivisions may be modified on the basis of new information, but if there is none, consistency can be sought by prorating the change in births that is required over all subdivisions. If fertility assumptions for one subdivision are more strongly based than for others, the adjustment can be assigned entirely to the other subdivisions.

In order to adjust mortality assumptions so that the number of deaths by subdivision will sum approximately to the national total, information about the effect on the number of deaths of incremental changes in assumptions is useful. It is suggested, therefore, that a special run of subdivisional projections be used to gather this information. Punch a duplicate of the projection instructions so that two sets of subdivisional projections can be made at the same time. For the second set, increase the mortality parameters exactly one percent. It does not matter which life-table index is used to express the mortality assumptions. Simply raise the values by one percent. The new values should be punched with as many decimal digits as necessary to express the one percent change precisely. Even though FIVFIV will only print two significant places after the decimal in its report, it will use the entire punched number for internal calculation.

After the special run is made, the effect of a one percent change in mortality parameters can be learned by comparing deaths in the two projections. Small adjustments in mortality do not have much effect on births, but fertility changes have a fairly strong effect on number of deaths when infant mortality is high. Therefore, it is better to postpone the adjustment of mortality assumptions until consistency is close at hand for fertility. In terms of sequence, that means handling the mortality on about the third trial, or possibly later.

Complete consistency cannot be expected, because the user is not allowed to vary every component of change for every cohort independently. Mortality schedules impose fixed patterns of deaths by age. It is not, therefore, even logically possible to generate a set of consistent subdivisional projections when different model life tables are used for different subdivisions. However, the analyst can come close to consistency and, if he wishes, force consistency at the end by treating one subdivision as a residual, or abandoning the controlling parent projection and substituting the sum of the subdivisional projections.

CHAPTER SEVEN: SOCIAL AND ECONOMIC PROJECTIONS _____

Social and economic variables are dependent in many instances upon the age, sex, and residential location of the population. Whenever that dependence is important in determining the value of social or economic variables, it is worthwhile to examine the effect on plans of population projections. If the relationship can be expressed by rates that are specific as to age, sex, or type of community (or some combination of these), a simple basis exists for deriving future values of the social or economic variable from population projections.

Types of social and economic variables that lend themselves to projection by the application of age-, sex-, and residence-specific rates are the following:

1. **Labor force.** Conventional labor-force participation rates may be used. Less conventional concepts of "available manpower" expressed in age-specific rates by sex and place of residence are equally acceptable to the computing routine. Separate estimates of labor supply by rural and urban areas are valuable for planning purposes.

2. **Housing units.** For each dwelling unit there is a household head (defining the social and housing units the same). Household headship rates are a direct means, therefore, of investigating the relationship between housing units and population projections. Forecasts of the demand for housing units can be linked to population projections for different residential locations such as rural and urban, and within the urban category by city.

3. **School enrollment.**   There is a fairly close correspondence between types of schools and the age and sex groups that are enrolled. Enrollment rates are used to express the numbers enrolled out of the relevant age and sex groups. Projections of future enrollment rates must have a clear definition: Either they are targets, or they are forecasts under specified conditions. Whatever the concept, the volume of enrollments is linked to population projections.

4. **Eligibles for health services.**   Health services often cater to well-defined groups in terms of age and sex. This is due, in part, to physiological and epidemiological associations of age and sex. It may also reflect the target groups selected to receive services. The effect of alternative population projections on the numbers of persons eligible for health services can be worked out by using age- and sex-specific rates of eligibility.

5. **Marital status of the population.**   Once given a set of age- and sex-specific rates for marital status, the number in each status category can be projected directly from population projections.

These examples refer to a few of the consequences of population growth. There are many more. Planning of commodity productions, investment, and public services all involve accommodation to future population change. When computing projections of economic and social variables by the application of age- and sex-specific rates, close attention must be given to the definition and estimation of the rates that are applied. Do they refer to projected demand or supply? What are the assumptions about income and prices? Are the projections forecasts, or do they only explore the implications of population change, leaving aside changes in other determinants of the final quantities of the variables?

Few planners would be satisfied to make social and economic projections based on a simple one-way derivation from population projections alone. Earlier, it was explained that PUNCH.FIVE and PUNCH.SINGLE can be used to transfer the results of population projections to planning models that are based on a wide range of variables, not population alone. This is to be encouraged. Concurrently, and with only a small investment in preparation of instructions, certain social and economic implications of population projections can be estimated approximately each time a projection is made. One can learn the implications of changes in the demographic assumptions with practically no effort at all, simply by re-running the projection with no change in the assumptions about the age- and sex-specific rates that determine social or economic variables.

AGE- AND SEX-SPECIFIC RATES

The subject AGESEXSPEC applies age- and sex-specific rates to a population projection to produce a projection of the corresponding variable. AGE-SEXSPEC is applicable equally to projections for urban, rural, regional, or other subdivisional populations. Rates that are specific as to residence may be used conveniently to make subdivisional economic and social projections. More than one variable is usually of interest and capable of being linked to population projections by age- and sex-specific rates. AGESEXSPEC can be given up to four times within a single projection.

Changes in rates may be projected over time by giving parameters for the linear segments shown in Figure 7.1. The rates must be less than 10.0

FIGURE 7.1   Rates for AGESEXSPEC

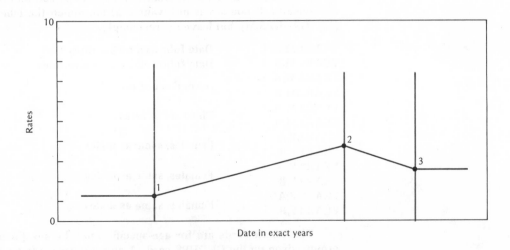

and not negative. A series of rates for up to three ascending dates specified in exact years may be given. The computer will assume a constant rate prior to the first date and following the last date given, which may be date 1, 2, or 3. Thus, if a rate is given for only one date, the rate will be constant for all dates. Between dates that are given, the computer will perform linear interpolation. The dates that are given need not necessarily fall on the dates at the beginning or end of the projections. SINSIN will compute rates midyear of years 0, 5, 10, and 15 and use the results for the projection.

AGESEXSPEC   **Optional subject (up to 4 times)**

TITLE.#.

A distinctive title for the AGESEXSPEC output is punched in columns 9–80. The symbol # must be replaced by a number or left blank. If SUBDIVIDE is used in the same projection, the following numeric codes will restrict printed output to the particular subdivision that has the age- and sex-specific rates of this subject:

0   No restriction; prints AGESEXSPEC for all subdivisions and parent population
1   Prints for PLACEONE only
2   Prints for PLACETWO only
3   Prints for parent population only

Only the first AGESEXSPEC is capable of producing projections from the PLACE-TWO (residual) population as well as from the PLACEONE and parent populations. The second through fourth AGESEXSPEC cannot produce projections for the PLACETWO population, although it can do so for either or both the parent and PLACEONE populations.

GROUPS.F.# #-# #.# #-# # etc., up to 12 groups (females)
GROUPS.M.# #-# #.# #-# # etc., up to 12 groups (males)

The age groups that are to be multiplied by the age- and sex-specific rates are given on the GROUPS cards. To specify a one-year age group, use, for example,

07–07. In order to include persons 75 and over, specify 75. Age 65 and over would be punched 65–75. The age group 0 cannot be taken alone, but persons under age 2 could be requested by 00–01. Different age groups can be used as a base for males and females. If one sex is not wanted at all, punch the label and include the card (e.g., GROUPS.M), but leave the rest empty.

YEAR1.M.A	Date followed by six rates
YEAR1.M.B	Date followed by six more rates
YEAR2.M.A	Second set of rates
YEAR2.M.B	
YEAR3.M.A	Third set of rates
YEAR3.M.B	
YEAR1.F.A	Females, same as males
YEAR1.F.B	
YEAR2.F.A	Females, same as males
YEAR2.F.B	
YEAR3.F.A	Females, same as males
YEAR3.F.B	

The YEAR cards are for age-specific rates by sex (M or F) to match the age groups given on the GROUPS card. A pair of year cards gives up to 12 rates for an exact year (hence the label YEAR). Both cards of the pair must be present, and the first numeric data field on both must contain the exact year. The year is always punched on the second card (B) of a pair whether or not the card contains rates. The string of up to 12 rates is arranged in the same order as the age groups on the GROUPS cards.

There must be a pair of YEAR cards for males and for females for at least one date, even if they are entirely empty for one sex. Whether or not additional dates are given is optional. Either male or female cards may be given first but should be kept together in pairs for each sex.

Digits beyond the fourth decimal place are rounded off and lost during computation. The acceptable range for rates is 0.0 to 9.9999.

AEND

The subject is always closed by an AEND card.

```
0         1         2         3         4         5         6         7         8
1234567890123456789012345678901234567890123456789012345678901234567890123456789012345678901234567890
                         EXAMPLES OF AGESEXSPEC

                *** RATES APPLIED TO SIX AGE RANGES WITH TWO DATES ***

AGESEXSPEC
TITLE. .'AVAILABLE CIVILIAN MANPOWER'  VALID 1972 TO 1981 ONLY.
GROUPS.F.15-19.20-24.25-29.30-54.55-64.65-74
GROUPS.M.15-19.20-24.25-29.30-54.55-64.65-74
YEAR1.F.A     1970.5       .22        .35        .20        .14        .11        .02
YEAR1.F.B     1970.5
YEAR2.F.A     1985.5       .25        .38        .29        .26        .11        .02
YEAR2.F.B     1985.5
YEAR1.M.A     1970.5       .58        .88        .98        .985       .855       .540
YEAR1.M.B     1970.5
YEAR2.M.A     1985.5       .49        .79        .98        .985       .765       .420
YEAR2.M.B     1985.5
AEND
```

(continued)

```
                         *** CONSTANT RATES ***

AGESEXSPEC
TITLE. .MALE LABOR FORCE
GROUPS.F.
GROUPS.M.15-19.20-24.25-29.30-54.55-64.65-74
YEAR1.F.A        2000.      (NOTE ANY YEAR WILL DO WHEN RATES CONSTANT OVER TIME)
YEAR1.F.B        2000.        (FEMALE CARDS INCLUDED EVEN THOUGH NO RATES)
YEAR1.M.A        2000.0      .58        .88        .98      .985      .855      .540
YEAR1.M.B        2000.0
AEND


             *** DIFFERENT AGE RANGES FOR MALES AND FEMALES ***
       *** PRINTING CONTROL ON TITLE CARD RESTRICTS APPLICATION TO PLACEONE ***

AGESEXSPEC
TITLE.1.HOUSEHOLDS ESTIMATED FROM AGE AND SEX SPECIFIC HEADSHIP RATES (THOUS)
GROUPS.M.30-64.65-69.70-75
GROUPS.F.50-69.70-75
YEAR1.M.A        1965.83      .95        .52        .15
YEAR1.M.B        1965.83
YEAR2.M.A        1977.5       .57        .20
YEAR2.M.B        1977.5
YEAR3.M.A        2000.        .97        .60        .30
YEAR3.M.B        2000.
YEAR1.F.A        1965.83      .16        .05
YEAR1.F.B        1965.83
YEAR2.F.A        2000.        .20        .10
YEAR2.F.B        2000.
AEND

12345678901234567890123456789012345678901234567890123456789012345678901234567890
```

CIVILIAN MANPOWER

An economist approached the author to request projections of "available civilian manpower" in urban areas of Turkey for 1972-1981. The concept of availability was broader than that of labor force participation, because the economist considered all males over age 15 to be available unless they were occupied as students, soldiers, prisoners, or were in other noncivilian pursuits outside the economy. Trends for the period were postulated on those definitions. Since he considered it a social objective to induce increased proportions of women to enter the labor market, rates of availability for women were assumed to rise over the period. The assumptions were punched as shown above in the first example following the explanation of AGESEXSPEC.

After preparing the subject AGESEXSPEC, it was included in the instructions for a projection for urban Turkey for 1970-1995. SINSIN processes 15 years at a time. It produced an urban projection, therefore, for "available civilian manpower" for 1970-1985. The results are shown in Example 7.2. Although not needed in this instance, it would be possible to extend the manpower projection additional years into the future by following the procedure explained in Chapter Four (page 68).

EXAMPLE 7.2   Available Civilian Manpower

REPORT OF ASSUMPTIONS FOR AGESEXSPEC

TITLE: 'AVAILABLE CIVILIAN MANPOWER'   VALID 1972 TO 1981 ONLY.

ASSUMED AGE-SPECIFIC RATES

F E M A L E S

AGE	1970	1971	1972	1973	1974	1975	1976	1977	1978	1979	1980	1981	1982	1983	1984	1985
15-19	0.220	0.222	0.224	0.226	0.228	0.230	0.232	0.234	0.236	0.238	0.240	0.242	0.244	0.246	0.248	0.250
20-24	0.350	0.352	0.354	0.356	0.358	0.360	0.362	0.364	0.366	0.368	0.370	0.372	0.374	0.376	0.378	0.380
25-29	0.200	0.206	0.212	0.218	0.224	0.230	0.236	0.242	0.248	0.254	0.260	0.266	0.272	0.278	0.284	0.290
30-54	0.140	0.148	0.156	0.164	0.172	0.180	0.188	0.196	0.204	0.212	0.220	0.228	0.236	0.244	0.252	0.260
55-64	0.110	0.110	0.110	0.110	0.110	0.110	0.110	0.110	0.110	0.110	0.110	0.110	0.110	0.110	0.110	0.110
65-74	0.020	0.020	0.020	0.020	0.020	0.020	0.020	0.020	0.020	0.020	0.020	0.020	0.020	0.020	0.020	0.020

M A L E S

AGE	1970	1971	1972	1973	1974	1975	1976	1977	1978	1979	1980	1981	1982	1983	1984	1985
15-19	0.580	0.574	0.568	0.562	0.556	0.550	0.544	0.538	0.532	0.526	0.520	0.514	0.508	0.502	0.496	0.490
20-24	0.880	0.874	0.868	0.862	0.856	0.850	0.844	0.838	0.832	0.826	0.820	0.814	0.808	0.802	0.796	0.790
25-29	0.980	0.980	0.980	0.980	0.980	0.980	0.980	0.980	0.980	0.980	0.980	0.980	0.980	0.980	0.980	0.980
30-54	0.985	0.985	0.985	0.985	0.985	0.985	0.985	0.985	0.985	0.985	0.985	0.985	0.985	0.985	0.985	0.985
55-64	0.855	0.849	0.843	0.837	0.831	0.825	0.819	0.813	0.807	0.801	0.795	0.789	0.783	0.777	0.771	0.765
65-74	0.540	0.532	0.524	0.516	0.508	0.500	0.492	0.484	0.476	0.468	0.460	0.452	0.444	0.436	0.428	0.420

'AVAILABLE CIVILIAN MANPOWER'   VALID 1972 TO 1981 ONLY.

F E M A L E S

AGE	1970	1971	1972	1973	1974	1975	1976	1977	1978	1979	1980	1981	1982	1983	1984	1985
15-19	135.1	146.4	158.9	172.1	185.1	197.4	208.7	219.2	229.6	241.0	254.3	269.3	296.2	304.5	323.4	342.2
20-24	187.2	201.5	215.7	230.4	246.4	264.0	282.7	303.2	324.8	346.1	366.0	385.0	402.6	420.0	439.0	460.9
25-29	83.5	92.8	104.0	116.5	129.6	142.9	156.5	172.0	184.1	198.9	215.4	234.1	254.8	276.6	298.2	319.0
30-54	207.1	231.3	257.5	285.9	316.9	350.7	387.3	427.2	470.2	516.1	564.7	616.3	670.8	728.9	791.5	859.2
55-64	37.5	38.4	39.3	40.0	40.8	41.7	42.8	44.0	45.6	47.8	50.6	54.1	58.3	62.9	67.7	72.6
65-74	4.2	4.4	4.6	4.9	5.1	5.4	5.6	5.9	6.2	6.4	6.7	6.8	7.0	7.2	7.3	7.5
TOTAL	655.	715.	780.	850.	924.	1002.	1084.	1170.	1260.	1356.	1458.	1566.	1680.	1800.	1927.	2061.

M A L E S

AGE	1970	1971	1972	1973	1974	1975	1976	1977	1978	1979	1980	1981	1982	1983	1984	1985
15-19	485.3	517.5	549.4	578.6	604.9	628.0	649.1	665.9	680.9	698.9	721.7	743.5	767.5	794.4	825.5	860.5
20-24	673.6	695.6	733.1	784.3	840.8	894.0	936.2	980.8	1030.7	1082.4	1129.2	1165.8	1194.6	1224.1	1262.4	1312.2
25-29	564.1	593.8	620.6	647.6	680.4	723.5	772.0	827.7	885.6	942.2	999.7	1070.6	1146.0	1215.9	1271.1	1312.4
30-54	1578.3	1659.7	1749.9	1845.8	1943.4	2040.9	2142.2	2242.9	2344.5	2451.0	2564.6	2685.2	2813.1	2949.4	3095.3	3248.7
55-64	289.5	293.6	296.3	297.6	299.0	302.0	306.1	311.3	319.9	333.7	352.9	377.3	406.4	438.1	470.2	502.2
65-74	90.3	95.0	97.8	99.9	102.4	106.0	105.6	109.3	115.3	121.9	128.3	123.4	122.4	123.2	125.0	126.0
TOTAL	3681	3855.	4047.	4254.	4471.	4694.	4911.	5138.	5377.	5630.	5896.	6166.	6450.	6745.	7049.	7362.

B O T H   S E X E S

AGE	1970	1971	1972	1973	1974	1975	1976	1977	1978	1979	1980	1981	1982	1983	1984	1985
TOTAL	4336.	4570.	4827.	5103.	5395.	5697.	5995.	6307.	6637.	6986.	7354.	7731.	8130.	8545.	8977.	9424.

FIGURE 7.3 Projections of Available Civilian Manpower and Employment, Based on Two Rates of Urbanization: Urban Turkey, 1972–1981

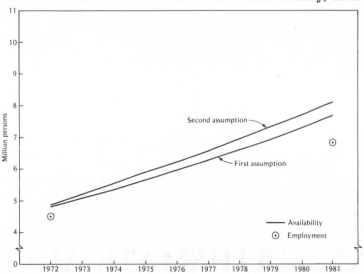

One of the advantages of linking manpower estimates to this particular urban projection is that the demographic effects of rural to urban migration and international migration are fully taken into account, at least insofar as assumptions can be made about them. The short-term effects on the urban manpower situation are substantial not only because the migration flows are large, but also because of their age- and sex-selective character, all factors that are incorporated into the modified cohort-component method of making demographic projections.

Estimates of excess civilian manpower are shown in Figure 7.3 to indicate the implications of certain demographic and economic assumptions. Employment estimates were made by Kemal Derviş using a Cobb-Douglas model developed by himself.[17] The estimates for 1972 (base date) and 1981 are median values resulting from a range of wage and investment policies that he considered. The curves for civilian manpower were projected with a single set of AGESEXSPEC instructions using two alternative assumption' about rates of urbanization in Turkey (see Chapter Five, pages 93–95).

One wonders how changes in West German economic policy wᵣ affect the urban labor market in Turkey. What would be the effect of elimı nating net exports of Turkish workers to Europe, as assumed in the laissez-faire national projection? Or if there were an increase in annual additions of Turkish workers to European labor markets, how would that affect the chain of projections leading eventually to estimates of urban labor supply?

Many questions about the effects of economic and social policy on the demographic determinants of population projections wait to be answered. Only migration, the most unpredictable of components, has been mentioned as a variable in this discussion. The long-term effects of policy on fertility and mortality should be considered as well. The consequences of changes in these demographic determinants can be studied by using FIVFIV and SINSIN. It is in the consequences of population changes that some of the motivation for social policies to shape the demographic future can be found.

---

[17] Kemal Derviş, "Substitution, Employment and Intertemporal Equilibrium in a Non-Linear Multi-Sector Planning Model for Turkey" (Ph.D. dissertation, economics, Princeton University, 1973), p. 75.

APPENDIX
ONE: MATHEMATICAL
APPENDIX _____

The computational procedures of FIVFIV produce population projections by the modified cohort-component method. The projection is made in five-year cycles. Each five-year cycle is independent of the preceding one, except that the initial population of each cycle is the terminal population of the preceding one. Different assumptions about fertility, mortality, and migration can be made for each five-year projection period. The total length of a projection may refer to as many five-year periods as desired by the user. For convenience, FIVFIV makes a projection of 35 years for each set of user instructions, but will extend that projection for as many additional 35-year periods as the user gives instructions.

The computations made by SINSIN follow those made by FIVFIV. SINSIN utilizes the first 15 years of output from FIVFIV as a basis. Distribution and interpolation are used to produce annual projections for the 15-year projection period. Options are available for the construction of nonstandard age groups, subdivision of the parent population, and computation of age- and sex-specific derivatives from the 15-year projection.

FIVE-YEAR PROJECTION CYCLES BY FIVFIV

The basic element of a population projection is a group of individuals whose common identification is that they were all born during the same period of time. They form a birth cohort. A population projection is made by projecting each cohort separately over time, keeping track of decreases due to deaths, increases due to in-migrations from outside the population, and decreases due to out-migrations. A new five-year cohort is created during the projection cycle by births.

Cohorts in the FIVFIV projection are designated as follows for each five-year cycle:

Cohort index (c)	Age at beginning	Age at end	Cohort index (c)	Age at beginning	Age at end
0	Born	0–4	9	40–44	45–49
1	0–4	5–9	10	45–49	50–54
2	5–9	10–14	11	50–54	55–59
3	10–14	15–19	12	55–59	60–64
4	15–19	20–24	13	60–64	65–69
5	20–24	25–29	14	65–69	70–74
6	25–29	30–34	15	70–74	75–79
7	30–34	35–39	16	75+	80+
8	35–39	40–44			

At the end of each projection cycle, the quantity of population estimated for cohorts 15 and 16 is combined to form an age group 75+. Thus, the five-year projection cycle always ends with the same set of 16 age groups with which it began: 0–4, 5–9, . . . 75+.

The projection is carried out in two major parts, one referring to the population alive at the beginning of the period ($c=1,16$), and the other referring to population born during the period ($c=0$). The cohorts alive at the beginning are changed only by deaths and migrations, not by births. Considering the effect of death alone,

$$(1) \quad C_{s,c}^5 = C_{s,c}^0 \cdot S_{s,c} \qquad (c=1, 16; \text{ and migration}=0)$$

C stands for population quantity of the cohort, c, having sex, s, and dated at the beginning of the period, or five years later, according to the superscript. S refers to the proportion in the cohort surviving from the beginning to the end of the five-year period. The survival rates, $S_{s,c}$, come from model life tables, which are explained in a separate section below. The projection is made separately for each sex because survival rates and other determinants differ by sex.

Migration makes additions or subtractions to cohort size during the period. The quantity of migration is specified in the user's set of instructions to FIVFIV. It is transformed into quantities by sex and cohort as explained in a separate section below. The resulting quantities are net balances of in-migrants minus out-migrants denoted by $M_{s,c}$. The balance may be positive or negative.

The proportion of migrants who survive to the end of the period, counting from the time of their migration, depends upon the length of time they are exposed to the risk of death after migration. It is assumed that all members of a five-year cohort have the same risks of dying per unit of time irrespective of age differences within the five-year age range of the cohort. Concerning date of migration, it is assumed that migrations are distributed equally over the five-year period. A consequence of this assumption is that migrants are exposed to the risk of death *after migration* for an average of one-half the projection period. The following expression, therefore, can be used to make the five-year population projection, taking migration into consideration:

$$(2) \quad C_{s,c}^5 = C_{s,c}^0 \cdot S_{s,c} + M_{s,c} \left(\frac{1+S_{s,c}}{2} \right) \qquad (c=1,16)$$

The final term, in parentheses, is the survival rate for migrants. The expression is only for those cohorts alive at the beginning of the five-year projection period.

The cohort born during the five-year projection period is projected separately with several intermediate computations. The first is to estimate the number of births that occur to women at risk during the period. The mean number of women at risk of bearing children by age group of the women (15–19, 20–24, . . . 45–49) is as follows, where W_i refers to women in the ith age group:

$$(3) \quad \overline{W}_i = \sqrt{W_i^0 \cdot W_i^5} \qquad \text{(where } i = 1,7)$$

The quantities of W_i^0 and W_i^5 are from the corresponding female population quantities found by age in the preceding stage of the projection.

Births, B, for the five-year period are obtained by using an age-specific fertility schedule provided by the user of FIVFIV for each five-year projection cycle. The schedule gives yearly births per woman of the ith age group, denoted by F_i. For the five-year period births are:

$$(4) \quad B = 5 \cdot \sum_{i=1}^{7} (F_i \cdot \overline{W}_i)$$

The total births of both sexes, B, are divided between the male and female populations according to an assumption about the proportion of births that are girls, denoted by g. The user supplies an assumption about the sex ratio of births that is used for this purpose. The youngest cohort, $c = 0$, is then projected as follows by sex, when there is no migration:

$$(5a) \quad C_{f,0}^5 = gB \cdot S_{f,0} \qquad \text{(migration} = 0)$$

$$(5b) \quad C_{m,0}^5 = (1-g)B \cdot S_{m,0} \qquad \text{(migration} = 0)$$

In this instance also, the survival rates come from model life tables that are described in more detail below. The survival rate for the birth cohort is defined differently, however, from those for cohorts alive at the beginning of the projection interval, $c = 1, 16$. In terms of standard life-table notation, the survival rates are as follows:

For $c = 0 : \dfrac{1}{5} \left({}_5L_0 / l_0 \right)$

For $c = 1,15 : {}_5L_{x+5} / {}_5L_x$

For $c = 16 : T_{80} / T_{75}$

where x refers to exact ages 0, 5, . . . 80.

In order to take into consideration the effect of migration on the size of the cohort born during the projection period, assumptions about the time distribution of migrations and the age distribution of migrants below age 5 at the time of migrations are necessary in order to define the survival rate. If migrations are distributed equally over the period and the distribution of migrants below age 5 gives equal numbers in each single-year age group (0, 1, . . . 4), then it follows that the appropriate survival rate is near to, but not exactly,

$$\frac{1 + S_{s,0}}{2}$$

Such a rate would be a good approximation if probabilities of dying declined linearly from birth to exact age 5. Since the condition is not closely approximated during the first year or so of life, the approximation of the survival rate for migrants just given is biased downward.

A further consideration is that the age distribution of migrants at the time of migration typically shows smaller numbers at very young ages of a few weeks or months than at slightly higher ages. Hence, a typical group of migrants under age 5 is exposed as a group more to the risks of dying that apply at higher ages than the risks that refer to very young infants. Therefore, the assumption, provisionally proposed above, that migrants are distributed equally by age below age 5, would impart a second downward bias to the survival rate in most applications.

Since information is seldom available with which to estimate accurately the age composition of migrants below age 5, and the curvature of the probabilities of dying below age 5 varies with the life table that is selected, there appears to be no better way of correcting for both biases than to adjust the survival rate, $S_{s,0}$, arbitrarily in a direction to reduce bias. Therefore, the amount of mortality shown by $S_{s,0}$ is reduced from one-half, as provisionally shown earlier, to one-third. The revised survival rate for migrants appears in parentheses as the last term in the expression for projections of the youngest cohort by sex:

(6a) $\quad C^5_{f,0} = gB \cdot S_{f,0} + M_{f,0}(.67 + .33S_{f,0})$

(6b) $\quad C^5_{m,0} = (1\text{-}g)B \cdot S_{m,0} + M_{m,0}(.67 + .33S_{m,0})$

This completes the five-year projection cycle. Certain of the variables are transformations of assumptions given by the user of FIVFIV. These are considered next.

Transformations of the Initial Population

The user provides an initial population by sex for 16 age groups, 0–4, 5–9, . . . 75+, or he instructs FIVFIV to select an initial population from the preceding population projection. Several transformations may be performed before the five-year projection cycles begin.

1. The population may be scaled separately by sex. The user supplies a new total for each sex that is used to scale all of the initial population values before any other operations are performed. This transformation is optional.

2. If the user does not provide a population quantity for the age group 75+ and there is a quantity given for a lower age group, the program will treat the lower age group that contains population and is nearest 75+ as an open age interval. If, however, all age groups are empty, FIVFIV assumes that the user meant to start with a zero population, as might be done when the projection is for an in-migrant population alone. When the open interval given by the user is below 75+, FIVFIV redistributes the population in the open interval to that age group and higher, so that the standard 16 age groups are filled. Redistribution is based on the stationary age distribution of the life table that has been selected to represent mortality during the first five-year cycle. The life-table values customarily denoted as $_5L_r$ are written here as $L_{s,a}$, where a is an index that refers to the five-year age groups, 0–4, 5–9, . . . 75+. The uppermost age group is 75+, denoted by $a = 16$, for which $L_{s,16}$ is the life-table value, T_{75}. If h is the highest age group for which the user provides age-distribution data, redistribution of the population quantity given for that age group, $P^*_{s,h}$ is as follows:

(7a) $\quad T^* = \sum\limits_{a=h}^{16} L_{s,a}$

(7b) $\quad C_{s,c}^0 = P_{s,a}^0 = P_{s,h}^* (L_{s,a} / T^*)$ $\qquad (a=h, 16; \text{ and } c=a)$

where P refers to population subscripted by an age index, and C to population subscripted by a cohort index. Values of $C_{s,c}^0$ below age group h are the same as those given in the untransformed initial population.

(7c) $\quad C_{s,c}^0 = P_{s,a}^*$ $\qquad (a<h; \text{ and } c=a)$

This transformation is made automatically by FIVFIV when required.

3. The initial population may be shifted to a date different from that represented by the input population.

Moving the Population by Date Shifting

The transformation that changes the date of the initial population is based on three pieces of information furnished by the user:

y^* Year of the input population. Specified by DATE.SHIFT.

w^* Week of the input population. Specified by DATE.SHIFT.

y Year from which the projection is to start. Specified by YEAR.TITLE.

When the date-shifting option is exercised, FIVFIV assumes that the user wants to initiate the projection from midyear of the yth year. Thus, the starting date is exactly, in years:

(8a) $\quad t_0 = y + .5$

The date from which the population is to be shifted is:

(8b) $\quad t^* = y^* + (w^* / 52)$

Hence, the amount of the shift, a, expressed in years, is:

(8c) $\quad \alpha = t_0 - t^*$

In order to shift the population by α, FIVFIV makes a trial five-year projection, starting from the input population and using all the assumptions about fertility, mortality, and migration that have been provided for the first five-year projection period. Continuous yearly rates of change, β, are then estimated for each sex and age group of the population.

(9) $\quad \beta_{s,a} = \dfrac{1}{5} \ \log (C_{s,(a-1)}^5 \ / \ C_{s,a}^0)$ $\qquad (a=1,16)$

The cohort subscripts are written in terms of the age index as $(a-1)$ and (a), respectively, to indicate that the rates of change, β, are computed "horizontally" across cohorts, rather than "diagonally" along them. Thus, the β rates refer to rates of change in age groups across the trial five-year projection array. If the initial population before date shifting is shown by values of $P_{s,a}^*$ and the initial population after shifting is shown by cohorts $C_{s,c}^0$, then

(10) $\quad C_{s,c}^0 = P_{s,a}^0 = P_{s,a}^* \ e^{\alpha \beta_{s,a}}$ $\qquad (a=1,16; \text{ and } c=a)$

Since there is no algebraic limit on α, it is possible to shift the initial population forward or backward in time as much as desired by suitable specification of y, y^*, and w^*. Shifting differs from projection, however, because it takes components of change into account indirectly through the trial projection for only a limited forward period of five years. Shifts for periods of more than a year should be avoided.

Shifts to starting dates different from midyear can be caused by the user by giving fictitious values of y^* and w^* to obtain the desired amount of shift. FIVFIV prints a message that mentions "midyear" whenever the date-shifting option is used, whether the values given for y^* and w^* were genuine or fictitious.

The user can provide different assumptions as a basis for date shifting from those used to make the actual projection from the new date. He makes one projection using assumptions for the first period that are to control the date shifting. Then he follows with a second projection that uses the date-shifted population of the first projection as the initial population. The second projection can have different assumptions for the first five-year period.

Mortality: Model Life Tables

Life-table survival rates and certain other variables from life tables are stored by FIVFIV at the beginning of each run. Normally, the user selects one of the regional families of model life tables prepared by Coale and Demeny to store, but other models can be substituted. Tables at any level within the range of the family are selected by linear interpolation between the 24 exact levels that are stored in the computer. Mortality is computed separately by sex to correspond with separate projections by sex of the population.

Whole models may be selected, or two models may be selected and combined to form a "split-level" model with mortality from one model below age 5 and mortality from the other above age 5. When split mortality is requested, FIVFIV joins segments of the two models at age 5. In effect, a new model is formed. Expressed in terms of survivors to exact age x, and with superscripts to indicate the models selected below age 5(*) and above age 5 (**), the new model is constructed as follows:

(11a) $\quad l_x = l_x^*$ $\qquad\qquad\qquad$ $(x \leq 5)$

(11b) $\quad l_x = (l_5^* / l_5^{**}) \cdot l_x^{**}$ $\qquad$ $(x > 5)$

On the basis of these two equations, it follows that survival rates can be read directly from the original two models, except for $S_{s,1}$.

(12a) $\quad S_{s,0} = S_{s,0}^*$

(12b) $\quad S_{s,1} = (l_5^* / l_5^{**}) \cdot \dfrac{{}_5 L_5^{**}}{{}_5 L_0^*}$

(12c) $\quad S_{s,c} = S_{s,c}^{**}$ $\qquad\qquad$ $(c = 2,16)$

Life-table indices that are printed in the output of FIVFIV are also found by relatively simple combinations or by reading them directly from the original two models. For the expectation of life at birth ($\mathring{e}_0$), at age 5 ($\mathring{e}_5$), and infant mortality (${}_1q_0$):

(13a) $\quad \mathring{e}_0 = {}_5 L_0^* / l_0^* + \mathring{e}_5^{**} \cdot l_5^{**} / l_0^{**}$

(13b) $\quad \mathring{e}_5 = \mathring{e}_5^{**}$

(13c) $\quad {}_1q_0 = {}_1q_0^*$

Fertility Transformations

The way in which yearly age-specific fertility rates enter the five-year projection cycle was described above (equations 3, 4, 5). The user provides the age-specific fertility assumptions in his instructions by giving a set of age-specific rates, F_i^*. The rates can be either the actual rates or a distribution of total fertility by age of woman that sums to any nominal total. The user gives separately an assumption for total fertility, T_F, which is accepted as a final assumption. The yearly age-specific rates are then multiplied by a constant, k, chosen so that the total fertility assumption is implemented and the relative age distribution of fertility is retained.

$$(14a) \quad k = T_F \, / \, (5 \cdot \sum_{i=1}^{7} F_i^*)$$

$$(14b) \quad F_i = kF_i^* \qquad\qquad (i=1,7)$$

If the user has given the actual age-specific fertility rates for his distribution instructions, k will be found to be 1.0 during computation.

Migration Transformations

Migration assumptions are given to FIVFIV in much the same way as fertility assumptions. The user provides the number of migrants by sex and age groups, $M'_{s,a}$, for each five-year projection period. The distribution of migrants that is given by age for each sex can sum to the actual total of migration for each sex or to a nominal total. The user gives independently an assumption about the total net balance of migrants for each sex, $T_{M,s}$, for the five-year period (quinquennial, not annual, quantities). Proceeding separately by sex, the age-specific migration quantities are then multiplied by a constant, k'_s, which will bring the age-specific distribution of migrants into agreement with the assumed total without altering the relative distribution among age groups.

$$(15a) \quad k'_s = T_{M,s} \, / \, (\sum_{a=1}^{16} M'_{s,a})$$

$$(15b) \quad M_{s,a}^* = k'_s M'_{s,a} \qquad\qquad (a=1,16)$$

If the user has given the actual quantities of migrants by age, rather than a distribution expressed in nominal quantities, the value computed for k'_s will be 1.0. Net balances of migration for particular age groups and for the total can be positive or negative.

Up to this point, the migration assumptions relate to age groups, where age is measured at the time of migration. The projection is made by birth cohorts, so migrants must be assigned to cohorts. It is assumed that migration is distributed equally over the projection period, and that there are equal numbers of migrants of each age within a five-year age group. It follows from these assumptions that one-half of those assumed to migrate at ages 10–14 belong to the birth cohort that was age 5–9 at the start of the period, and half to the cohort age 10–14 at the start. Generalizing, the following assignment of migrants from age groups to cohorts can be made, where the subscripts of M refer to cohorts, and the subscripts of M^* to age groups:

$$(16a) \quad M_{s,0} = .5M_{s,1}^*$$

$$(16b) \quad M_{s,c} = .5M_{s,a}^* + .5M_{s,(a+1)}^* \qquad (a=1,15; \text{ and } c=a)$$

$$(16c) \quad M_{s,16} = .5M_{s,16}^*$$

The correspondence between the indexes c and a is as follows: ($c=1$) refers to a birth cohort aged 0–4 at the beginning of the period; ($a=1$) refers to a five-year age group, 0–4, at any time. The distribution to the first cohort (equation 16a) comes from "one side" only, since there are no persons who migrate with ages 0 to minus 4. The distribution to the oldest cohort (equation 16c) is arbitrarily restricted to one-half of the persons who migrate with ages 75+ on the assumption that their age distribution is skewed toward the lower bound of the open age interval.

Migration Rates in Place of Quantities

When migration assumptions are given in the form of rates per thousand population by age and sex groups, they are used to compute quantities of migrants as a first step. Since migration rates refer to five-year periods, the appropriate base for the computation of quantities of migrants is the mid-period population. A preliminary five-year projection cycle is executed with no migration as in equations (1) and (5a,b). The resulting values of the population by age and sex group at the end of the five-year period are $P_{s,a}^{5,p}$, where the superscript p indicates a preliminary value without the effect of migration. Rates of migration, $R_{s,a}$, per thousand population are multiplied by the preliminary midperiod population values to obtain quantities of migrants, $M_{s,a}^{*}$.

$$(17) \quad M_{s,a}^{*} = \frac{R_{s,a}}{1000} \sqrt{P_{s,a}^{0} \cdot P_{s,a}^{5,p}} \qquad (a=1,16)$$

The quantities of migrants by age and sex, $M_{s,a}^{*}$, are then allocated to projection cohorts as in equations (16a,b,c). Thereafter, migration enters the projection as in equations (2) and (6a,b,c).

Finding Instead of Assuming Total Migration

When the FINDMIGRATION option is used, the total population to be reached at the end of each five-year projection cycle is assumed, rather than found as a result of the population projection. Any terminal population can be produced by varying the migration assumptions, holding all other assumptions unchanged. The FINDMIGRATION option causes this to be done.

In order to obtain unique migration quantities by age and sex, the user furnishes an age distribution of migrants for each sex the same as before. The total of each distribution is considered to be nominal. The sex ratio of migrants is also fixed by an assumption, provided by the user, concerning the ratio of males to females among migrants of all ages. The ratio for totals by sex, when given with the age distributions by sex, fixes the sex ratio in every age group. Only the total migration of both sexes combined for the five-year projection cycle is unknown.

When FINDMIGRATION is requested, an iterative convergence routine is used to find the unique quantity of migration that will produce the population "target" at the end of the five-year projection cycle. After finding the migration, FIVFIV assumes migration in the regular way and executes the projection once more. The final pass through the projection cycle confirms the population projection that was already known as a result of the convergence routine. If there is any failure in the convergence process, which is conceivable when assumptions with unacceptable consequences are given, FIVFIV prints a message.

When date shifting is requested along with FINDMIGRATION, the trial projection cycle for date shifting includes the finding of migration. The reason is that the user has specified, in effect, certain rates of population change during the first five-year period when he gives an assumption about the size that the total population will reach at the end of the cycle. Since the user has specified a shifted date for the start of the projection, the "target" population for the first cycle refers to a date exactly five years from the shifted date. The trial projection, however, is made from the date of the input population, not the shifted date. Therefore, a trial population target is computed for use in the trial projection when FINDMIGRATION has been requested. The total population "target" for the trial, T_P^{5*}, is computed from the total population given as input, T_P^{0*}, and the total population assumed as a "target" for five years from the shifted date, T_P^5.

$$(18a) \quad z = \frac{1}{5+\alpha} \log (T_P^5 / T_P^{0*})$$

$$(18b) \quad T_P^{5*} = T_P^5 \, e^{(-az)}$$

where α is from equation (8c) above. The results of FINDMIGRATION within the trial projection are not used for the final projection. They were computed only as an intermediate step to learn at what rates (β values in equation 9) the population was changing, in order to shift the initial population to a new date.

DISTRIBUTION AND INTERPOLATION BY SINSIN

The projections produced by FIVFIV are transformed into annual population estimates by SINSIN. The user can also request that SINSIN produce, in addition to estimates by standard five-year age groups, estimates by special age groups that he defines. An intermediate step in the production of annual estimates is to distribute the five-year age aggregates of FIVFIV among single-year age groups, and then to interpolate between the years 0, 5, 10, and 15, to produce annual estimates for the intervening years. In effect, it is necessary to produce a "single-single" projection of the population from age 0 to 75+ annually for the 15-year SINSIN projection. In order to retain consistency between FIVFIV and SINSIN projections, the aggregates for five-year age ranges must be distributed among single years of age without changing the totals for each five years of age.

The distribution and interpolation methods used by SINSIN are shown schematically in Figure 1.1 according to the following symbols:

A. Distributions at years 0, 5, 10, and 15

-    Accepted as computed by FIVFIV

| Vertical distribution using Sprague multipliers[18]

◯   Vertical distribution using stable model

---

[18] Thomas Bond Sprague, "Explanation of a New Formula for Interpolation," *Journal of the Institute of Actuaries* 22, no. 270, pp. 1880–1881. See also Shryock and Siegel, *The Methods and Materials of Demography*, pp. 688, 876.

B. Interpolation at lowest and highest ages

—— Horizontal interpolation in logarithms using La Grange coefficients[19]

C. Interpolation of single-year cohorts as they age

╲ Diagonal diminishment in logarithms using LaGrange coefficients

▨ Shaded areas show linear interpolation in logarithms

⊘ Diagonal diminishment with decrements from a stable model

⟩ The first set of distributions (A) splits the five-year age groups from FIVFIV into single-year age groups. Sprague multipliers perform this task well in the middle range of ages, creating a sequence of single-year age groups that reflects the changing size of the population above and below. At the lowest ages, however, the multipliers can only use information from the age distributions at higher ages to determine curvature, which is misleading for ages 0, 1, . . . 4, where early childhood mortality creates a special shape.

An alternative solution is to use stable population models, because they represent the curvature at early ages more satisfactorily. Therefore, SINSIN calculates stable models from the mortality and fertility assumptions of the projection and uses them to distribute population among age groups 0 to 5. For years 5, 10, and 15, the assumptions of the projection about mortality and fertility during the preceding five years are used to calculate the stable. For year 0, it is necessary to estimate the stable from mortality and fertility immediately following that date, because information about years preceding the projection is not available.

Person-years lived in the selected life table are calculated from the proportions surviving to age x by single years from age 0 to 5. The resulting stationary distribution is then transformed into a stable distribution with the rate of increase in the birth sequence during the five-year period. The rate of increase of births is given by the rate of increase in female population of childbearing age during the five-year period, when each age group is weighted by its corresponding age-specific fertility. The stable age distribution, L_j, for single-year age groups from 0 to 5, indexed by j, is given by

$$(19) \quad L_j = L_j^* \cdot e^{-jb} \qquad (j=0,5)$$

where L_j^* is person-years lived in the stationary life-table population, and b is the rate of increase in the birth sequence.

The stable models below age 5 and Sprague multipliers above age 5 are used to distribute the five-year age estimates to single-year age groups at years 0, 5, 10, and 15. The two systems are allowed to overlap and give different estimates for the population of age 5. The difference is distributed above and below age 5 so as to form a relatively smooth connection between the two segments while still retaining the original size of the estimates by five-year age groups.

---

[19] Milton Abramowitz and Irene Stegun, eds., *Handbook of Mathematical Functions*, Applied Mathematics Series 55 (Washington, D.C.: US National Bureau of Standards), p. 879.

FIGURE 1.1   Distribution and Interpolation Procedures for SINSIN

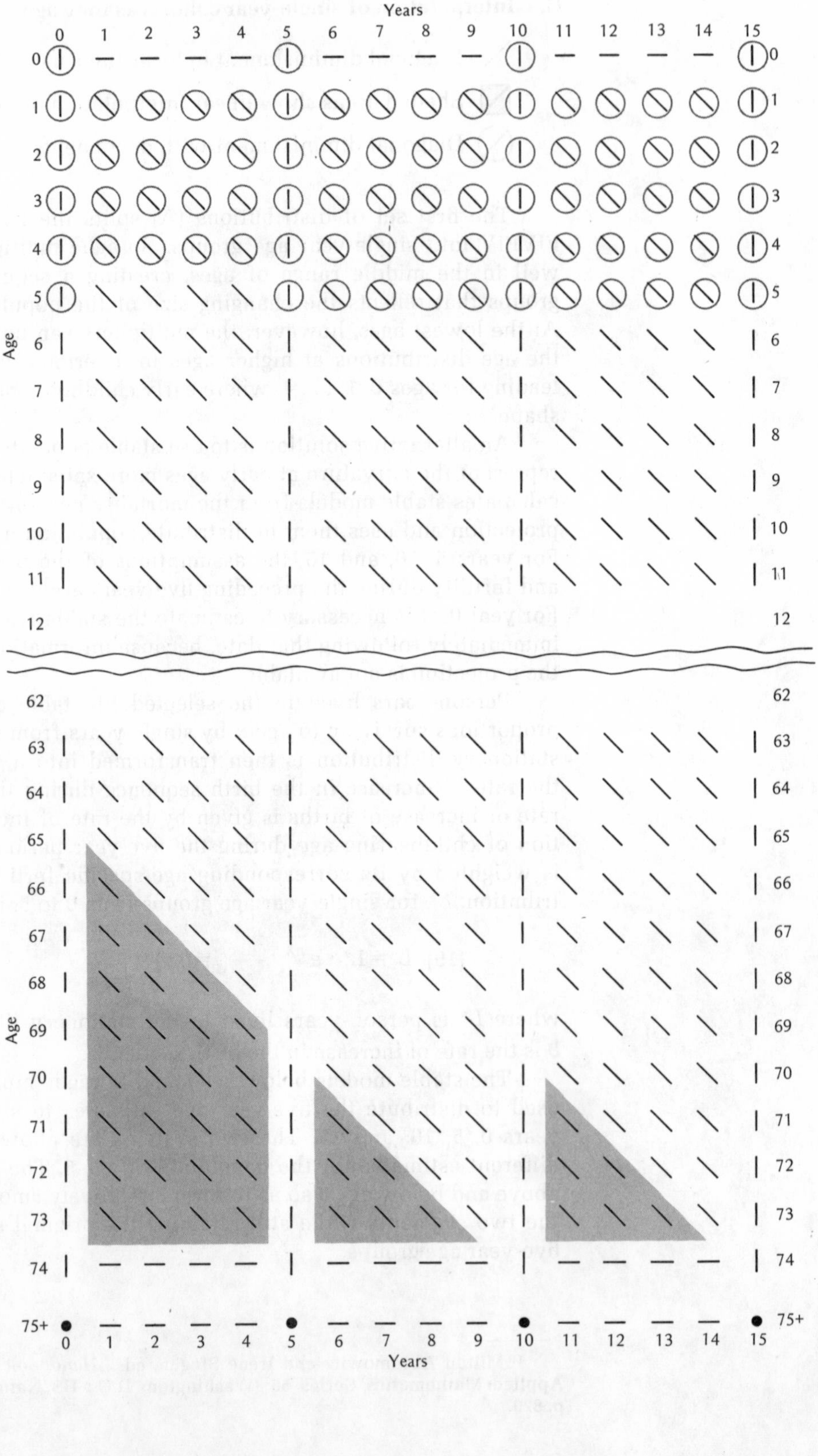

The upper and lower boundaries of the projection array (Figure 1.1) are fixed by horizontal interpolation as indicated above under (B). Four-point LaGrange interpolation coefficients are applied to logarithms calculated from the estimating values given by preceding steps for years 0, 5, 10, and 15. The logarithm transformation reflects the assumption that population change is continuous.

The rest of the interpolations are performed diagonally by single-year cohorts. The single-year age quantities on the boundaries of the array and at the intermediate year dates of 5 and 10 are accepted as fixed. Consequently, re-aggregation of the single-year age groups by five-year age groups will be the same in SINSIN tables and FIVFIV tables. Minor discrepancies that arise between the two are due to loss of precision during computation.

Interpolation is done along the diagonals by application of LaGrange interpolation coefficients to logarithms of the estimating values. Throughout most of the array, four estimating values are available. Wherever the diagonal traverses less than 10 years, linear interpolation is substituted for the LaGrange coefficients. The shaded areas at the highest ages of the distribution in Figure 1.1 show where this happens.

Below age 5, the stable model that was calculated for the immediately preceding vertical distribution is considered a better guide for interpolation than the LaGrange curve of values. Consequently, the stable distribution is imposed on the LaGrange curve by a system of weighted averages that increases the importance of the stable as one moves from higher to lower ages. This procedure is not as effective for diagonals that have fewer than five values below age 5. In particular, no attempt to smooth the resulting curve across the overlap of the stable and the LaGrange curve at age 5 is made. A shaded triangle is shown in Figure 1.1 covering certain values in the lower ages that are affected by this limitation.

Although the entire array of single-single values is acceptable for most purposes, results for the second and third five-year panels (dates 5 to 15) are strongest. Therefore, when 15-year annual projections are overlapped to obtain a 35-year annual projection, as explained in Chapter Four, the user is advised to discard estimates for dates 0–5 in panels (B) and (C) of the 35-year projection.

Occasionally, SINSIN will fail to produce distributions that are fully representative of actual processes of population change. Losses of precision in computation and the arbitrary nature of mathematical distribution and interpolation may cause single-year cohorts to appear to increase with age, rather than decline, in the absence of migration. Within the precision of the basic data available for projections, such anomalies may be accepted as reminders of the approximate nature of such population projections.

SUBDIVIDING BY THE RATIO METHOD

The classical ratio method of making projections for local populations is available as an option with SINSIN. The projection for a subdivision of a "parent" population is made by ratioing the five-year age and sex groups of the parent population. Ratios of the subdivisional to the parent population are specified by the user. Up to four parameters for each age group, and for the total population, separately by sex, are given by the user. SINSIN computes ratios, denoted as $\gamma_{s,a}^{t}$, from these assumptions. The subscript a

is an index for the conventional 16 age groups defined earlier, plus one more, denoted by $a = \pi$, which stands for the total population of one sex. Assumptions are given by sex for each age group and for the total population. Four acceptable combinations of assumptions that may be given by the user are indicated as alternatives (a) through (d) below.

Assumptions Given by User		Acceptable Combinations			
		a	b	c	d
1. Ratio and first date	$\gamma^{t'}_{s,a}, t'_{s,a}$	x	x	x	x
2. First slope	$d'_{s,a}$		x	x	x
3. Second date	$t''_{s,a}$			x	x
4. Second slope	$d''_{s,a}$				x

Corresponding with the four combinations of assumptions recognized by SINSIN are the following equations with which to find values at the projection dates:

(20a) $\quad \gamma^t_{s,a} = \gamma^{t'}_{s,a}$

(20b) $\quad \gamma^t_{s,a} = \gamma^{t'}_{s,a} + d'_{s,a}(t - t'_{s,a})$

(20c) $\quad$ same as (20b), where $t < t''_{s,a}$; and

$\qquad \gamma^t_{s,a} = \gamma^{t'}_{s,a} + d'_{s,a}(t''_{s,a} - t'_{s,a})$, where $t \geq t''_{s,a}$

(20d) $\quad$ same as (20b), where $t < t''_{s,a}$; and

$\qquad \gamma^t_{s,a} = \gamma^{t'}_{s,a} + d'_{s,a}(t''_{s,a} - t'_{s,a}) + d''_{s,a}(t - t''_{s,a})$, where $t \geq t''_{s,a}$

Sets of ratios are calculated from the above for each of the four dates defined by the FIVFIV projection that is used by SINSIN. The four dates, t, in exact years are: $(y + .5)$, $(y + 5.5)$, $(y + 10.5)$, and $(y + 15.5)$, where y is the year (integer) from which the projection starts. The values of $\gamma^t_{s,a}$ calculated in this manner are assumptions about the ratios for each projection date.

At each of the four projection dates, t, the subdivisional population, denoted by $X^t_{s,a}$, is found from the parent population, $P^t_{s,a}$, as follows:

(21a) $\quad k^t_s = \dfrac{\gamma^t_{s,\pi} \cdot P^t_{s,\pi}}{\sum\limits_{a=1}^{16} (\gamma^t_{s,a} \cdot P^t_{s,a})}$

(21b) $\quad X^t_{s,a} = k^t_s (\gamma^t_{s,a} \cdot P^t_{s,a}) \qquad (a = 1,16)$

The purpose of equation (21a) is to find a constant, k^t_s, which can be used in (21b) to force the sum of the subdivisional age groups to equal a total population for the subdivision that is found by ratioing the parent population's total. Thus, the following condition is fulfilled:

(21c) $\quad X^t_{s,\pi} = \gamma^t_{s,\pi} \cdot P^t_{s,\pi} = \sum\limits_{a=1}^{16} X^t_{s,a}$

The computing strategy is to split the original population projection passed by FIVFIV to SINSIN by equations (21a) and (21b). The $X^t_{s,a}$ values are substituted for the original $P^t_{s,a}$ values, and SINSIN processes the substitute FIVFIV projection as if it were the original FIVFIV projection. Stable models that are used for the distribution of population below age 5 are based on the fertility and mortality of the parent projection.

When the user requests that the residual population be printed as well as the subdivisional one, it is computed by subtracting the single-year subdivisional projection from the original single-year projection that was made for the parent population. Fresh interpolation and distribution are not done by SINSIN for the residual population.

AGE- AND SEX-SPECIFIC DERIVATIVES

SINSIN computes quantities of any description that can be derived by applying age- and sex-specific rates to the population estimates. Examples are quantities of married persons, school attendance, labor force, numbers of households, and numbers of clients for a benefit such as old-age insurance. Only the population parameter enters such calculations. Other determinants must be reflected in the selection of the age- and sex-specific rates. The user names what he is estimating, specifies a set of age groups to which rates will apply, and provides assumptions about the rates. Each sex is handled separately.

The age- and sex-specific rates are denoted as $\theta^t_{s,u}$, where t refers to the date of applicability, s to sex, and u to an index for up to 12 age groups whose ranges are defined by the user. The user furnishes rates for one, two, or three dates. Ratios are assumed to be constant prior to the first rates and after the last rates given. Between the first and second rates a linear function is assumed, and between the second and third a linear function is assumed. If only one set of rates were given, they would be held constant over time. Specifically, if a second set of θ values is not given, then,

$$(22a) \quad \theta^{t'''}_{s,u} = \theta^{t''}_{s,u} = \theta^{t'}_{s,u} \qquad \text{(where } t''' = t'' + j; t'' = t + j)$$

The symbol, j, is any positive constant selected arbitrarily. If only the third set of rates is omitted,

$$(22b) \quad \theta^{t'''}_{s,u} = \theta^{t''}_{s,u} \qquad \text{(where } t''' = t'' + j)$$

For any date, t, ratios are then computed according to the following expressions:

$$(23a) \quad \text{where } t < t', \qquad \theta^t_{s,u} = \theta^{t'}_{s,u}$$

$$(23b) \quad \text{where } t' \leq t < t'', \qquad \theta^t_{s,u} = \theta^{t'}_{s,u} + (t - t') \left(\frac{\theta^{t''}_{s,u} - \theta^{t'}_{s,u}}{t'' - t'} \right)$$

$$(23c) \quad \text{where } t'' \leq t < t''', \qquad \theta^t_{s,u} = \theta^{t''}_{s,u} + (t - t'') \left(\frac{\theta^{t'''}_{s,u} - \theta^{t''}_{s,u}}{t''' - t''} \right)$$

$$(23d) \quad \text{where } t > t''', \qquad \theta^t_{s,u} = \theta^{t'''}_{s,u}$$

Once rates have been computed for all 16 dates from year 0 to 15 in the SINSIN projection, they are applied to the annual population projection, and regrouped according to the age groups, u, specified by user. The age- and sex-specific quantities that are derived are denoted as $D^t_{s,u}$.

$$(24) \quad D^t_{s,u} = \theta^t_{s,u} \cdot P^t_{s,u}$$

Each sex is handled separately, so the definition and indexing of u may vary by sex if the user specifies.

APPENDIX TWO: INSTALLATION OF FIVFIV AND SINSIN

The first runs on a computer with FIVFIV and SINSIN should be made under the supervision of a programmer. Each system has unique features that need to be taken into consideration when the programs are first prepared for use. A programmer familiar with the local system can make the programs ready and supply the user with system control cards to run his jobs. Thereafter, users with no prior knowledge of programming or the local system should be able to prepare job decks and submit them without assistance. This appendix is written for a programmer who will supervise preparation and initial use of the programs.

FIVFIV-SINSIN PACKAGE

The FIVFIV-SINSIN package is supplied either as a magnetic tape of card images or as a box of physical cards. The tape is easier to mail and cards can be punched from the tape at the destination. The package can be requested in either form (see back of book for ordering instructions). The following description refers to tape. Normally, the package is written on a 300-foot, 9-track tape at a density of 800 bpi. The tape contains two successive unlabeled files of card images. The cards are represented by logical records of 80 bytes in EBCDIC coding written 50 cards per block of 4,000 bytes. Tapes can be supplied with different specifications, coding, and blocking to meet the requirements of all systems.

There are two source programs, FIVFIV and SINSIN, written in standard (ANS) FORTRAN IV. In addition, the package contains test data and model life tables. The arrangement of the files on tape (or the box of cards) is as follows:

File 1:   FIVFIV source deck

Test data for FIVFIV consisting of 'East' model life tables and instructions for one projection

SINSIN source deck

Test data for SINSIN consisting of sample card output from FIVFIV to be used as input for SINSIN

'South' model life tables

'West' model life tables

'North' model life tables

Cards for user's own life tables MY LT

File 2:   Programmer's documentation. If this file of card images is dumped on the printer, 80 characters per line, it will provide programmer's documentation for FIVFIV and SINSIN. (Supplied as a listing if cards are ordered.)

The first file should be dumped on cards and the cards used to install and test the two programs. The length of the file is approximately 2,500 cards. The second file will produce approximately 3,000 lines when dumped on the printer.

The package requires a computer with an in-core memory of 64K bytes for installation without modification. FIVFIV may be used alone on some machines with only 32K bytes of in-core storage by using overlay. The minimum necessary computer configuration to use both programs is a card reader, a printer with a print line of 120 characters or more, and a means for passing data from FIVFIV to SINSIN. An on-line card punch, disk, or tape unit will suffice.

TESTING THE PACKAGE

When the package is received, it should be tested to verify that it is in good order. Make no changes in the programs or test data. FIVFIV and SINSIN are each tested separately. The following streams of system control cards, programs, and test data show the job set-up for an IBM 360/40 Disk Operating System. Programmers at different kinds of installations will recognize the changes necessary to adapt the job stream to their system. Note that the FORTRAN unit numbers for the card reader and printer are 5 and 6, respectively.

```
0         1         2         3         4         5         6         7
1234567890123456789012345678901234567890123456789012345678901234567890123

        JOB STREAMS FOR IBM 360/40 DISK OPERATING SYSTEM
                  TO TEST FIVFIV AND SINSIN

// JOB TESTFIV
// OPTION LINK,NODECK
// EXEC FFORTRAN
   < SOURCE PROGRAM FIVFIV >
```

(continued)

```
/*
// EXEC LNKEDT
// ASSGN SYS002,X'00C'
// ASSGN SYS003,X'00F'
// EXEC
      < TEST DATA CONSISTING OF 'EAST' MODEL LIFE-TABLES
        AND INSTRUCTIONS FOR ONE PROJECTION.  CONCLUDES
        WITH A CARD LABELED HALT >
/*
/&
// JOB TESTSIN
// OPTION LINK,NODECK
// EXEC FFORTRAN
      < SOURCE PROGRAM SINSIN >
/*
// EXEC LNKEDT
// ASSGN SYS002,X'00C'
// ASSGN SYS003,X'00E'
// EXEC
      < TEST DATA FOR SINSIN >
/*
/&

123456789012345678901234567890123456789012345678901234567890123456789012345678901234567890123
```

Printed output from the test runs of FIVFIV and SINSIN should be identical with Examples 2.9 (pages 42–45) and 4.1 (page 64), respectively. During these two tests the programmer will see the results of compilation at his particular computer. On one computer it was discovered that a DATA statement had more continuation cards than could be accepted, so the statement was divided into two. On another, the compiler failed to accept one particular double-precision Hollerith string of eight characters, so that card was retyped with a literal string in quotes. The FORTRAN of FIVFIV and SINSIN has been successful enough times to predict success in the future, but the programmer must try for himself.

ALTERNATIVE JOB STREAMS

One of the programmer's tasks is to select among several alternatives the most satisfactory way of using FIVFIV and SINSIN under local conditions. He will prescribe control cards for the particular computer system that is used. He will also point the user to the particular job stream that should be used. A job stream is a sequence of cards that the user must follow in order to submit his job to the computer. Once the user knows the job stream, he is on his own and will require no further assistance from the programmer.

In addition to control cards, the user needs a life-table deck. Four decks corresponding with 'West,' 'South,' 'North,' and 'East' model life tables are furnished with the programs. In addition, there is a deck labeled MY LT that a user can make into a set of life tables of his own. Each deck consists of 144 cards. The programmer can duplicate the life-table decks and users may select from among them. Only one family of life tables is submitted during a single run on the computer.

Job Stream 1: FIVFIV at a "Small" Computer Installation

The job stream for FIVFIV described below is appropriate when the analyst wants to use only FIVFIV, or when the computer system is not large enough to execute both FIVFIV and SINSIN as a single job. This is the simplest installation.

JOB STREAM 1

** System control cards
FIVFIV object deck
** System control cards
Life-table data   (One family; either sex first)
Instructions for one projection
Instructions for additional projection(s)
HALT card   (Punch HALT in columns 1–4)
** System control cards

Note that the user should have an object deck, rather than a FORTRAN source program. The programmer should provide the user with such an object deck, because it will enable runs to be made quickly at minimal cost in computer time. Of course, a FORTRAN source program can be used with appropriate control cards instead of the object deck, but computer time will increase greatly.

An improvement of Job Stream 1 becomes possible if the programmer can place the object deck in the computer's direct-access library. In that event, the user submits control cards instead of the object deck itself. Considering that the object deck is nearly a thousand cards, a few control cards in its place is a great convenience.

Job Stream 2: SINSIN at a "Small" Computer Installation

When SINSIN is run separately from FIVFIV, it uses input that is prepared by FIVFIV. Assuming a successful run has been made with FIVFIV and that FIVFIV provided card output for use by SINSIN, the job stream is as follows:

JOB STREAM 2

** System control cards
SINSIN object deck
** System control cards
Punched output cards from FIVFIV
** System control cards

The punched output cards that come from FIVFIV provide the link that is needed between FIVFIV and SINSIN. The card output of FIVFIV should be given to SINSIN exactly as it is and in the order that it was punched by the computer. Blank cards or system identification cards at the beginning or end should be discarded. In order to be certain that the card deck is in order, inspect the first card. It should have a sequence number 1 punched in column 80. The last card should have HALT punched by FIVFIV in the middle of the card. No completely blank cards should remain at the beginning or end. The number of cards that are passed by FIVFIV to SINSIN depends upon the SINSIN options that are used.

This job stream, like the preceding one, can be simplified if the programmer can place the object deck in the system library. In that event, the object deck is not given by cards but is called into the system by a few system control cards.

Job Stream 3: Minimum Effort at a "Small" Computer Installation

The programmer may be able to provide for communication between FIVFIV and SINSIN without punched cards. This is done by using a temporary sequential file on disk or tape as a regular part of the routine. The job stream is divided into two logically separate jobs, but they are run by the operator one immediately after the other. The operator must be told effectively not to separate the two jobs.

In the job stream that follows, it is assumed that the programmer has placed the FIVFIV and SINSIN object decks in the system as part of its library. The control cards include calls to the library.

JOB STREAM 3

Job A (FIVFIV)
** System control cards
Life-table data   (One family; either sex first)
Instructions for one projection
Instructions for additional projection(s)
HALT card   (Punch HALT in columns 1–4)
** System control cards
Job B (SINSIN)
** System control cards

Although shown as two jobs to be executed sequentially, some operating systems would allow them to be combined as two steps within a single job. This would be preferable if acceptable as a routine job stream.

Job Stream 4: Minimum Effort at a "Moderate-Sized" Computer Installation

At a moderate-sized computer center, where the in-core memory or partition is on the order of 110K bytes or more, FIVFIV and SINSIN can be joined in a single program called FIVSIN. The programmer provides either an object deck or load module in the system library, which is brought into action by control cards alone. As usual, a programmer must prescribe the control cards, and after that the user is on his own.

JOB STREAM 4

** System control cards
Life-table data   (One family; either sex first)
Instructions for one projection
Instructions for additional projections(s)
HALT card   (Punch HALT in columns 1–4)
** System control cards

This completes the illustration of alternative job streams. In order to make any one of them operational, the programmer will need to change certain cards in the FORTRAN programs to fit the selection of job stream. This is explained below.

LOGICAL UNIT NUMBERS

The READ and WRITE statements in the FORTRAN programs refer to logical units (e.g., card reader or printer units) by variable names rather than by number. These variables are initialized with reference numbers at the beginning of each program by a DATA statement. As supplied, FIVFIV and SIN-SIN have reference numbers that may be used (see Table 2.1), or the programmer may change them by repunching the relevant DATA statements. There is one DATA statement near the beginning of FIVFIV and another near the beginning of SINSIN.

```
0          1          2          3          4          5          6          7          8
123456789012345678901234567890123456789012345678901234567890123456789012345678901234567890

            DATA STATEMENTS FOR FIVFIV AND SINSIN

    DATA KIN,KOUT,KSPOOL,KPFIV,KPSIN /5,6,0,0,0/                          FIV4  11
    DATA KSPIN,KOUT/5,6/                                                  SIN4  20

123456789012345678901234567890123456789012345678901234567890123456789012345678901234567890
```

The choice of unit numbers is determined by the job stream that is selected, the means for communication that will be used between FIVFIV and SINSIN, and the local default values for card reader, printer, and punch (if any). In order to minimize the use of assignment cards, initialize KIN and KOUT with the system default numbers for the card reader and printer, respectively. Next, choose a means of communication between FIVFIV and SINSIN.

TABLE 2.1   Logical Unit Numbers

Logical unit	Variable name	Reference number as supplied
UNITS FOR FIVFIV		
Card reader	KIN	5
Printer	KOUT	6
Output for SINSIN (card punch, disk, or tape unit)	KSPOOL	0
Output from PUNCH.FIVE	KPFIV	0
Output from PUNCH.SINGLE	KPSIN	0
UNITS FOR SINSIN		
Input from FIVFIV (card reader, disk, or tape unit)	KSPIN	5
Printer	KOUT	6

1. **FIVFIV alone:** For many purposes, and particularly for teaching and student exercises, FIVFIV is sufficient alone. Select Job Stream 1 and do not change the DATA statement in FIVFIV. If subjects that require output on devices other than the printer are accidentally given to FIVFIV, the reference numbers as supplied (zeros) will cause the computer to skip them automatically. If a wide variety of uses is planned, it may be convenient to install Job Stream 1 for FIVFIV tasks and provide a second job set-up for applications that require the capabilities of both FIVFIV and SINSIN.

2. **Communication by cards:** Although card communication is most easily understood by newcomers to computing (one can see the cards), it does require that two completely separate jobs be executed, one to obtain card output from FIVFIV and the other to submit the cards to SINSIN. If card communication is used, select Job Streams 1 and 2 for FIVFIV and SINSIN, respectively. Initialize KSPOOL with the unit number for the card punch and KSPIN for the card reader.

3. **Communication by magnetic disk file:** The most efficient means of communication is disk. It should be used if the system permits direct access to a working area on disk. Allocate file space for 2,000 80-byte logical records. This is enough to communicate as many as 20 to 80 separate projections all in one run. If Job Stream 3 is used, the file must be passed automatically from the FIVFIV job or job step to the SINSIN job or job step. If Job Stream 4 is selected, the working area is used within a single job and no passing of the file is necessary. Reference to the disk file is accomplished by initializing KSPOOL and KSPIN with the same disk file unit number.

4. **Communication by magnetic tape file:** The procedure for using tape is similar to that for disk. The differences are that no space allocation is necessary on the assignment control card, but provision must be made to have a scratch tape mounted and on-line whenever a FIVFIV-SINSIN job is run. Since few systems are operated with a scratch tape always accessible, the use of tape for communication places the burden on the user of including special instructions with his job to mount a tape. As with disk communication, it is necessary to provide for passing the tape between job steps or jobs. Initialize KSPOOL and KSPIN with the same tape unit number.

When communication between FIVFIV and SINSIN is by disk or tape file (alternative 3 or 4 above), provision must be made for correct positioning of the read and write operations, irrespective of which job stream is selected. The files are sequential. To meet this requirement, the programmer should delete the comment symbol C from the ENDFILE and REWIND statements that appear near the end of SUBROUTINE READIN. Deletion of the C will activate both statements. (Do not alter the statement CALL SINSIN at this stage. It will be discussed below.)

```
0         1         2         3         4         5         6         7         8
1234567890123456789012345678901234567890123456789012345678901234567890123456789012345678901234567890

              DELETE 'C' IF COMMUNICATING BY DISK OR TAPE

C     ENDFILE KSPOOL                                              PIV4 518
C     REWIND KSPOOL                                               PIV4 519

1234567890123456789012345678901234567890123456789012345678901234567890123456789012345678901234567890
```

It is not usually necessary to keep data passed from FIVFIV to SINSIN. Hence, if a disk file is used, delete the file following execution of SINSIN. Provision in the preestablished job stream to delete the file *before* each FIV-FIV job is a safe way to make sure that the file can be opened for write operations. The programmer should try in this and other respects to equip the user with a set of system control cards that will function properly whether or not the user decides to utilize the full program capabilities.

The commands PUNCH.FIVE and PUNCH.SINGLE cause output to be produced by FIVFIV and SINSIN, respectively, in a machine-readable form. These outputs are for use with special computer programs written by or for the analyst. The future use of the output determines how the form of output should be planned. If PUNCH.FIVE and PUNCH.SINGLE will never be used in the future, do not change the initialization of KPFIV and KPSIN. References to zero unit numbers will cause the computer to ignore any commands to produce special output.

The most flexible form for machine-readable output is punched cards. If the system has a card punch, initialize KPFIV and KPSIN with the unit number for the card punch. If it is necessary or preferable to save special FIVFIV and SINSIN output on disk or tape, initialize KPFIV and KPSIN with the corresponding tape or disk unit number.

For routine processing of jobs that do not include the commands PUNCH.FIVE or PUNCH.SINGLE, it does not matter what unit numbers have been specified on KPFIV and KPSIN. It is not necessary to include corresponding assignment control cards in the job stream until PUNCH.FIVE or PUNCH.SINGLE are used. Thinking ahead to the time when users may wish to have special output, the following initialization plan is suggested:

1. If the system has a card punch, initialize KPFIV and KPSIN with the card punch unit number.

2. If the system does not have a card punch, initialize KPFIV and KPSIN with an unassigned unit number such as 9. Inform users that they must add an assignment control card for number 9 to the job stream whenever they want to use PUNCH.FIVE or PUNCH.SINGLE. The assignment control card should point to the tape or disk unit where the user's personal tape or disk file will be located and on which he will save the special output. The logical unit should be different from the one used for KSPOOL and KSPIN. Also, different devices (tape or disk drives) should be used since there is no way to provide a general plan in advance for communicating between FIVFIV and SINSIN, and saving special output, on the same device.

If the local FORTRAN compiler allows an option of END= in READ statements, punch the parameter END=995 on the READ statement in SUB-ROUTINE READIN. This may be done at the same time as the unit numbers are being fixed.

```
0          1          2          3          4          5          6          7          8
1234567890123456789012345678901234567890123456789012345678901234567890123456789012345678901234567890

          SPACE FOR OPTIONAL PARAMETER 'END=995'

    10 READ (KIN,5020       ) SECT,REST,REST2                              FIV4 122

1234567890123456789012345678901234567890123456789012345678901234567890123456789012345678901234567890
```

After punching the END= option, the HALT card may be eliminated from Job Streams 1, 3, and 4. Or, if retained, execution of FIVFIV will not be affected. If the means of communication between FIVFIV and SINSIN is cards, the user may notice that a special form of HALT card is generated by FIVFIV. It should continue to be passed.

SINSIN AS A SUBROUTINE

On systems large enough to place FIVFIV and SINSIN in core at the same time (about 110K), SINSIN may be converted to a subroutine and executed within the same job. Job Stream 4 is the relevant one, and communication between FIVFIV and SINSIN is by disk or tape file. The following changes are made in the FORTRAN source programs:

1. Delete the comment symbol C on the CALL statement in FIVFIV. This card appears near the end of SUBROUTINE READIN and immediately before SUBROUTINE OUTPUT.
2. Delete the comment symbol C on the SUBROUTINE declaration at the beginning of program SINSIN.
3. Place the FIVFIV and SINSIN decks together in one source deck.

```
0         1         2         3         4         5         6         7         8
12345678901234567890C123456789012345678901234567890123456789012345678901234567890

        DELETE 'C' TO CONVERT SINSIN TO SUBROUTINE

C     CALL SINSIN                                                       FIV4 520
C     SUBROUTINE SINSIN                                                 SIN4   4

12345678901234567890C123456789012345678901234567890123456789012345678901234567890
```

TESTING THE JOB STREAM

After all the changes in FORTRAN statements have been made, it is time to produce object decks or to load the object code directly into the system library. FIVFIV and SINSIN take substantial computer time to compile, but they execute rapidly. It is a serious waste of computer time to give source decks to users. Every effort to provide users with access to object code should be made. At some installations it will be possible to create load modules and keep them in on-line libraries.

Once the job stream is completely established, a sample job deck of control cards, programs (if not in system library), and FIVFIV test data should be prepared for the user. Only the FIVFIV test data are needed. The SINSIN test data on cards may be abandoned at this stage. From now on, input given to FIVFIV will generate output that serves as input for SINSIN. The test deck for FIVFIV in the package contains commands that will cause communication between FIVFIV and SINSIN to occur, unless the test refers to FIVFIV alone with KSPOOL initialized by zero.

The job deck that is given to users must be tested by a final test run. If communication between FIVFIV and SINSIN is by disk file, run the complete sequence twice in order to be certain that the disk file is deleted routinely between successive executions of FIVFIV. In order to be certain that SINSIN is reading a newly created file the second time, alter one of the test data cards on the second run. Near the end of the FIVFIV test data, there is a card labeled GROUPS on which a decimal point may be added immediately after the label in column 7. As a consequence, the SINSIN output will no longer include as many special age groups. The printed pages numbered page 5 and above will have noticeably less output on the second of the two final test runs.

```
0         1         2         3         4         5         6         7         8
1234567890123456789012345678901234567890123456789012345678901234567890123456789 0

          FOR SECOND OF TWO FINAL TEST RUNS ADD DECIMAL
               ON THE TEST DATA CARD 'GROUPS'

     *** LAST FIVE CARDS OF TEST DATA ARE SHOWN HERE ***
MEND
REGROUP
GROUPS        <ADD A DECIMAL IN COLUMN 7>
END PROJECTION
HALT

1234567890123456789012345678901234567890123456789012345678901234567890123456789 0
```

Users will need to have copies of the life-table data. In most countries one family, usually 'West,' will be the principal one used. However, all four regional families and the special MY LT should be made available and duplicated as needed.

APPENDIX THREE: ERROR DIAGNOSIS: MESSAGES AND CODES _____

Errors must be taken seriously, but not all errors are true ones. The first error that occurs in a run is always a true error, and the reason for it must be found. Sometimes additional error messages are given that have logical reasons, but which will disappear if the first error is corrected and the job is rerun.

The error message, *****INVALID SUBJECT HEADER: is often repeated several times. This occurs when FIVFIV wants a valid subject header, does not find one, and has to pass through a series of cards looking for one. The first card it tried might have been a mispunched header. The next cards could be valid information cards, but the computer will continue to report failure card by card until it finds a good subject header. Then it will stop giving error messages and continue processing in the normal way. Therefore, treat the first message as serious and those immediately following as possibly not serious. However, search thoroughly for additional errors if there is any break or change in the sequence of messages given. Then try again, and find out whether the corrections that have been made eliminate the error messages.

The computer sometimes cannot detect all errors in a single run. One error may cause subsequent cards to be processed incompletely, thus hiding errors. Therefore, additional errors may be revealed after the first errors are corrected and the job is rerun.

FIVFIV detects and diagnoses many of the errors that users make. There are some types of errors, however, that FIVFIV cannot detect itself. They may cause the computer system to print its own message and to terminate the job at that point. Some computer systems will print an image of the offending card for you. If so, study the card image carefully. The most likely reason for failure is a non-numeric character in a numeric data field. Or there might be an extra decimal point. Cards given in wrong order also could be a reason. If no card image is printed, the user can still determine which card or cards are causing trouble by examining the sequence of header cards that have been printed on the first page of output. On that page, header cards are listed as they are read by the computer. The erroneous or misplaced card comes after the last header that was successfully read. It may come anywhere afterwards. Probably the error is located among the information cards for the last subject header that is printed on the page.

If trouble occurs before any subject headers are printed, it is certain that the error occurred before the first set of instruction cards were read by the computer. Probably something is wrong with the very first header card. Or the life-table data may be mispunched. Also inspect the life tables carefully for correct sequence. As a last resort, list the life-table data on the printer and compare with the list supplied with the package. If *all* subjects have been printed on the first output page for one projection, including END PROJECTION, and trouble occurs before any output is printed, the life-table data may be defective.

If trouble occurs after some subject headers are printed but before all are printed, it is certain that the error follows the last valid subject header. Probably it comes prior to the next valid subject header in your deck, although this is not certain. The error sometimes, although seldom, comes in the next subject. The first step in error diagnosis is to find the place in the job deck where the trouble is logically located. Then look for the specific error on the cards themselves.

If it is very difficult to identify the location of the error in the deck, try changing the sequence of subjects (any sequence is allowable) on the chance that the new error messages will provide more clues concerning the exact location of the trouble.

It is possible for the projection to be made successfully, but for the output to be strange. If so, something is wrong with the assumptions. Study the fertility and mortality assumptions that are printed on the first numbered page of output, and look over the migration assumptions on page 2, if there are any. If surprisingly large figures appear, input data may have been incorrectly placed in the numeric data fields so that empty columns were read by the computer as extra zeros. If unexpected assumptions are printed, the user may have failed to include assumptions that he had planned. In certain circumstances, FIVFIV will fill gaps in assumptions with assumptions from a previous projection, and the results are meaningless.

Never place completely blank cards in a FIVFIV deck. When searching for punching errors, look carefully at the column positioning. If you suspect a particular card but cannot see an error in the printing along the top of the card, punch it again (do not duplicate). Occasionally two characters are punched in the same column, with the result that an erroneous card code is given to the machine. The card reader of the machine itself may detect such errors by flashing the message, "validity check." Never completely trust the printing along the top of a card, since the computer reads the key punch holes, not the printing. That is why it is better to list a deck of cards on the printer

```
                   * SUBJECT HEADER INIT.POP OMITTED. HENCE SEARCH  *
                   * MADE FOR A VALID HEADER WITH REPEATED MESSAGES *

DURING INPUT THE FOLLOWING CARDS WERE READ AS SUBJECT HEADERS:

YEAR.TITLE
INIT.F.A       2761.7
***** INVALID SUBJECT HEADER: INIT.F.A
INIT.F.B       1054.9
***** INVALID SUBJECT HEADER: INIT.F.B
INIT.F.C        232.7
***** INVALID SUBJECT HEADER: INIT.F.C
INIT.M.A       2791.4
***** INVALID SUBJECT HEADER: INIT.M.A
INIT.M.B       1116.4
***** INVALID SUBJECT HEADER: INIT.M.B
INIT.M.C        225.2
***** INVALID SUBJECT HEADER: INIT.M.C
DATE.SHIFT
MORT.SPLIT
FERTILITY
END PROJECTION


                      * INFORMATION CARDS WERE OUT OF SEQUENCE *

FERTILITY
***** INFORMATION CARD ERROR IN SUBJECT FERTILITY        ERROR TYPE C.


                * MESSAGE FROM SYSTEM:  EXTRA DECIMAL POINT PUNCHED *

YEAR.TITLE
INIT.POP

IHC215I CONVERT - ILLEGAL   DECIMAL   CHARACTER .
INIT.F.B        49.7       40.0     .31.8     24.7      18.6       13.4        8.9


            * APPARENTLY NORMAL BUT NO PROJECTION.  PROBABLY OLD.POP WAS  *
            * USED AND THE PRECEDING PROJECTION FAILED TO PROVIDE A POP   *

YEAR.TITLE
INIT.POP
SCALE
FERTILITY
MORTALITY
END PROJECTION


           * SINSIN MESSAGE.  PROBABLY A BAD PROJECTION WAS PASSED FROM  *
           * FIVFIV.  CORRECT THE PROJECTION AND MESSAGE WILL DISAPPEAR. *
           * INSPECT SEQUENCE NUMBERS IF COMMUNICATING BY ACTUAL CARDS.  *

THE DATA SAVED FROM FIVFIV ARE OUT OF ORDER; EXPECTED CARD NUMBER  9 BUT FOUND
CARD NUMBER  1


            * THE FOLLOWING MESSAGE IS FOUND ON PAGE 3 OR 4 WHEN FIVFIV  *
            * PASSES DATA ONWARD TO SINSIN.  IF MESSAGE NOT FOUND, SINSIN *
            * SUBJECTS WERE NOT REQUESTED OR THE PROJECTION FAILED TO PRO-*
            * DUCE SUITABLE OUTPUT FOR SINSIN.                            *

RESULTS FROM THIS PROJECTION WERE SAVED FOR SINSIN
```

for inspection than to look only at the printing on the cards themselves. Most errors can be found by inspecting cards themselves, however, and suspicious cards can be punched a second time to make sure a good card is used.

IF SINSIN FAILS

All that has been said so far applies to the execution of FIVFIV jobs. SINSIN rarely fails after successful execution of FIVFIV, because all the instructions for SINSIN are given first to FIVFIV and it does the error checking. However, SINSIN can fail under certain circumstances.

If SINSIN is terminated with a message that signifies "read check," or indicates in some other way that the input data for SINSIN cannot be read successfully, check for the following possible sources of trouble:

1. Assumptions for AGESEXSPEC or SUBDIVIDE may be out of range. The permissible ranges are described in the instructions for AGESEXSPEC and SUBDIVIDE.

2. Population size may have become too large for FIVFIV to pass the numbers to SINSIN. Individual age-sex groups of one million or more cannot be passed. Totals are not passed.

If cards are used to pass results from FIVFIV to SINSIN, you can inspect the cards. Asterisks on any of the cards except the title card and the HALT card indicate numbers too large to be passed. Remedy: If the offending numbers appear to refer to population, increase the size of units in which population (and migration) is expressed. Otherwise, check once more the assumptions for AGESEXSPEC and SUBDIVIDE.

When a defective projection is made by FIVFIV, the data passed to SINSIN are coded so that SINSIN will recognize the error and skip the projection. The user may learn whether complete data for a SINSIN projection were passed from FIVFIV by looking for a message on the last page of the printed FIVFIV output. It should say that the results of the projection were saved for SINSIN. Whenever FIVFIV does not pass data, or passes incomplete data for a projection, no such message is printed. SINSIN itself may print messages to indicate that the data it received are incomplete or out of order, but it will continue and, if the data for the next projection are satisfactory, SINSIN will make the next projection successfully.

Since SINSIN cannot handle extremely large or very small numbers, look for such extreme values in FIVFIV output as a possible source of SINSIN failure. The remedy usually is to change the units in which population is expressed for the FIVFIV projection. An initial total population of zero for a projection is acceptable to FIVFIV, but not to SINSIN.

Error Messages and Symbols

SOMETHING WRONG WITH LIFE TABLES: The message will compare what was expected with what was found and thus identify where in the deck of life-table data there is a missing card, a card out of order, or a card from a different family. Check that the first and last cards are present. There are 72 cards for each sex.

*****INVALID SUBJECT HEADER: This message is followed by 20 spaces in which are printed whatever was found in the first 20 columns of the card. Is the card content valid and correctly spaced? Does it begin in column 1? Compare the spelling with the description of headers in the text. Other possible errors are:

1. **Missing header card.**   This will cause the first information card to be read as if it were a header, and its label will appear in the message. Additional messages will follow even for perfectly good information cards until a valid header is located. Correct the first error and the rest will disappear.

2. **Too many information cards.**   FIVFIV may be looking for the next subject and will object if it finds more information cards. The message will report the label of the "extra" information card. Some earlier card may be the extra one that needs to be removed.

3. **Misplaced closing card.**   Certain subjects are closed by a final information card. Closing cards that might be in the wrong place are: FEND, MEND, SEND, AEND. If out of place, and if information cards that should precede the closing card actually follow it, FIVFIV will object to each of the following information cards one by one and will report the labels. Put the closing card in the correct location and the other messages will disappear.

*****INFORMATION CARD ERROR IN SUBJECT: This message will be followed by the name of the subject. First make sure that no information cards have been left out of that subject. If that is not the source of trouble, use the error code (given by the message) to determine the type of error. Check each information card for the subject to try to find the error. Compare cards carefully with directions given in the text.

If a series of messages about invalid subject headers follows immediately after INFORMATION CARD ERROR, disregard them. Probably FIVFIV is looking for a valid subject header or for instructions about another projection, so it can get back to work.

***ASTERISKS where numbers are expected in the printed output. When the computer tries to print a result that requires more space than is available, it fills the space with asterisks. Probable causes of the trouble are:

1. Population assumptions were punched without decimals or not right-justified so that extra spaces caused the computer to add zeros. Check INIT.POP, SCALE, MIGRATION, and FINDMIGRATION.

2. Too many births were generated because TOTAL.FERT was punched incorrectly.

3. Too large a population was assumed and it grew beyond the size limits allowed by the program. Remedy: Use larger units for population and migration quantities.

Error Codes for Information Cards

A   **FIVFIV could not recognize the label.**   The sequence of letters, decimal points (periods), and numerals is punched wrong or belongs to a type of information card that was not expected. Compare labels with instructions in the text. Look especially for wrong positioning of letters and other characters in columns. Punching always starts in column 1. If labels on the cards are correct, are the cards arranged in correct order? Do they belong to the subject whose header precedes them?

B   Sex.   Possible errors are: M or F was not punched in the correct column. Compare the column positioning on your cards with the text. Was information given twice for one sex and not for the other?

C   Consecutive numbering.   A string of cards that is supposed to be in numerical order is not. Common location of error: FERDIST, column 8; or MIGR, column 6.

D   Seven projection periods.   Certain types of data must be supplied for all seven projection periods. Check column 10 of FERDIST and column 8 of MIGR for each sex. Do the numbers add to 7?

E   Consecutive letter sequence.   Strings of information cards that are lettered A, B or A, B, C are involved. The entire string of cards must be present and must be together in the correct sequence. Check the letter sequences.

F   Numerical values.   If the subject is MORTALITY or MORT.SPLIT, the assumption for females for the first period was zero, which is illegal on the female card. Possibly the numeric data field was accidentally left empty. If the subject is AGESEXSPEC, probably different years were specified on a pair of cards when they should be the same, or a year >9999 was used. If the subject is SUBDIVIDE, a year >9999 was used. An empty or zero first field is not allowed for total fertility (subject FERTILITY) or for total population (subject FINDMIGRATION).

APPENDIX FOUR: DIRECTORY OF SUBJECTS FOR INPUT_____

Rules for punching: Start all cards with a label in column 1. Numeric data fields are 10 columns wide, located in columns 11-20, 21-30, . . . 71-80, except where placement is shown by # # symbols. Right-justify numbers. Numeric data appear only on information cards, not on the header (first) card of a subject. Punch decimal points (periods) exactly as shown.

Ordering of subjects: Any order is acceptable except that END PRODUCTION must be last.

*Required subject.
†Alternative to required subject.
( ) Page references to explanations and examples in text. Numbers in bold face indicate the main reference.

* **YEAR.TITLE**
  YR.# # # #. Starting year; title in columns 9-80.
  (pp. **10-11**, 31, 41)

* **INIT.POP**
  INIT.F.A ⎫ Females by 16 five-year age groups in continuous
  INIT.F.B ⎬ string on 3 cards (7/7/2). If open interval below
  INIT.F.C ⎭ age 75 +, leave higher age groups empty.

  INIT.M.A ⎫ Males. Male cards may be placed ahead of female
  INIT.M.B ⎬ cards provided sets of 3 kept together.
  INIT.M.C ⎭ (pp. **11-12**, 33-34, chap. 3, 75-82)

† **INIT.POP** Alternative
  OLD.POP.# # # # Year label of the population in the preceding projection that will be used as the input population for this one.
  (pp. **13**, 32, 55)

DATE.SHIFT
  YR.# # # #.WEEK.# # Date of actual input population by year and week of the year.
  (pp. **14**, 31, 33, 40)

SCALE
  TOTAL.F Female population total at date of input. Columns 11-20.

  TOTAL.M Males. Either males or females may be given first.
  (pp. **15**, 50, 55)

* MORTALITY

MORT.LV.F } or { MORT.EZ.F   Select life tables by level (LV)
MORT.LV.M } or { MORT.EZ.M   or by $\mathring{e}_0$ (EZ). Either sex first.
                                (pp. **16**, 26-29, 41, 56)

† MORT.SPLIT

CHILD.LV.F. } or { CHILD.IM.F   Select under age 5 by level
CHILD.LV.M   } or { CHILD.IM.M   (LV) or by infant mortality
                                  (IM). Either sex first.

ADULT.LV.F   } or { ADULTS.E5.F   Select over age 5 by level
ADULT.LV.M.   } or { ADULTS.E5.M   (LV) or by $\mathring{e}_5$ (E5). Either sex
                                    first.

Keep child and adult pairs of cards together,
either pair first.
(pp. **17-18**, 26-29, 34-36, 41)

* FERTILITY

TOTAL.FERT   First information card; total fertility for 7 periods.
FERDIST1.# } n age-specific fertility schedules 15-19, . . . 45-49.
FERDIST2.# } Each schedule applies to # periods. Sum of #
FERDISTn.# } totals 7 periods.
FEND   Last information card; no data.
               (pp. **18-19**, 36-37, 41, 48-49, 54, 110)

SEXRATIO

MPERHUNDF   Males per hundred females in first data field.
               (pp. **20**, 41, 50-51)

MIGRATION   Quantity option.
MIGLEVEL.F   Yearly migration levels for 7 periods. Females.
MIGLEVEL.M   Males. Either sex first. These 2 cards must be first.
MIGRFn.#.A } Female distributions of migration for 16 age
MIGRFn.#.B } groups. n sets. Each set applies to # periods.
MIGRFn.#.C }
MIGRMn.#.A }
MIGRMn.#.B } Male distributions. Keep sets of 3 cards together.
MIGRMn.#.C } Either sex first. Sum of # totals 7 periods.
MEND   Last information card; no data.
               (pp. **20-21**, 37-40, 41, 82-88, 108)

MIGRATION   Rates option. Alternative to quantity option.
RATES   First information card; no data.
MIGRFn.#.A } Yearly migration rates per thousand population
MIGRFn.#.B } for 16 age groups. Females. n sets of rates. Each
MIGRFn.#.C } set applies to # projection periods.
MIGRMn.#.A }
MIGRMn.#.B } Male migration rates. Keep sets of 3 cards to-
MIGRMn.#.C } gether. Either sex first. Sum of # totals 7 periods.
MEND   Last information card; no data.
               (pp. **22**, 41, 82-88)

FINDMIGRATION

TARGETPOP   Assumed population total at dates   } This pair,
               5, 10, . . . 35.   } either order,
MPERHUNDF   Migrant males per hundred fe-   } comes first.
               males, 7 periods.

MIGRFn.#.A MIGRFn.#.B MIGRFn.#.C	Female distribution of migration for 16 age groups. n sets. Each set applies to # periods.
MIGRMn.#.A MIGRMn.#.B MIGRMn.#.C	Male distributions. Keep sets of 3 cards together. Either sex first. Sum of # totals 7 periods.
MEND	Last information card; no data. (pp. **23-24**, 88-99, 108-109)
STABLEXTEND	Include as many times as desired. No information cards. (pp. **24**, 47-48, 55)
PRODUCTION	Use only once. Applies to all subsequent projections. (p. **25**)
PUNCH.FIVE	Include as many times as decks desired. (pp. **25**, 42, 67, 108, 112, 139)
REGROUP GROUPS.##-##.##-##.##-##	Required for all SINSIN projections. up to 7 age ranges; right-justify single digits. (pp. 64, **65-66**, 69-70)
PUNCH.SINGLE	Include as many times as decks desired. (pp. **67**, 106, 108, 112, 139)
SUBDIVIDE PLACEONE.	Title in columns 10-80.
PLACETWO.	Empty if no residual wanted; otherwise provide title.
TOTALONE.F TOTALONE.M	Ratio, date, slope, termination date, second slope. Same for males. Either sex first.
RATIOS.F.A RATIOS.F.B RATIOS.F.C	16 age-group ratios, one date for females.
SLOPE1.F.A SLOPE1.F.B SLOPE1.F.C	16 slopes and, if second segment follows, termination date for the first linear segment; no SLOPE cards required if ratios are constant over time.
SLOPE2.F.A SLOPE2.F.B SLOPE2.F.C	16 more slopes if there is a second segment; otherwise cards may be omitted.
RATIOS.M.A RATIOS.M.B RATIOS.M.C	Males, same as females. Either sex first.
SLOPE1.M.A SLOPE1.M.B SLOPE1.M.C	Males, same as females.
SLOPE2.M.A SLOPE2.M.B SLOPE2.M.C	Males, same as females.
SEND	Last information card; no data. (pp. 100-106, **102-104**, 113)
AGESEXSPEC	Subject may be used up to three times in one projection.
TITLE.#.	Printing control # may be blank; provide title, columns 9-80.

GROUPS.F.##-##.##-## Define up to 12 age groups for females; right-justify single digits.

GROUPS.M.##-##.##-## Males, same as females. Either sex first.

YEAR1.F.A	Date; six age-specific rates; use as many fields as needed.
YEAR1.F.B	Date; six more rates (always 2 cards; always both dated).
YEAR2.F.A	Second date; six age-specific rates.
YEAR2.F.B	Second date; six more rates (2 cards, both dated).
YEAR3.F.A	Same for third date (2 cards, both dated).
YEAR3.F.B	Cards for second and third dates are optional.
YEAR1.M.A ⎫ YEAR1.M.B ⎬	Males, same as females. Either sex first.
YEAR2.M.A ⎫ YEAR2.M.B ⎬	Males, same as females.
YEAR3.M.A ⎫ YEAR3.M.B ⎬	Males, same as females.
AEND	Last information card; no data. (chap. 7, pp. **113-115**)

* END PROJECTION   Always placed last.
(p. **26**)

Summary of Error Codes

A   Labels: Punched correctly? Correct order of information cards?

B   Sex: Two sets of data for one sex only? M and F punched correctly?

C   Consecutive numbering: Order numbered cards. FERDIST or MIGR.

D   Seven projection periods: Are FERDIST or MIGR data given for 7 periods?

E   Consecutive letter sequence: Order cards A, B, . . .

F   Numerical values: First value missing? Year invalid?

CUT HERE TO REMOVE

APPENDIX
FOUR: DIRECTORY
OF SUBJECTS
FOR INPUT_____

Rules for punching: Start all cards with a label in column 1. Numeric data fields are 10 columns wide, located in columns 11-20, 21-30, . . . 71-80, except where placement is shown by ## symbols. Right-justify numbers. Numeric data appear only on information cards, not on the header (first) card of a subject. Punch decimal points (periods) exactly as shown.

Ordering of subjects: Any order is acceptable except that END PRODUCTION must be last.

*Required subject.

†Alternative to required subject.

( ) Page references to explanations and examples in text. Numbers in bold face indicate the main reference.

* **YEAR.TITLE**		
YR.####.		Starting year; title in columns 9-80.
		(pp. **10-11**, 31, 41)
* **INIT.POP**		
INIT.F.A	⎫	Females by 16 five-year age groups in continuous
INIT.F.B	⎬	string on 3 cards (7/7/2). If open interval below
INIT.F.C	⎭	age 75 +, leave higher age groups empty.
INIT.M.A	⎫	Males. Male cards may be placed ahead of female
INIT.M.B	⎬	cards provided sets of 3 kept together.
INIT.M.C	⎭	(pp. **11-12**, 33-34, chap. 3, 75-82)
† **INIT.POP**		Alternative
OLD.POP.####		Year label of the population in the preceding projection that will be used as the input population for this one.
		(pp. **13**, 32, 55)
DATE.SHIFT		
YR.####.WEEK.##		Date of actual input population by year and week of the year.
		(pp. **14**, 31, 33, 40)
SCALE		
TOTAL.F		Female population total at date of input. Columns 11-20.
TOTAL.M		Males. Either males or females may be given first.
		(pp. **15**, 50, 55)

* **MORTALITY**

MORT.LV.F } or { MORT.EZ.F } Select life tables by level (LV)
MORT.LV.M }   { MORT.EZ.M } or by $\mathring{e}_0$ (EZ). Either sex first.
                                       (pp. **16**, 26-29, 41, 56)

† **MORT.SPLIT**

CHILD.LV.F. } or { CHILD.IM.F } Select under age 5 by level
CHILD.LV.M }   { CHILD.IM.M } (LV) or by infant mortality
                                      (IM). Either sex first.

ADULT.LV.F } or { ADULTS.E5.F } Select over age 5 by level
ADULT.LV.M. }   { ADULTS.E5.M } (LV) or by $\mathring{e}_5$ (E5). Either sex
                                      first.

                                    Keep child and adult pairs of cards together,
                                    either pair first.
                                    (pp. **17-18**, 26-29, 34-36, 41)

* **FERTILITY**

TOTAL.FERT   First information card; total fertility for 7 periods.
FERDIST1.# }   n age-specific fertility schedules 15-19, . . . 45-49.
FERDIST2.# }   Each schedule applies to # periods. Sum of #
FERDISTn.# }   totals 7 periods.
FEND   Last information card; no data.
                                    (pp. **18-19**, 36-37, 41, 48-49, 54, 110)

SEXRATIO

MPERHUNDF   Males per hundred females in first data field.
                                    (pp. **20**, 41, 50-51)

MIGRATION   Quantity option.
MIGLEVEL.F   Yearly migration levels for 7 periods. Females.
MIGLEVEL.M   Males. Either sex first. These 2 cards must be first.
MIGRFn.#.A }
MIGRFn.#.B }   Female distributions of migration for 16 age
MIGRFn.#.C }   groups. n sets. Each set applies to # periods.
MIGRMn.#.A }
MIGRMn.#.B }   Male distributions. Keep sets of 3 cards together.
MIGRMn.#.C }   Either sex first. Sum of # totals 7 periods.
MEND   Last information card; no data.
                                    (pp. **20-21**, 37-40, 41, 82-88, 108)

MIGRATION   Rates option. Alternative to quantity option.
RATES   First information card; no data.
MIGRFn.#.A }
MIGRFn.#.B }   Yearly migration rates per thousand population
MIGRFn.#.C }   for 16 age groups. Females. n sets of rates. Each
                                    set applies to # projection periods.
MIGRMn.#.A }
MIGRMn.#.B }   Male migration rates. Keep sets of 3 cards to-
MIGRMn.#.C }   gether. Either sex first. Sum of # totals 7 periods.
MEND   Last information card; no data.
                                    (pp. **22**, 41, 82-88)

FINDMIGRATION

TARGETPOP   Assumed population total at dates } This pair,
                                    5, 10, . . . 35.   } either order,
MPERHUNDF   Migrant males per hundred fe- } comes first.
                                      males, 7 periods.

MIGRFn.#.A ⎫ MIGRFn.#.B ⎬ MIGRFn.#.C ⎭	Female distribution of migration for 16 age groups. n sets. Each set applies to # periods.
MIGRMn.#.A ⎫ MIGRMn.#.B ⎬ MIGRMn.#.C ⎭	Male distributions. Keep sets of 3 cards together. Either sex first. Sum of # totals 7 periods.
MEND	Last information card; no data. (pp. **23-24**, 88-99, 108-109)
STABLEXTEND	Include as many times as desired. No information cards. (pp. **24**, 47-48, 55)
PRODUCTION	Use only once. Applies to all subsequent projections. (p. **25**)
PUNCH.FIVE	Include as many times as decks desired. (pp. **25**, 42, 67, 108, 112, 139)
REGROUP GROUPS.##-##.##-##.##-##	Required for all SINSIN projections. up to 7 age ranges; right-justify single digits. (pp. 64, **65-66**, 69-70)
PUNCH.SINGLE	Include as many times as decks desired. (pp. **67**, 106, 108, 112, 139)
SUBDIVIDE PLACEONE.	Title in columns 10-80.
PLACETWO.	Empty if no residual wanted; otherwise provide title.
TOTALONE.F ⎫ TOTALONE.M ⎭	Ratio, date, slope, termination date, second slope. Same for males. Either sex first.
RATIOS.F.A ⎫ RATIOS.F.B ⎬ RATIOS.F.C ⎭	16 age-group ratios, one date for females.
SLOPE1.F.A ⎫ SLOPE1.F.B ⎬ SLOPE1.F.C ⎭	16 slopes and, if second segment follows, termination date for the first linear segment; no SLOPE cards required if ratios are constant over time.
SLOPE2.F.A ⎫ SLOPE2.F.B ⎬ SLOPE2.F.C ⎭	16 more slopes if there is a second segment; otherwise cards may be omitted.
RATIOS.M.A ⎫ RATIOS.M.B ⎬ RATIOS.M.C ⎭	Males, same as females. Either sex first.
SLOPE1.M.A ⎫ SLOPE1.M.B ⎬ SLOPE1.M.C ⎭	Males, same as females.
SLOPE2.M.A ⎫ SLOPE2.M.B ⎬ SLOPE2.M.C ⎭	Males, same as females.
SEND	Last information card; no data. (pp. 100-106, **102-104**, 113)
AGESEXSPEC	Subject may be used up to three times in one projection.
TITLE.#.	Printing control # may be blank; provide title, columns 9-80.

CUT HERE TO REMOVE

GROUPS.F.##-##.##-## Define up to 12 age groups for females; right-justify single digits.

GROUPS.M.##-##.##-## Males, same as females. Either sex first.

YEAR1.F.A — Date; six age-specific rates; use as many fields as needed.

YEAR1.F.B — Date; six more rates (always 2 cards; always both dated).

YEAR2.F.A — Second date; six age-specific rates.

YEAR2.F.B — Second date; six more rates (2 cards, both dated).

YEAR3.F.A — Same for third date (2 cards, both dated).

YEAR3.F.B — Cards for second and third dates are optional.

YEAR1.M.A ⎫
YEAR1.M.B ⎬ Males, same as females. Either sex first.

YEAR2.M.A ⎫
YEAR2.M.B ⎬ Males, same as females.

YEAR3.M.A ⎫
YEAR3.M.B ⎬ Males, same as females.

AEND — Last information card; no data.
(chap. 7, pp. **113-115**)

* **END PROJECTION** — Always placed last.
(p. **26**)

Summary of Error Codes

A — Labels: Punched correctly? Correct order of information cards?

B — Sex: Two sets of data for one sex only? M and F punched correctly?

C — Consecutive numbering: Order numbered cards. FERDIST or MIGR.

D — Seven projection periods: Are FERDIST or MIGR data given for 7 periods?

E — Consecutive letter sequence: Order cards A, B, . . .

F — Numerical values: First value missing? Year invalid?

Ordering Tape or Cards

The package is supplied on tape unless requested on cards. The charge for reproduction and mailing is US$25.00, payable in advance in US currency only. Please make your remittance payable to The Population Council and send it, along with this form, to The Population Council, Comptroller's Office, 245 Park Avenue, New York, N.Y. 10017. The charge will be waived if the order is made on behalf on a recognized institution in a developing country.

Tapes are readily shipped by international airmail. They are usually admitted upon arrival in the same class as international letters. If cards are requested, provide exact instructions concerning the preferred means of shipment and address for the package.

Provide the following information about the computing facility on which the package will be used:

1. Computer manufacturer _____
   (e.g., I.B.M.; C.D.C.; I.C.L.; D.E.C.; etc.)

2. Model of computer _____
   (e.g., 360–40; 1130; 1901; 11/45; 8e; etc.)

3. Type of operating system _____
   (e.g., DOS/360; VOS/370; BATCH; etc.)

4. Is FORTRAN available? No_____ Yes_____ Level of compiler(s)_____
   (e.g., E;F;G;H; Version 10)

5. Available memory—indicate base (decimal, octal), units (words, bytes), and bits or digits per unit.

   _____

   (e.g., 16K decimal words, 8 digits per word; 32K octal words, 32 bits per word)

6. Are 7-track tape drives available? No_____ Yes_____
   Check all available _____ _____ _____
   228   556   800

7. Are 9-track tape drives available? No_____ Yes_____
   Check all available _____ _____ _____
   800   1600   6250

8. Is disk available? No_____ Yes_____ Manufacturer and model_____

9. What is the character width of the line printer? _____
   (i.e., 80; 120; 132; etc.)

10. Location of the computer installation _____

   _____

   _____

(Please print)

Your Name _____

Your Full Mailing Address _____

   _____

DATE DUE

DATE DUE		
... ... 1975		
MAR 2 5 1975		
NOV 1 4 1977		